Joseph grew up in deep, dark Berkshire. He has been a busy professional actor for over twenty-five years, having played leading roles at most of the major theatres in England including the National Theatre, the Royal Court, Almeida, Hampstead Theatre, the Old Vic, Donmar Warehouse and the RSC (where he is an associate artist). He has appeared in West End musicals and has won several awards for his stage work including the UK Theatre Award and Whatsonstage Awards. He has appeared in a dozen feature films including *Angel Has Fallen* and *Casino Royale*. His extensive and varied television career has included regular leading roles in *The Last Kingdom, Banished, 24, Campus, Holby City, The Sarah Jane Adventures* and *Peak Practice,* among many others.

Joseph has taught in several of the leading drama schools in the UK; he is patron of the Actors Centre London and is a fellow of the Rose Bruford College.

This is his first book.

http://www.josephmillson.com
Twitter: @josephmillson
Instagram: @millpotts

Praise for *Work ... and other four-letter words*

'This is wonderful. It's the proper story of an actor's life – not the champagne and air-kisses, but the graft, the doubt, the debt, and sometimes, just sometimes, the bliss.'

– Russell T. Davies

'If you are interested in the real life and challenges of a working actor, then this book is absolutely essential. Joe Millson writes in an engaging, honest but highly optimistic tone, and his passion for the craft and the life he obviously loves so much shines through those pages. For fellow creative professionals like myself who have to engage with those beautiful nutters, *Work* demystifies many of the things actors do, and how they need to think about this strange undertaking. Therefore it should also be required reading for anyone crazy enough to want to join their ranks.'

– Irvine Welsh

'A funny, authentic and sometimes painful account of starting off as a professional actor.'

– Sir Richard Eyre

'A breathless and highly entertaining backstage chronicle of what it's like to be a young actor making his way in the shark-infested waters of showbiz. Lots of laughs, setbacks galore, and enough juicy anecdotes to keep the most ardent celeb spotter happy...'

– Michael Simkins

'Millson writes about the craft of acting with the tireless ardour of a besotted lover. Beneath the hilarious (and sometimes deliciously indiscreet) anecdotes lies the story of a boy becoming a man. A joy to read.'

– Mark Ravenhill

'Joseph Millson looks back on the bluster and blunders of his early career with a candour that sometimes seems dangerously unfiltered. From dole queues to dramatic heights, he captures the randomness of the acting profession while bristling with enthusiasm for the job.'

– Dame Harriet Walter

'Joseph Millson shares with us a vivid and fascinating insight into the breathtaking highs and the excruciating lows of "An Actor's Life For me", and he's still smiling.'

– Dame Celia Imrie

'This book is a scream! Filled with the real-life adventures of a very funny, ridiculously handsome and very naughty actor. Read, giggle, blush, you will have a ball.'

– Andy Nyman

'Please buy this book – it will give you useful queasy insights into the reality of our bonkers profession, and if Joe gets some paid gigs as a writer it might serve to keep him off our screens and stage. Truly – it's hilarious and also unique – it's not the humble-brag of a Huge Star (yet) it's a lot like what it's actually like…'

– Ian Kelly, playwright, author and actor

'The shelves are full of actors' biographies, memoirs, anecdotes and filled with books about acting. But this book is a must-read: a unique, at times hilarious and at times searingly honest personal take on what it really means to be a working – or not – actor. It's funny, wise, generous and has a big beating heart, a passionate account that gets right to what the work feels like, what it, in all its many guises, asks of the actor, and how one survives. Joseph Millson is that wonderful, romantic and maybe unusual these days animal – "stage-struck". This love affair, for that is what it is, is optimistic, demanding, deluded, disappointing, triumphant and consuming. But it also has to be balanced with his other significant relationships – girlfriends, wife, children, parents and it is the honesty with which Joseph describes these relationships and how they inform his work that makes the book so moving and so recognisable. There are moments when he describes the physical sensations of acting as transformative that made me cry with joyful tears! Full of humour and wisdom. Young actors venturing on this capricious life will find it both inspiring and enlightening.'

– Anni Tyson, senior acting tutor RADA

'I have absolutely devoured this book! A fantastic, open-hearted, emotional (I laughed, I cried), educational and utterly authentic ride. The best thing I've read in a very long while. I can't wait for Volume 2.'

– Craig Baxter, playwright

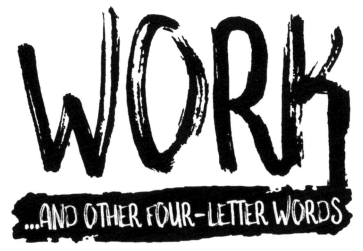

...AND OTHER FOUR-LETTER WORDS

EVERYTHING YOU'VE NEVER HEARD ABOUT BECOMING AN ACTOR!

JOSEPH MILLSON

Edited, designed and produced by Tandem Publishing
http://tandempublishing.yolasite.com/

Cover design by Paul Burgess Graphic Design.
Author photography by Alex Bourne.

10 9 8 7 6 5 4 3 2 1

A CIP catalogue record for this book is available from the British Library.

For Jessica and Gabriel

'There is no short cut, no patent tram-road to wisdom: after all the centuries of invention, the soul's path lies through the thorny wilderness which must be still trodden in solitude, with bleeding feet, with sobs for help, as it was trodden by them of old time.'
George Eliot – *The Lifted Veil*

But also…

'Fuck it…'
Jeff Grosso – skateboarder

Contents

Prologue: The Bahamas — xi

1995 — 2
1996 — 20
1997 — 56
1998 — 84
1999 — 126
2000 — 144
2001 — 162
2002 — 194
2003 — 218
2004 — 250
2005 — 276

Epilogue — 333

Thanks — 335

print would be a tiny foothold; evidence of something – of a campaign fought at the very least. And if by any chance I got a positive review, then it was proof that at least one person didn't think I was shit.

I think *The Times* used a nice adjective like 'splendid' about my performance, and a lady on a Radio 4 arts programme, when talking about how well we had caught the style of the period, said something like, 'The way they stand … Joseph Millson "makes a leg" so well'. Little did she know that's how I stand when I'm making a cup of tea but I was thrilled.

CROCKER GOLD

Towards the end of the run, Ben asked if I'd mind auditioning for MTC's next show, which was to be *Loot* by Joe Orton. It would begin rehearsals in the spring of the following year. *Mind?* I was over the moon he might want to work with me again and desperate to be in such a great play. He explained that the Arts Council who funded his tours had recently advised him to branch away from performing just the obscure 'lost' comedies, and to present other classics from British playwrights. *Loot* was to be the most modern play he had produced and a fairly sure-fire hit with audiences.

So, audition I did, and I repaid his interest in me by doing a great deal of homework. I expected no favours just because I'd already worked for him and I was over the moon to get an offer. After the last night of *The Dramatist* I was able to enjoy Christmas with the luxury of a job in the bank for the year ahead.

1996

Dolly, the world's first cloned sheep, took her first 'BAAA', Charles and Princess Diana got that divorce, the Dunblane massacre saddened the nation, as did IRA bombings of the Arndale shopping centre in Manchester and the Docklands in London; the Spice Girls got their first number one with 'Wannabe', beating the rivalling Britpop gods Blur and Oasis, *The English Patient* and *Independence Day* were the big films, and Mad Cow Disease swept the nation and led some away from beef forever.

Driving myself
to set

La Belle Dame Sans Merci by John Keats
Short Film

I had a few months to wait before rehearsals for *Loot* began and, with no luck finding short-term work, I dutifully signed on for unemployment benefit every week at Greenwich dole office, where I was a figure of hate for an enormous deaf man who seemed to always be just behind me in the queue. I tried to vary my arrival time to avoid bumping into him, but, each week, there he'd be, stepping into the queue just behind me. He would stare at the back of my head and then as soon as I turned around, come right up to my face and say, 'You. Big. Wanker,' in an incredibly loud voice. I had no luck establishing how I'd offended him, so tended to opt for a smile and a 'thank you', before making my exit.

My girlfriend, Cath, and I would forgo certain foods to share the fairly high cost of subscribing to *PCR*, the *Periodical Casting Report*. It would arrive printed on red paper (to prohibit photocopying and sharing) every Monday, and I would be standing by with stamped envelopes, our photos and our very brief CVs to feel proactive and perhaps get us some work. I say 'work'. Most of what was advertised was unpaid – student films or low-level, bring-your-own-costume fringe theatre stuff. But it was experience that I was after. I had no children, no credit card debts and no mortgage. The only real responsibilities were rent and food and we were living in a damp basement flat in the least desirable part of South London, so outgoings were as low as they could be. We called this weekly enterprise 'Joey's Jobs' and it did occasionally pay off.

My first real experience in front of a camera was a short film of the John Keats poem, 'La Belle Dame Sans Merci', which I had seen advertising for actors in *PCR*. The advertisement said it was to be shot in and around Brighton, on film, not video, with extremely high standards of production, and directed by an 'award-winning young director'. For once, *PCR* was not exaggerating. I got the job as the young knight at arms, the film was beautifully made, and it transpired to be a very fateful experience in my life.

ALONE AND PALELY LOITERING

There was a small snag in that the filming dates were smack in the middle of rehearsals for *Loot*. But Ben Crocker was kind enough to give me a couple of days off so that I could go down to Sussex for a long weekend of filming.

When I think back to that first real experience in front of a film camera I remember truly loving it and being fascinated by this new element of the craft I had to conquer, acting for a lens instead of a big hulking human audience. But mainly, I remember the *cold*. Cold like I'd never known before.

It was January and the location was on and around the banks of a beautiful reservoir in the Sussex countryside. Ice covered much of the water and snow was all around us. I was costumed in a beautiful suit of steel armour for most of the film. This looked fantastic but weighed a tonne. It took three people to get me into it and more to get me out of it, so toilet breaks were rare. It was impossible to walk in too, so I was transported to and from set in the front of a dumper truck.

The metal had another quality which I will never forget: it conducted cold. The majority of the film required me to

Prologue

The driver asks me if I want to go to my hotel or 'straight to the party'.

'What party?' I ask.

'It's Daniel's birthday today and the producers are throwing a little party.'

'Oh,' I say. 'Let's go to that.'

We drive for a long time and though I've been too excited to sleep for twenty hours, I eagerly try to glimpse what I can of the Caribbean world through my blurry vision (my only pair of glasses has been written off under a business-man's foot on the flight).

The sun is setting. I crack open the window to breathe in the tropical air, and try to take stock.

I try, but fail.

It's too much to grasp: I'm on my way to Daniel Craig's birthday party, in the bloody Bahamas... I'm playing a cool little part in a James Bond film... I'm here on a break from rehearsing my dream role of Benedick in *Much Ado About Nothing* for the Royal Shakespeare Company, *and* I've only just finished performing a leading role in the Ibsen play, *Pillars Of The Community*, at the National Theatre...

We eventually pull up at the edge of a beach where a

party is in full swing. A Bahamian band is playing an irresistible 'rake and scrape' beat at incredible volume. Strings of coloured lights illuminate beach bars and tables of exotic-looking food.

The car door is opened for me and I'm immediately met by a very merry Daniel Craig, who marches towards me screaming, 'Yes! Another fucking actor! Welcome!'

He stuffs a fat cigar into my mouth, slaps my back and bounces off towards the dance floor. I laugh and stammer, 'Happy birthday' as I follow.

The fruit punch is delicious, highly alcoholic and I'm suddenly very thirsty. I drink glass after glass after glass. By the time I meet our producer, Barbara Broccoli, I am utterly pissed, but it's fine. I feel like I've known her all my life. Within an hour, I'm skinny dipping with the cast and crew in the Atlantic Ocean; within three hours, I'm unconscious.

I awake in an enormous bed with absolutely no idea of where I am or how I got there. The sensation doesn't pass for what feels like an age. Then, slowly, as my head and stomach alert me to their fragility, I'm able to finally take stock.

I am indeed in the Bahamas. I am doing that Bond film and my career is rather shiny right now. But as I lurch my way towards what I pray is the bathroom, I recall, with every heave of my stomach, the long and difficult road I've travelled to get here...

1995

John Major was Prime Minister, Clinton was President, Oklahoma got bombed, Japan got earthquaked, O. J. Simpson was found innocent, Christopher Reeve was paralysed falling from his horse, Peter Cook died, Princess Diana gave her famous 'people's princess' interview to Martin Bashir, Bond was back in the shape of Pierce Brosnan in *GoldenEye,* the cool kids were listening to Alanis Morissette or The Smashing Pumpkins, Pizza Hut introduced the stuffed crust and fish and chips cost £1.60 a portion.

Liverpool Empire. 1995

David Copperfield – The Musical
Liverpool Empire, Manchester Palace

NO YAWNING!

My first day as a professional actor was arse-clenchingly scary. I'd somehow been cast in a musical; if the singing scared me, the dancing *terrified* me and dancing was all we did on day one. Barely an hour into the day, the director screamed at some poor actor in the corner of the room, 'NO YAWNING!' My overwound work ethic heartily approved, and I immediately took this as a 'rule' of the theatre that I'd never heard before. It turned out it was just this one man's pet hate, but it's stuck as a rule with me ever since. In rehearsal rooms or on television sets, I'll still be found hiding behind furniture, under tables or running to the loo if I have to yawn.

FIRST DIGS

By now, I must have stayed in hundreds of strange rooms in people's homes and every variation of hotel and bed and breakfast, for anything from one night to several months, following this job of mine around the country and then the world. The cheap room I rented for my time in Liverpool that year was a few stops out of town on the metro to the coastal suburb of Blundellsands. A small, dark, child's room at the top of a large unfriendly family home; a quiet family, who seemed a little resentful at having me there and not at all sure how to take the long-haired, smiling, bouncy, bespectacled beanpole of an actor, who was suddenly making endless rounds of toast in their kitchen and whistling in their mouldy bathroom.

Only the father seemed at all friendly, partly because he

was the one I gave my money to once a week and partly because he seemed to quite enjoy looking at me as I went to and from the shower.

The room was mine though, a space where nobody I knew could reach me (this being many years before mobile phones or internet). It was my laboratory, where I learned lines and scribbled notes until I collapsed every night, then woke so full of energy I had to do press-ups on my few square feet of carpet before taking a shower, so excited was I to be an actual paid actor, earning my own suppers away from everyone I knew.

Dickens begins *David Copperfield* with the following lines:

> Whether I shall turn out to be the hero of my own life, or whether that station will be held by anybody else, these pages must show.

I couldn't help feeling I was finally writing the first pages of my own life.

SPINAL TAP SETS AND ELEVATOR ORCHESTRAS
The fact that the show was an absolute stinker didn't register for quite some time, so high was I on the ever-present miracle of having a job. But the signs were there, if I'd been looking.

I always love that moment early in rehearsals when the designer shows the cast the model box of what the set will look like. And indeed, the designs for *David Copperfield: The Musical* looked fantastic, from the opening, where young David Copperfield would step out of the pages of an enormous book flown in from the ceiling, to stained-glass windows and an enormous upside-down boat, amongst other grand designs.

Well, something got lost in translation. Some measurements weren't converted into metric perhaps, because the actual set we all saw when we excitedly arrived at the theatre to begin our technical rehearsals was – how can I put this? – tiny. Really tiny.

The Liverpool Empire seats 2,348 people. It's one of the biggest theatres in Europe and has the widest stage I've ever performed on (84 feet across to be precise). As we began the technical rehearsals I snuck out into the auditorium to watch the opening of the show. When I saw the child actor playing young David Copperfield stooping to look smaller than the 'giant' book he was supposed to step out of, I wondered if we might be in trouble.

There were also musical clues that this wasn't going to be *West Side Story*. Before going up to Liverpool, I'd been sent a cassette tape of the music for the show for me to practise and learn my songs. It was awful. That special, cheap, synthesised sound, which tries but fails to reproduce a full orchestra. I knew it was only a guide and told myself it would sound much better on real instruments – with real strings, brass and percussion.

We rehearsed for weeks with our musical director on his lone keyboard and were often told how wonderful the 'orchestra' was going to sound. My default optimism faced quite a challenge, however, when the day before we opened we had our first rehearsal with the 'orchestra'. There were no strings, no brass; just an electric drum kit and not one but three synthesisers now helping to bring the same elevator muzak up to an incredible volume. It was identical to my cassette tape. Identical, just really, really loud.

But I still believed. Hell yes, I still believed it was going to be a hit!

FIRST NIGHT TO END ALL FIRST NIGHTS

Somehow or other, over 2,000 seats had been sold for the opening performance. Little did we know we were rarely to achieve even a quarter of that audience again. It was an awful lot of people to be presenting a staggeringly under-rehearsed show to. We'd not managed to squeeze in a dress rehearsal and only hurriedly finished the technical rehearsal, so there were costume changes and scene changes that had never been performed 'at speed'.

My main role was the complicated young cad Steerforth, but before I got to him I had other roles to play.

My first appearance on a stage as a professional actor was a scene and a song with me as the evil Mr Murdstone who hovered over David's early childhood, accompanied by Miss Murdstone, who did most of the talking and singing in the first scene. I'd worked out a lovely line in frightening grunts and harrumphs, which would hopefully distract from the appalling ageing make-up, and the curly black wig.

It was chaos backstage, but I was ready. A musical number called 'This Is Just A Dream' finished, and the audience applauded. The *audience* – they were real! It went dark, very dark. Pint-size scenery was heard shifting around and I walked out to sit in Mr Murdstone's chair, deep in character and ready to begin my life on the stage.

When the lights came up, I was alone.

I'll remind you of the Liverpool Empire's 84 foot of stage width as you picture this. Let's also keep in mind those 2,000 strangers sitting out there staring at me.

I was eventually joined by our ten-year-old David Copperfield, who came running across the football pitch of a stage to sit opposite me, red-faced and terrified, but we were still a Miss Murdstone short of a scene – and she had the first line.

An especially thick kind of silence descended. If I listened hard, I could just make out some hushed swearing and crying in the down-stage left wing. But out on stage, silence.

Though I say so myself, I was brilliant. I'm not sure who gives out the awards for meaningful grunting and growling but those two minutes (which felt like an hour) were inspired. I made noises like a cow in labour and faces like a bulldog chewing a wasp until Miss Murdstone arrived and we could sing our duet, 'Spare The Rod'.

I had no time to fret about any of this after the scene ended. I was needed in another corner of the theatre in totally different make-up and costume, for a bit of cheeky cockney chorus work in a big crowd scene and song. I secretly loved this number: milling about, pretending to sell potatoes from a wheelbarrow with my mucky urchin face, clutching my braces, singing and dancing my little heart out.

That number went surprisingly well. In the wings a few minutes later, I stopped in a dark corner to drink it all in. I watched a scene change that I hadn't seen before, a beautiful stained-glass window was being flown in and the music suddenly *did* sound wonderful. Then one of our leading actresses began singing and it was superb. I was transfixed, elated, full of pride and joy to be part of it all.

Until, the applause faded and the music and scenery started moving into the next scene. I had ten seconds before my first entrance as the educated, rich and immaculate Steerforth. I'd been so busy watching the show, I'd entirely forgotten to change out of my street urchin costume and mucky make-up. I had no time to do anything except take my cap off, get in position, enter up stage centre and give it my best – right up to the interval.

THEY LOVE ME!

The second half stuttered along in its own frenetic way. The audience loved Alvin Stardust as Uriah Heep, particularly his rock number 'Umble', which he performed energetically in an orange wig and prosthetic knuckles. (I shit you not about the knuckles. He was very proud of them. He thought they were essential to playing Uriah Heep and paid for them with his own money.)

When I finished my only solo number, 'Lovely Lady', I was totally unprepared for the sound of 2,000 people clapping. Don't get me wrong, they didn't cheer, or throw knickers at me. But that many people – none of whom were friends or family – clapped. Not dutifully, but enthusiastically. At me. At me, *singing*!

Fate wasn't going to let me get cocky. I'd finished my contributions to the show and stood in the wings watching the last scene, willing it to go well. Norman Rossington as Mr Micawber had the big plot-resolving number where the baddie was cornered, proved to be a villain and David could thus live a free man.

I've had easier times watching real-life car crashes. Norman couldn't remember a word of the song, a song loaded with important plot details, revelations and resolutions. But, he could remember all of the moves (performed as well as he could with his new plastic hip) and he could remember the bad guy's name. He didn't miss a move or a note as the principal cast looked on and tried to react in the right places while he loudly sang: 'Dee dum, dee dum, dee dum, dee dum, dee dum, dee dum dee HEEP! Dee dum, dee dum, dee dum, dee dum, dee dum, dee dum, dee dum, dee HEEP!''

I was horrified to hear the song receive the same kind of applause as my charming ballad. Norman left the stage, walked past me in the wings, put his hand on my shoulder and said in his broad Liverpudlian accent, 'They love me.'

The ordeal wasn't quite over yet. We took our curtain calls, and yes, unbelievably the audience was still there. We even walked back down to the front of the stage for a modest encore. I was mesmerised, elated, I'd arrived.

The next thing I felt was a thud on the back of my neck, as the largest theatre curtain in Europe knocked me to the ground, leaving the departing audience looking at my dazed and sweaty face sticking out from under a sea of red velvet.

'WHY MUST THE SHOW GO ON?'
Somewhere in the middle of our two-week run at the Liverpool Empire, a company meeting was called. Cast, crew and of course our enormous 'orchestra' assembled in the circle bar. Rumours had been flying. We were doing decent business: surprisingly, a few hundred stumbled in and stumbled out every night, but the atmosphere was growing increasingly tense whenever management were around or mentioned.

It seemed certain people weren't getting paid. Cheques had started to bounce although, so far, not mine. After living on gruel for three years at drama school I'd been gleefully spending most of my wages the minute they arrived in my account at the end of each week.

To be fair to my first agent, she'd warned against accepting this job as it was a 'non-Equity' contract but, clearly, there was to be no stopping me accepting. 'Somebody wants to pay me to act? Where do I sign?' It's a philosophy I've found hard to shake to this day.

A non-Equity contract means actors are unprotected in situations like this. As our composer/author was led into the room trembling and weeping on her husband/producer's arm it soon became clear the company had gone broke. They were full of apologies, praise, and love – but all out of cash.

Apollo Leisure, who owned the six theatres around the country we were booked to appear in over the next few months, didn't want their theatres to go dark. So, we were offered a bizarre deal to continue with the tour on a large, and unspecific, pay cut and effectively share out whatever the takings were each week of the tour – after our amazing orchestra had been paid their full wage of course as *they* were working on union contracts!

The pervading opinion in the room was that '*the show must go on*'; that we were a 'family' and we all loved the show. I felt heartbroken and angry. I'd worked hard for years and made many sacrifices to be a professional actor. This wasn't amateur dramatics. When the vote was taken whether to 'go on with the show', my hand stayed down.

Things got worse when I went to a phone box outside the theatre and called my agent. She investigated the monies she'd received from the company, which she'd been paying into her accounts monthly, and it soon transpired that for several weeks she'd been sending me good money from her account and now was out of pocket herself.

For three years at drama school in London, I'd worn the same clothes, worked cash jobs between terms ('landscape gardening' aka digging ditches), never went out and had lived on milkshakes and baked potatoes. Yet I'd somehow achieved the impossible and got through the whole thing without a wealthy family or taking a student loan. It felt like I was the last person in the country to do this, but now, here I was broke again and over a thousand pounds in debt to my agent.

MUTINY IN MANCHESTER, OR, 'UP THE WORKERS'. OR, 'FUCK THIS, I'M OFF'

We shuffled on from Liverpool to the Manchester Palace Theatre, where we played a few shows and then our self-governed pay day approached. I was now definitely the most out-of-pocket member of the entire cast and I'd asked to receive my backdated wages that night to bring me level with everyone else.

A queue of actors filled the staircase outside the dressing room of the elected actors' rep, who had the cash to share amongst us. I'd got myself there an hour early to be at the front of the queue, to put in my request while the going was good, but I was only offered the hundred pounds or so that everyone else was getting. Though polite, it was a clear stalemate: the pressure to just 'muck in' like everyone else was huge. I knew the only card I had to play.

I was the only principal character who'd not been allotted an understudy. Young buck that I was, they presumed I'd never get ill. So, despite being led to understand I was a traitor to show business, I told them I was going to stay in that corridor in my own clothes until the money I was owed was given to me. I felt up against the wall, literally – characters from the world of Dickens started to float past me towards the stage for the opening number, tutting and cursing at me as they went.

The curtain was held. We were twenty minutes over the time the show should have begun. Then the producer arrived (no doubt wearing a bullet-proof vest). I was ushered impatiently into a dressing room, handed a brown envelope with a few extra hundred pounds in it and told to 'keep my mouth shut and get on the fucking stage'.

We performed the show that night but I'd started a ball rolling. By the end of the evening a couple of other actors had had enough. By the next day it was over.

I've been tough about money ever since. Really tough. Not about how much I get paid, but about *getting* paid. It still amazes me how long it can take to get paid for acting work. If you took that long to pay a plumber or a builder for building your new kitchen, they'd be back to rip the whole lot out from the wall.

The Dramatist by Frederick Reynolds
The Magnificent Theatre Company
Middle-Scale National Tour

My first proper, *proper,* professional job. You know, with wages and stuff.

A slightly optimistically titled theatre company ... but one that I had actually heard of. MTC specialised in digging up long-forgotten 'gems' – unperformed, unknown plays from hundreds of years ago, predominantly comedies – dusting them down and serving them up with energy if not finesse. An Equity contract too, albeit an Equity minimum wage of £214 a week. But after several months out of work and signing on at Greenwich benefits office, I was ecstatic.

The Dramatist is a cracking little play, genuinely funny, and incredibly inventive for the time it was written (1820s–1830s). The central character, Vapid, is a playwright, obsessed with stealing ideas from all he meets for his tawdry creations. But over the course of the play he begins to get the lines between fiction and reality very blurred, seems to slip into one of his own farces and has to write his way out. Stoppard would have been proud.

I was playing the fairly thankless role of the young juvenile in love with the wrong gal, but this was *such* an exciting job to me. I'd trained to be a classical actor, sort of (that was what it said on my graduation certificate anyway), and here I was, soon to be wearing tights, a sword and trying to make old-fashioned language understandable and amusing for an audience, nightly.

Even more exciting to me was the sheer length and workload of the tour. I was delighted to read in my contract that I'd have to be involved in the 'get in' and 'get out' of the set from each theatre. My country boy's working-class ethic/guilt complex would relish any heavy lifting they could throw at me.

Shortly before rehearsals began, I was at home in the damp basement flat I shared with my girlfriend in New Cross, when through the letter box dropped an excitingly full envelope containing the script, along with the flyer that advertised the show. I sat on the floor and studied the tour schedule on the back of that shiny A5 flyer until I knew it by heart, until my eyes went dry.

The Arts Council of England subsidised the company

and the remit was clearly to perform in as many different theatres and arts centres up and down the British Isles as was humanly possible in three months. There must have been thirty tour dates, all over the country. Sometimes a few nights, often only a one-night stand. Then pack the set up into the truck and get back on the road. The tour culminated in two weeks at a theatre in London. It looked exhausting... Perfect!

DARLING

It's a well-known fact that actors call people 'luvvie' and 'darling' only because they can't remember their names. The brain sponge is so full, or finally exhausted, from learning hundreds of thousands of lines of dialogue over the years that there is nothing left for inconsequential details like people's real names. (Although, interestingly, actors are fantastically good at remembering casting directors' names.)

These days, I've fallen into the cliché and am terrible with names. Try as I might, it's not my strength, and actors who I adored working with only a few months before will look at me with appalled faces as I flounder around after bumping into them, and finally fail to introduce them properly to my wife or kids. But as I sit here thinking about some of these early jobs, I remember the names as well as the faces: early experiences, like first loves, seem to use indelible ink to write their stories upon us.

Rehearsals for *The Dramatist* were in a church hall in the middle of Richmond Green. It was late summer. I'd be there nearly an hour early to sit on a bench outside the church and walk through the previous day's work, to ensure that this day's work would please the Gods of

Thespis... I exaggerate only slightly.

The cast were not only lovely but really good, experienced, professional actors, with the exception of our intrepid director, who ran the company and had given himself the lead role.

I think it's worth pausing to paint a little picture of our valiant leader, as he featured in much of the next year or two of my working life. Ben Crocker was childlike in many ways; he was still in his thirties, just, but his taste in clothes and cigars made him seem older. I might be imagining that he drove an old Jag, but it fits the image.

Ben had, until a few years previously, worked in the City, a stocks and shares man who really enjoyed his high-end amateur dramatics at the weekend. The story I was told was that he'd had an incredible windfall with some shares, cashed them in and started the company. His father (or grandfather?) had been a kind of actor/manager back in the day, and I think it was a romantic attachment to this legacy that led him to not only direct, but also cast himself in a leading role in all of the company's productions. Don't get me wrong, he was doing a great job of running that company, all credit to him. But, his directing style could best be described as 'impatiently gag led', and his acting style was that of an excited amateur.

I didn't care, I was grateful. The play was well written. It worked. We could, and often did direct ourselves. I was chuffed to bits to be on board.

FIRST CIRCUS FAMILY

The tour took off and I found myself learning at a pace. From the spaces we were playing, each theatre requiring a different energy and vocal attack, I learnt a great deal from the length of the run. I had never had to play the same part for more than a few weeks before. I had to get 'show legs' for the first time. I also learnt from the audiences. They varied from the tiny and silent to the enormous and raucous. (We also encountered the enormous and silent variety, which were scariest of all.)

But mostly I learnt from the actors and stage managers surrounding me. We were living, and working and travelling together non-stop for many months. It was my first experience of a real circus family, all for one and one for all; conversations seemed endless, always available and always surprising. I wonder how different this might have been had we all had mobile phones and email ever ready? Laughter was littered through my days.

Here, I was an equal. Age didn't mean anything, it was what you did on stage that mattered. Respect was earned, and post-show cheese and wine was consumed.

A TIME MACHINE IN NORTH YORKSHIRE

Some people collect autographs, others soap, or stickers from apples, or belly button fluff, or beermats. But, I've always collected theatres – visits to new theatres. And I may have picked up the habit on these early tours.

The insides of theatres have always taken my breath away and altered my state of mind, much in the way a lot of people feel when walking into a beautiful church or cathedral for the first time. Deep down, that's what these buildings are to me: churches, sculptures of hope and communion, where collections of strangers come to share an experience, to see the shaman shake the story stick. Happy atheist that I am, this has always moved me and given me hope.

Only a middle-scale tour like this would have been booked in to some of these little hidden theatres, arts centres and converted chapels and churches, scattered across the country. Without these jobs, I may never have known of their existence.

The absolute gem from this whistle-stop tour of England had to be the Georgian Theatre Royal in Richmond, North Yorkshire. Look it up on the internet, please, otherwise you might think I'm exaggerating. Built in 1788 by the actor/manager Samuel Butler, it is the oldest totally original working theatre in the country. It is teeny-weeny and utterly beautiful. A tiny, chocolate box of a theatre, with wooden benches in the stalls below and a small circle of audience above that you felt you could reach out and touch. We were to play a couple of nights there and one of them was to be a unique experience.

The Dramatist was, in 1995, an unknown play, but back in the 1800s it'd had a brief moment of popularity and had gone into the repertoire of a few acting companies up and down the land. It just so happened that the last recorded performance of *The Dramatist* was in Richmond, North Yorkshire. They had a lovely little museum attached to the theatre and there, for all to see, was a Georgian playbill advertising a performance of *The Dramatist* at The Georgian Theatre Royal, Richmond in 1830 (something). This blew my mind a bit, but not nearly as much as the gala performance later that night – lit only by old-style footlights and with many of the audience in Georgian costume. They also happened to be a brilliant audience who laughed loudly and when the play took flight, it really was as if we had turned that theatre into a time machine for a couple of hours. I felt I could reach out and touch the ghosts of ham actors past and felt sure they approved heartily of my performance as young 'Neville'. A performance that in other venues, if I was being honest, had begun to smell a little ripe.

LONDON BABY

We finally arrived in London for our run at the Lilian Baylis Theatre; a 180-seat studio theatre attached to the famous Sadler's Wells Dance Theatre in Islington.

After the companionship of the road, it felt strange for us all to fly straight off after each show to catch a bus, tube or train home to our girlfriends, boyfriends, children or pets. But I was finally a professional actor performing in London – where who knew who might be watching, and friends and, more importantly, critics were coming to see us.

It wasn't just vanity that had me excited about the chance of being mentioned in reviews, or in national papers. There was a pragmatic desire for these things too. I've always subscribed to Paul McCartney's approach to being reviewed: 'if you believe the good ones, you have to believe the bad ones.' And I do, though it's often a little painful. But back then, it meant something more. I'd somehow chanced upon this thing called acting a good deal later in life than most people catch the bug; it was a way of life totally out of the ken of anyone I grew up with and I was keenly aware that I was starting out as near the bottom rung of the ladder as you could get. I wasn't looked after by a powerful agent; I had no friends or family in the business; no family money or any other way of earning a living to fall back on. This was *it*. I bloody loved it, and wanted to stay, thank you very much, so every column inch that mentioned my name in an actual piece of public

lie injured (or 'sojourning' as Keats would put it) on the snow-covered bank of the lake. The lovely costume lady had generously donated the one and only hot water bottle to me but, by the end of a full day in that suit on the snow, I couldn't feel any sensation in my fingers or toes and had to get help doing up laces and buttons. My toes itched like they were on fire for weeks afterwards. Lucky it was only a three-day shoot or they might have dropped off.

But it was a great first film. The director of photography and camera operator were brothers, who I really clicked with – Howard Ford operating the camera, and Jon Ford lighting it all. Roughly seventeen years later this connection would bear some extraordinary fruit – in India of all places!

Loot by Joe Orton
Magnificent Theatre Company, National Tour

I'm certain Gary Oldman got his performance spot on as the playwright Joe Orton in the movie *Prick Up Your Ears*. That permanent naughty twinkle in his eyes. The more serious the situation, the funnier life seemed to him. Well, I believe his writing contains an actual magic. It's really, really good writing, on every level. But more than that, when you read it, and especially when you perform it, his naughtiness travels unfiltered and undiluted from the Islington bedsit he was writing it in, to the rehearsal room the actors are working in many decades later. It feels like he's there; a mate, a naughty, non-judgemental pal giggling away in the corner of the room as you work, and you daren't look at him because you know you'll never be able to stop laughing.

CENTRE MIDFIELD, DOWN STAGE RIGHT

A small footballing detour as I try to explain why this was such a happy and fulfilling job for me. I played a great deal of football for many years when I was younger, to a fairly high level. I was never flashy, goals were rare, and overhead kicks and other trick shots didn't interest me. What I loved was reading the game, connecting a useful, accurate pass at the right time to someone who *could* do the wonder stuff that got the goals. Taking the ball from an opponent before he'd even seen me coming.

I eventually found the perfect place to play, or it found me. Centre midfield; an exhausting position that required running the entire length of the pitch again and again as part of both defending and attacking play. But I was always needed, always 'useful'. 'He's a useful player, Mr Millson,' my father would occasionally hear from those who knew. (Dad knew next to nothing about football but never missed a game.)

Playing the part of Dennis in *Loot* was a perfect centre midfield acting gig. He was not the lead role, in fact he said relatively few lines, but he was almost always on stage, part of the action and always part of the comedy. Over the course of the tour, night after night, week after week, I took a perverse amount of pleasure in the long stretches of the play where I was on stage, but only called upon to speak every few pages. It fascinated me how much my focus, my listening, the timing of my reactions and looks, even my position on the stage, could help others get 'their' laughs. I would secretly make experiments, tiny adjustments, and see if I could help make another person's line get an even bigger laugh the following night if I listened harder, stayed in the moment more, or planned my reaction less. How genuinely surprised could I be? If I tune out slightly during this section but start *really* listening just before that section, will it help focus the audience for that moment there etc etc? It was *fun*. A secret science that made every night a joy.

My son, Gabriel, has developed (through no nudging from me) into a very fine footballer. He plays for the town team, and is far better than I was at his age. His favourite position is, you guessed it, centre midfield, and the coaches often tell me what an incredibly 'useful' player he is.

HOLDING THE CORPSE
All that lovely stuff about the craft of comedy I was learning was only of use when I was able to stand there, listening and following the action of the scene. It wasn't quite so great when I was shaking with laughter or crawling off stage on my hands and knees, begging the stage manager to slap me hard to stop my uncontrollable giggles.

I don't think I've ever known a company that corpsed as much as this one. I blame Joe Orton's twinkle. Even during rehearsals, it was ludicrous. No one was trying to make anyone else laugh but it seemed an ever-present danger. Orton requires fairly silly things to be said very seriously for it to work. We also had a leading man, Philip Dunbar, playing Inspector Truscott, who had a ridiculous level of twinkle. It was very hard to look him in the eye.

Ben Crocker's finest hour as a director might just have been the way he finally dealt with this incredibly giggly company of actors. We had only one dress rehearsal before we opened the show at the first venue of our tour, which I think was the Wilde Theatre, Bracknell. I know, it's terrible when actors keep showing off about the glamorous places they've travelled to but I can't help it...

We were maybe half an hour from the end of the dress rehearsal and had entered a vortex of painful laughter, which none of us seemed able to pull out of. Suddenly, mid-scene, mid-struggle, our director was on stage, amongst us. He calmly sat down on part of the set and said, 'It's half past five now and you all need to eat, so we should probably just forget about this dress rehearsal and take a dinner break. Good luck tonight, have a lovely first show.' No bollocking could have had the same effect. He looked so disappointed, it was awful. None of us were trying to be naughty. It was like a disease.

Without any discussion we all began a campaign of professionalism. The first night went well, a solid performance of a really great play. In fact, weeks and weeks went by of solid performances. Audiences were reasonably large, but not exactly taking the roof off with laughter.

I can't remember which theatre we were in but I do remember the precise line of the play where it all went wrong. It was in the second half, where I spent most of my time down stage right, holding, aptly enough, the mummified corpse of the man whose funeral the play is set around. We hadn't had a big audience for a while but this night was packed and they were loving it. We were a well-oiled machine – until…

TRUSCOTT: 'It reminds me of the case of the limbless girl killer.'
HAL: 'Who'd kill a limbless girl?'

Pause.

TRUSCOTT: 'She was the killer.'

Not that funny a line? Agreed, and there are way funnier in the play. But live theatre is a strange thing and on this night, in that theatre, that line of dialogue *really* tickled them. A large laugh rolled in, where we weren't used to it, but, pros that we were we waited, and when it was calming down we tried to get back on track. But something wouldn't let us; the entire audience seemed to have felt our surprise, and Philip Dunbar's face was just bloody funny at the best of times so the laugh rolled again. Again we paused. Again it rolled. We waited, then breathed in to restart the play. But Joe Orton's twinkle had crept out of its box and was sneaking up our trouser legs.

It was a perfect circle of laughter between the audience and us. Unexplainable; wonderful and *terrible*. It went down in the stage manager's notes as a six-minute corpse. Weeks of suppressed giggles came pouring out. The brilliant Celia Nelson, who was playing Nurse McMahon, only made the whole thing funnier for audience and cast by somehow never laughing, just watching serenely as actors all around her variously slid to the floor, faced walls, cried for help or slapped themselves in the face.

I was in real trouble with giggling for the rest of the tour. Indeed the ghost of that night didn't leave me for many years. I've learnt to embrace all that happens on stage now and positively invite the unexpected, but for years and years I was afraid of losing control like that in front of people who had paid real money to see professionals. The shame of it was awful. But I have learnt to celebrate the magic of it. On the rare occasions that I direct I am always secretly thrilled when my actors get to the stage of rehearsals where they start to get the giggles; not through 'secret' practical jokes but through trust, connection with each other and the fun of it all, like children playing at the back of class. It's a good sign. It is human. It is joyful, but needs to be shared with the audience, harnessed and poured back into the play.

MY DAD SETS ME FREE IN BURY ST EDMUNDS

Apart from the night I forgot to put my protective cricket box down my pants for the scene where Truscott grabs me hard by the balls while he interrogates me, and poor Philip Dunbar, in front of a packed house, sent one of my bollocks out of all reach for nearly a week – apart from that I have only one other clear memory and ever-present lesson from this job.

My parents were always rock-solid pillars of support, but in a very non-interfering way. Money rarely flowed freely in our family, in fact it was often in very short supply, but I could fill a book with the unexpected, generous and inventive ways they found to encourage me and keep me moving through drama school and these early years of being an actor.

They came to see almost everything I did and, sometimes, my dad would find a way to see even the stuff he wasn't supposed to. Through private showings of end-of-term work at college and then at drama school, Dad's booming laugh was somehow always out there. He didn't care who had to be bribed, or tickled with jokes, to let him in.

One brief tale to illustrate: one of my final shows before leaving the Rose Bruford College of Speech and Drama was playing Romeo in *Romeo and Juliet* – an honour, a joy, and a tour around the South of France to boot! An amazing experience, but hard work in incredible heat. We were scheduled to play a week at the Agen Shakespeare Festival 1994, a week in which I had already passed out mid balcony scene from heatstroke and got drunk for the first time in my life after being spurned by our beautiful stage manager, for whom I had secretly held a bit of a torch for three years. I remember during the next day's hungover performance hearing a laugh out in the audience that sounded incredibly like my dad's. But it couldn't have been. I was in a tiny town in the middle of nowhere in the South of France and he was busy trying to make ends meet at home.

The laugh came again – and there was no mistaking it. It was him.

My smile could have lit up the theatre. My parents had planned a surprise flying visit of support; as part of a cheap holiday they had carefully not told me about, they had driven the whole way and, before internet and mobile phones, had somehow found the sweaty, converted warehouse we were performing in and snuck into their seats. I can only imagine how exciting this must have been for them.

Back to 1996 then, where 22-year-old me was so looking forward to seeing his mum and dad who were coming to watch *Loot* at the Theatre Royal, Bury St Edmunds. I hadn't seen my parents for a little while and was especially excited to see my dad who had recently finished a long and nasty course of chemotherapy. His first. There were more to come. He was only forty-three years old when he had been diagnosed the year before with Non-Hodgkin Lymphoma.

We finished that evening's show, a pretty average performance with no serious laughter spasms from anyone, on stage

29

or in the audience. I met Mum and Dad in the theatre bar afterwards and I must have been saying something about what a daft and silly job acting was, when Dad suddenly stopped me. He grabbed me by the arm, looked me in the eye and said, 'Oi, never, *ever,* think what you do isn't useful, or important. You just helped to make hundreds of people laugh for over two hours. In this shitty world, Joe, that is priceless. So don't let me hear you apologising for what you do again.'

That was it, we moved swiftly on. I'm not sure Dad ever knew what a gift those words were. What they unlocked. I was incredibly close to my father. I idolised him and had watched him work his fingers to the bone almost 365 days a year my entire childhood. My mum too. Hard, hard work, sometimes for very little reward. Despite their support, I felt strong, working-class guilt at what a joyful thing my job was when I was doing it, and how simple it must look to the untrained eye.

Sometimes, at a social occasion or at one of my children's school concerts with lots of 'grown-ups' around with 'real' jobs, I can still slip into this self-depreciating habit. Less and less as the years go by, but I know my dad's smiling spirit is always standing by, ready to clip me round the ear and set me straight.

Joe's Story
Bournemouth Film School

Three days in Bournemouth playing a disabled chap in a wheelchair, for travel expenses and a copy of the film. That's all you need to know about that one.

Artaud at Rodez by Charles Marowitz
Finborough Theatre

STAGE DOOR JOHNNIE

After *Loot*, I was out of work again, with very thin audition prospects. The government had recently made changes that made it effectively impossible to reapply for unemployment benefit. I tried to find some kind of job that would let me take time out to attend any auditions that might come in. The obvious job for actors is evening bar work but I was keeping that at a long arm's length. I grew up in a pub. I'd had a wonderful time living in one, but working in one has never appealed to me. Perhaps if my mum and dad had been actors I'd have run straight off to work in a pub.

I had experience as a stage manager and as a theatre flyman so went from stage door to stage door at every West End theatre, leaving my contact details, and was eventually offered a temporary job for a couple of months as the stage door keeper at the Ambassadors Theatre.

I rather liked the cupboard I occupied beside the stage door and the work was numbingly simple. I kept myself busy with 'Joey's Jobs' and read a lot of books sitting in that little sentry box.

I would gaze out of my tiny window at the stage door of the theatre opposite, where lucky actors were wandering in every evening to perform *The Mousetrap*. Their lives seemed like a dream to me; yes, it was a cheesy old thriller but those people were getting paid to *act* in the *West End* for a *year!* I was nakedly jealous.

The show I was keeping door for was a very different number; it was a musical called *Dames at Sea!* It starred

Peter Duncan of *Blue Peter* fame. I had, as it happened, spent a long summer with Peter when I was seventeen as an assistant stage manager on a musical called *The Card* at the Watermill Theatre, Newbury, near where I grew up. He'd been friendly enough with me back then but had no idea who I was anymore and 'didn't really fancy a chat about acting'.

I was pretty much invisible to the entire cast as they returned their dressing room keys to me. I quietly noted this and vowed to always be decent to stage door keepers, wherever I worked. But I enjoyed the job and, like a hungry animal, was kept alive by the mere whiff of the performances happening so close to me every night.

I was searching for acting work every single day. Something eventually came in for me.

'I'll show them,' I said to myself. 'They can shove their stage door up their arses – I'm off to do an obscure play by Charles Marowitz for no money, above a pub, for a student director for a whole week's run!'

THEATRE OF CRUELTY – OR, WHY DON'T WE GET A DISCOUNT AT THE BAR?

There is not a great deal to tell about *Artaud at Rodez* except that it was a surprisingly good production. There was, I'm ashamed to admit, yet again, rather a lot of giggling on stage from me. A couple of good friends I knew from drama school were in it with me and the material was, to put it mildly, insane: a play written by a self-confessed madman about a collection of madmen in theatres and mental institutions, and many of us were dressed in tight, tank-top vests, so we were up against it.

What was significant, and perhaps meant to be from this

experience, was that a new friend and ally emerged in one of my cast mates, Stuart Mullins. We were to go on to become great friends and also to create and run the theatre company *PURSUED BY A BEAR* together for seven years, a theatre company that's still going strong today.

The Fantasticks by Harvey Schmidt and Tom Jones
King's Head Theatre, Islington

UP ON THE ROOF

I'm going to take you on a brief detour: a jump cut to the year 1990.

When I was just sixteen years old, living on a farm in the middle of nowhere in Berkshire and busy having too much fun on a performing arts course at the now bull-dozed Newbury College, I was faced with having to find theatre-related work experience for a couple of weeks during the summer holiday as a component of the course. I had some leanings towards stage management, carpentry and set building. I can't remember what led me there or who gave me the phone number, but I called and somehow persuaded The King's Head Theatre in Islington, London, to take me on as very definitely unpaid stage management help. They seemed more than happy to have me there, with promises that I would get plenty of opportunity to practise my set-building skills.

My brother, Pete, was living in London and trying to make it as a rock star. When I arrived to squat on his floor, it seemed to me incredibly bohemian, cool and grown up. In retrospect, it must have been a significant pain in the arse for him; an annoyingly upbeat, appallingly dressed, sweaty teenager taking up valuable privacy and floor space in his tiny room in a shared flat in Muswell Hill.

What was only supposed to be two weeks' gentle work experience turned into many more weeks of a very British kind of child exploitation. Upon arrival at the theatre, I was quickly put to work every day, and long into several nights, in a basement under a pub at the other end of Islington, helping to build and paint the sets for the next show, *Here Come the Clowns*. The show's designer / set builder / prop master / costume wrangler (this was fringe theatre after all) was a lovely, quiet man, who took me under his wing for that first week. Until I arrived, he was building and painting a complicated circus-themed set single-handedly. So he was delighted to have a hard-working, if unskilled, assistant.

We would climb up from the basement to take tea breaks in the sun, both covered in sawdust, paint and sweat. Islington wasn't then the clean and trendy spot it is now, but I loved it.

By the end of the week, the set was built, painted, and installed in the theatre. We even had time for him to drive me to a pub theatre in Deptford, South London where another show he was designing was opening. I can still see myself struggling to get the perspective right on the telegraph wires I was painting on top of the beautiful sky-scape he had created. He didn't talk much but he looked after me, fed me whenever possible, respected me, and taught me a lot. I was beginning to think that this set-building malarkey might do as a career for me.

Sadly, he was not a permanent member of the theatre staff and after a little over ten days together, he was on his way, back to wherever he'd come from to look for more shows to design. This was fringe theatre and he was as poor as a church mouse, but somehow he found a few pounds to give me as we parted and warned me to watch out for myself at the King's Head…

The King's Head Theatre of 1990 was a strange beast. A 'supper theatre', where ticket prices included a three-course meal at tables in the tiny auditorium, followed by the show. I saw the disgusting kitchen the meals were prepared in and was amazed more people weren't poisoned. The whole operation was overseen by the infamous and now deceased Dan Crawford. An American by birth, Dan was a wild-haired, wild-eyed spirit who flew through rooms and never looked anyone in the eye. He had opened up this music and theatre venue decades before and it was probably the very first 'fringe theatre' in London. Over the years, it had been host to a few important productions, and a few commercial successes that had transferred to the West End and even Broadway, but it was always authentic in its threadbare qualities. The building was freehold, not answerable to any brewery, landlords or higher authority. The massive and noisy till behind the bar still added things up by shillings and guineas and the bar staff were taught to make the conversions. Dan was rumoured never to have had a bank account or to have paid tax. He was also rumoured to be a practising wizard or warlock or druid (or some such) in his spare time. I doubted it not.

I was put to work in the office. My duties were few: answering the rarely ringing phone and taking whatever rambling, nonsensical message was left. If Dan was in the room, I had to write down the name of whoever was calling and pass the paper over for him to see. If he shook his head then I was to state clearly that he wasn't in the building and I didn't know when he would return.

Another duty was 'filing' the letters from actors. I had no strong leaning towards acting myself at this point so felt no pain in following my orders. Hundreds upon hundreds of shiny ten-by-eight photographs of desperate actors were either put straight into the specific dustbin with 'Actors' written on it (I wish I was making this up), or, if they had included a large stamped addressed envelope, sent back to them with the stock, 'nothing for you at this time' letter. I wonder how many sixteen-year-old hands were to dispose of my own hopeful letters in later years? Apart from these duties I was bored to death, and spent much of my time staring out of the window at the birds flying around the beautiful church over the road.

I wasn't always alone in the office. Every other day or so, a woman in her late thirties was in there with me, who was some kind of administrator. We talked a little, she seemed lovely and I enjoyed making her laugh whenever she was there. She discovered how poor I was, thought it awful that I couldn't afford to get out and see London and kindly offered to take me out at the weekend to take in some of the sights. This we duly did: a bus tour, a gallery somewhere, and then she offered to cook me dinner back at her place in Islington. I wasn't entirely green and had noticed her looking at me slightly hungrily. I thought it flattering, funny even, but nothing serious. She knew I was sixteen.

I soon thought differently when back at her flat I was left sitting on a sofa for an unusually long time while she 'popped to the loo'. She re-entered in the full clichéd seduction uniform of black stockings, suspenders and some kind of basque. She lowered herself onto the sofa next to me. Whatever fantasies I may have occasionally entertained about encounters with an older woman vanished. Without a word, or a backward glance I was out of that door and away down the road.

I was certainly learning a lot on this 'work experience'. I desperately didn't want to run into that lady again – I felt awful for letting her down as much as anything. So I found the boss and begged to get back to some set building. As it happened, there was nothing being built at the moment but, if I wanted some similar experience, Dan had a 'great idea … just great'. Without ever agreeing myself that it was a 'great idea', I was, before I knew it, up in the windowless loft of the building converting the dark and filthy Victorian squalor into a 'pretty' bedroom for Dan's nine-year-old daughter, Katy.

A handyman was with me for the first day or two. He spoke barely any English and was a far cry from the lovely man I'd worked with only a week or two before. He put the stairs and wooden braces in place for room dividers while I cleaned hundreds of years of bat shit and clutter into bags and boxes. I was then left alone for a couple of days to fit the insulation into the floor cavities and nail the floorboards down.

Once the loft was complete I was moved back into the theatre to work for a week or so as assistant stage manager on a fantastic play called *Deceptions*. Then back to Berkshire I went. Little did I know that six years later I would return to that building to work on its stage.

CUT TO…

Six years later, back in dear old 1996 after yet another audition won by 'Joey's Jobs', I found myself reading and singing for that same shifty-eyed old wizard, Dan

Crawford. I had no real desire to be in musicals but they were so much easier to get auditions for than straight plays. I could hold a tune and was determined to work, so had applied in earnest to be seen for the young lead in *The Fantasticks*. I knew this musical had been running just off Broadway for over fifty years but had never enjoyed real success in London.

I sang my little heart out and read in my best cheesy American accent. Dan and the musical director seemed impressed, or desperate, but I was still in the room.

Some small talk was entered into, so I asked, 'Do you not remember me, Dan?'

Shifty-shifty, shift-shift, went his eyes under those enormous wizard's eyebrows…

'Er, no. Should I?'

'Well, no, probably not, but, when I was sixteen you got me to convert your loft into your daughter's bedroom, for no money…'

Silence.

Followed by even less eye contact. Followed by a long journey home.

Where was that filter most people seem to be born with? I often used to think of a sign one of my teachers had above his desk at school. It read, 'Always make sure brain is engaged before opening mouth'. Great advice. Couldn't do it. I still have trouble. I like David Mamet's version of the same motto even more: 'Silence builds a fence for wisdom.' I might get that as a tattoo.

Well, they must have been desperate because I got the job. It was a non-Equity, fringe contract paying £115 a week, but it would be a high-profile show, seen by many and reviewed by all. And Matt was a great, if soppy, part.

I had a couple of beautiful songs and a wonderful duet in the show. I couldn't wait.

It was therefore something of a shock on the first day of rehearsal to discover that the very young actress playing my lover was none other than the 'Katy' whose bedroom I had laid the floorboards for six years previously.

VIOLET ELIZABETH BLOT

Katy was a sweet girl, but it was hard to become her pal. This was an important job for me. All my scenes were with her and she was not an actress. She was a fifteen-year-old schoolgirl with a fairly serious lisp, who fancied having a go at singing in musicals, and whose daddy ran a theatre. She was also close to tone deaf. Some of her harmonising made me shiver. She was also clumsier than a clown and suffered from acute halitosis. Many weeks later, I overheard her proudly telling someone backstage how she never brushed her teeth and that it drove her 'momma' mad. Lovely. It was a build-up of plaque and tartar that I was enjoying every night when we had to 'freeze' in a kiss at the end of one of our songs. How kind she thought I was to keep offering her my mints. I was just trying to survive.

The rest of the cast were excellent, experienced pros and I loved working with them, including the extraordinarily long-haired and very 'showbiz' Jonathon Morris playing our narrator. I had grown up watching him in the 1980s sitcom *Bread*. He had just finished playing the same role he was playing for us now in a big budget movie of *The Fantasticks* made by MGM, and had recently appeared in a West End run as Frank-N-Furter in *The Rocky Horror Show*. Thanks to him, we were getting lots of press attention leading up to our first night. I wondered if somehow he might be getting more than £115 a week. Curiously, the movie of *The Fantasticks,* which he really did star in, has never been released.

Jonathon had actual fans. I sat next to him in the unbelievably small dressing room we all shared backstage. During our opening week, he would get a daily delivery of fan mail, mostly from the *Rocky Horror* fans who were a dedicated breed. He plopped one letter onto my desk with a smirk and said, 'You open it. I recognise the handwriting, you open it.' I duly did so – and discovered a Polaroid photograph of a particularly sweaty and unkempt vagina. It had the words, 'PLEASE help yourself' and a telephone number written underneath.

Jonathon also had kirby grips in his hair, hundreds of them. They sparkled under the stage lights and I wondered aloud if he had any other way of keeping that mane of hair out of his face. It was an odd look and a very small theatre. He told me no one would notice. They did. Those kirby grips got more column inches in the reviews than any of us.

But the show was a bit of a hit, despite a press night where I managed to land squarely on one critic's foot after my dramatic leap off the stage during a chase. It was my first real London Press Night, with all the papers in and a scattering of famous faces out there. As I finished one of my big numbers, which I sang under a spotlight in the aisle of the theatre, Michael Winner stood up right next to me to applaud my efforts and literally spat in my face as he shouted, 'Very. Bloody. Good!'

After another performance, I was introduced to Burt Bacharach, who had loved the show and told me I had a 'beautiful voice'! He must have been jet-lagged.

I got my first personal and unkind reviews in amongst the raves, but managed to take them with a pinch of salt. Especially the funny ones. 'Joseph Millson joins a long line of juvenile leads who fade into the King's Head wallpaper' was a personal favourite.

Our director was thrilled and the run was extended, twice. I think it may have been one of the longer runs in the theatre's history. We were sold out, so I was intrigued as to why we couldn't perhaps be paid a little more than £115 a week, a figure that could barely keep my head above water. 'You will all get fantastic money when we transfer to the West End,' Dan would assure me, as he looked at my nose, my ears, anywhere but my eyes. My agent had heard nothing about a West End transfer, however, and I had begun to take note of another phenomenon…

BUCKET MONEY

Every night of every single performance of every single production in that theatre, once the audience were in their seats, Dan Crawford would take to the stage in his deliberately shabby clothes, holding a large bucket, and give a well-designed, witty little speech about how the theatre wasn't funded; how the room they were all sitting in was nearly two hundred years old, the roof was in a terrible state of repair and they were 'lucky it wasn't raining' (cue laughter). 'Could y'all dig deep into your pockets and give whatever you can towards our roof renovation fund…?'

I often saw that bucket filled halfway to the brim with paper money. And I'd seen Dan make this exact same speech, with the exact same bucket, several times six years before when I was there on work experience. So, after some investigation, I discovered that to the best of anyone's knowledge, no maintenance work had *ever* been performed. I smelled a rat. And not just the dead one we'd found in the backstage toilet.

I'm not sure I would have taken matters into my own hands had Dan not been so unsympathetic when I told him one day that my treasured make-up box, which had been a gift from my parents and contained expensive make-up and a host of personal knick-knacks, had been stolen from the dressing rooms. He didn't care. Well, I didn't miss a beat. I told him it was fine, not to worry, but, 'Listen, Dan, is it OK if I start doing my pre-show warm-ups up in your flat? It's just so cramped down here on that stage…' 'Of course, of course,' said the wizard of Islington. 'The keys are in the office, just lock up after you're done.'

That bucket money had to be somewhere. Singing, 'mee, mee, mee, la, la, la,' loudly as I went, I searched the flat. I discovered tightly rolled wraps and envelopes of cash. Some of them covered in dust. Behind cereal packets, in cupboards, behind books, underneath dusty awards. I thought about it carefully, and did some sums. Over the next few weeks, I became very dedicated to my warm-ups and gradually brought my wage up to Equity minimum, throwing in a couple of hundred for work on the loft for good measure.

The Rivals by Richard Brinsley Sheridan
Magnificent Theatre Company
National Tour

A few weeks into the run of *The Fantasticks,* good old Ben Crocker came through with an amazing offer. He wanted me to play the lead role of Jack Absolute in a National Tour of *The Rivals*, a play I'd loved ever since watching a BBC TV production of it, starring Michael Hordern and Patrick Ryecart, on video in the library at drama school. It was a part that leapt off the page at me. I felt I could really shine in it and I'd read about so many great actors' performances in the role. I accepted at once, and even persuaded Ben to let my girlfriend, Cathy, who though a great actress hadn't yet had a decent job since leaving college, audition for the small but perfectly formed role of Lucy. She got the job and all was suddenly roses. Cathy's contract included performing some stage management duties whilst on tour, but we were thrilled. We'd been poor for so long and now we would not only be working on a great job together but earning two wages.

There was a slight problem when the original short run of *The Fantasticks* kept getting extended due to its success. When Dan Crawford asked us all to stay for an extra month, I had to tell him I couldn't as I was booked to start rehearsals. He was horrified. 'But I'm absolutely certain we'll be transferring to the West End straight after this. You can't go on tour. It'll ruin this for everyone and it's *such* an important role for you to play in the West End.'

'But, Dan, my agent hasn't heard anything about this.'

Shifty-shifty, shift-shift, went that eye contact again. 'No, no, I'm just waiting for the final deal to be done but, I'll call her this afternoon…'

Evidence of a run in the West End remained thin and I wasn't going to let a chance to play in one of the greatest comedies ever written slip by for a 'maybe'.

JOEY TWO JOBS

The Fantasticks was keeping me busy every night, with matinées on Saturdays, for three out of the four weeks of rehearsal for *The Rivals*. These two gigs were, of course, occurring at different ends of London and I lived near neither of them. I was exhausted, but happy as the proverbial pig in shit. I leant in towards the heavy workload with a smile. I was in a hurry to clock up experience and here I was, rehearsing a bit of classical theatre by day and performing in a musical by night. I kept a box of neat glucose powder in my dressing room at The King's Head and would shovel the stuff into my mouth to give me energy to get through.

But even this wasn't enough to sate my thirst for work. On the first day of rehearsal for *The Rivals,* when Ben said to us all at the read-through that he would read in the small part of The Coachman (who appears only in the opening scene of the play) as it hadn't yet been cast, I immediately announced, 'I can do it. Jack doesn't appear on stage for ten pages, I'll have plenty of time to change.'

Ben let me read the part that day and at a tea break asked me if I was serious. I told him I was. 'But, Joe, you are playing the leading role. The coachman is a tiny part meant for a burly old man.' He'd been planning to employ an extra assistant stage manager nearer the opening week who could act well enough to perform this small scene too. I told him he could save himself a wage, promised him the audience would never know it was me and that I'd be helping Cath backstage whenever I could anyway. I was suddenly more excited about this possibility than about playing the handsome young lead. I've always felt freer to express myself the less I've felt like me on stage.

God love him, he said yes. I think the saving a wage thing swung it.

'LORD, IT'S HARD TO BE HUMBLE WHEN YOU'RE PERFECT IN EVERY WAY'

It's a fascinating experience writing some of these chapters, reaching back into the soggy grey matter to scrape out these memories. Thus far it has been enjoyable. I've had a smile on my face a lot of the time as I remember the excitement and struggle of these early jobs.

But I find myself not wanting to look this particular younger me in the eye. If I met him tomorrow, I'm not sure how much I would like the 22-year-old Joseph Millson. In fact I'm fairly certain I'd want to slap him. Or at least pull his chair out from under him as he went to sit down.

I see a young man in such a hurry. A hurry to do what? To test himself? To prove himself? To create his own 'legend'? I was almost insanely certain of my potential. Like a racehorse smelling a big track for the first time. I had read the play so often I could see and hear exactly how it should play. There it is: that toxic word, 'should'. How much easier might life be if we erased its existence and replaced it with 'could'.

My behaviour in rehearsals verged on the autistic. The 'correct' timing of the dialogue, positioning of the actors, even the pacing of the scene changes seemed so obvious. Each wrong note and inflection pained me. I would bite my lip, twitch, sigh, grunt and shake, as actors mumbled and tip-toed through rehearsals. I don't think I said anything out loud but I can only imagine the pained expression I was wearing all day long.

The lovely actress playing opposite me as Lydia Languish

burst into tears one day mid-rehearsal, apparently for no reason. I thought she was just struggling with the lines, but later at home Cath told me she was upset because she thought I thought she was a bad actress. I had no idea what had given her that impression, and sadly, absolutely no sympathy. This wasn't a 'love-in'. I wasn't there to make friends and if she couldn't stand the heat she should get out of the kitchen.

Oh, Millson.

I've always had to learn things the hard way, through falling flat on my face, through actual physical experience. Even if I could teleport back to 1996, to take that barrel-chested young man for a pint and gently suggest that it might be healthy to stop looking for perfection, to remember kindness, that acceptance is the key to work on stage and in front of the camera, that theatre is a moveable feast, will be different every night and is, more importantly, always a *collaborative* art form, he wouldn't have listened.

I do, however, remember the moment I noticed my own behaviour and I still often think of this small event with shame.

NOTE TO SELF

It is often said that, 'If you can't spot the arsehole in the company, it's probably you.' And it might just be true. We'd been on tour for a few weeks. My perfectionist side was having a few sleepless nights but the play was working. Our intrepid director hadn't seen the show for a while and turned up somewhere to watch a matinée. He called a note session for the entire company backstage before the evening show. It seemed perfunctory to me; he was only giving us notes because he felt he had to. I was now on my third production with Ben, all too aware of his taste. I was frustrated by everything he said. When he asked me, in front of the whole company, not to do some little new thing he'd noticed in that afternoon's show, I blew my top. I was way ahead of him. Surely he knew I was always making small experiments with every scene and was already aware that it (whatever 'it' was, I really can't remember) didn't work and I had no intention of repeating it; I didn't need to be told. Without engaging brain, I opened my mouth…

'For Christ's sake Ben, if you are going to give us notes, can you give us real notes?'

I wasn't aware I'd just shat all over the floor in front of everyone but that is exactly how the company responded, and rightly so. Nobody, least of all my girlfriend, spoke to me for days.

Years later, directing some theatre for the first time, I learnt a valuable lesson whilst giving one of my first note sessions. I loved my actors, wanted to help them be even more brilliant, but, as I delivered my notes, many of those actors wore expressions on their faces much as if I had just called their mother a c*nt. I suddenly remembered my outburst at poor Ben Crocker. He was just trying to help.

This is how I learn.

I over-compensated for years after this revelation. When a director gave me notes, I became a nodding dog. 'Thank you, yes, brilliant!' I would chirp. Even if I didn't agree, I was on a mission to at least look grateful and to just 'take the fucking note'. I wonder how I seem to directors these days…

BILLINGHAM AND OTHER GHOST STORIES
It wasn't a benchmark production of *The Rivals*, but, do

you know what? It wasn't bad. I honestly think I might have been slightly better in the role of The Coachman than I was as Jack. I certainly had more fun. I loved that opening scene with my old ally from *The Dramatist,* Jon Atkins, playing 'Fag'. I was disguised under a fat suit, a thick Berkshire accent, a tri-cornered hat, oversized floor-length coat, stick-on warts and an eye-patch. I had to hold an eight-foot riding whip throughout the scene and always entered through the auditorium at the top of the show, shouting my way to the stage. The eyepatch, combined with my own poor eyesight in the useable eye, and that enormous riding crop in my hand, made tripping over in front of the audience an almost nightly occurrence.

But, as the saying goes, 'leading roles make leading actors'. As Jack Absolute, I was carrying a great deal of the story every night. It's not better or worse to play a leading role, but it is different. It requires a different skill set, a drip-by-drip, ever-developing relationship with the audience. There is a responsibility not to let the ball drop. Energy and stamina are essential. I was lucky to have a crack at big parts like Jack Absolute in smaller produc-tions; to make my mistakes without the nation's press watching. We weren't expecting too much press at any of our eight or so venues; we weren't likely to see critics from the *Guardian* at the De La Warr Pavilion, Bexhill-on-Sea, and certainly not at the Forum Theatre, Billingham!!

Oh, sweet Jesus of the Christ. The Forum Theatre, Billingham. A theatre which shared its box office and entrance foyer with the town's ice rink. And, believe me, there were far more people out on the ice every night than in the theatre.

This was a particular low spot in my touring life. I mean

no offence to the good people of Billingham when I say it really is an armpit of a place. An entire town originally constructed to house the employees of the enormous ICI chemical plants that used to dominate the area. I'm guessing ninety per cent of the houses and municipal buildings were built in the 1960s, in a hurry, from an endless supply of the same grey cement. The ICI factories were long closed by the time we arrived, unemployment was at staggering levels and an air of depression and anger hung over that town like nothing I've ever felt.

Everything was grey for our week there: the weather, the people, the tea, the audiences, the eggs that Cathy and I ate every morning as part of our deal at the worst bed and breakfast in Great Britain. Our relationship was already a little strained. We had been living together for three years and Cathy was a great friend who I adored, but we weren't finding life on the road together the joy we had anticipated. Having to try to sleep in a damp room above the constant noise of the roughest pub in Tyneside, with a constantly moaning, unhappy, egotistical actor, whose costume you also had to wash every night as part of your contract, was a lot to ask of anyone. I wish I'd been kinder.

We made it though, and were still hanging on in there at the end of the three-month tour as we returned to our equally grey and equally damp basement flat in New Cross.

Cinderella
Buxton Opera House

BEING ALIVE

I was thrilled to get this little job. It followed another spell of unemployment and no money but I was also starting to feel a little claustrophobic, both in the relationship and in the tiny basement we shared. I have no doubt it was me using up most of the oxygen.

A job that took me away for five weeks to the highest town in England seemed a perfect way to get some space and perspective, literally and figuratively. Prince Charming in *Cinderella* at the beautiful Opera House in Buxton, Derbyshire, opposite some old actor who hadn't exactly starred in the TV series, *'Allo 'Allo*. My showbiz credentials were really getting going now!

We rehearsed the entire show in one week! In the cellar of the lovely hotel opposite the theatre. I enjoyed those rehearsals so much more than I did for *The Rivals*. There wasn't room for debate. You come on here, you stand there, you say this, then you get off; learning a few songs and a few dances as you go.

I couldn't believe my luck when I was told my solo number as Prince Charming was to be 'Being Alive' from Stephen Sondheim's musical, *Company*. I was a recent and devoted convert to Sondheim's musicals; I'd played John Wilkes Booth in *Assassins* as my final production at drama school, which slightly blew my mind with its brilliance. I'd also recently seen *Company* at the Donmar Warehouse and loved it, so, getting to sing 'Being Alive' with a little orchestra in a beautiful theatre eleven times a week would be real soul food.

Or, you know, maybe it wouldn't…

I got busy learning this amazing song all about the agonies of love and lost hope, and saw how it actually fitted the Prince Charming story really well at that point of the show and I was ready to add a little depth to the panto. At my song's big moment in that one week's rehearsal, I gave it my all. There may have been tears rolling down poor Prince Charming's cheeks, I couldn't say. The company actually clapped, which meant the world to this nervous singer.

Then our lovely director, Philip, asked me very graciously if I would do it again, 'but, if you don't mind, you absolutely must smile, all the way through'.

He was serious. He wanted teeth visible whenever possible. If you know the song, please, give it a go. Not easy and fairly hilarious. But I 'took the note' and it was fine. In fact it was fun. Everything about this job was fun and that over-sized giggle monster was bubbling away and getting me in trouble again. Especially as my beautiful Cinderella was a terrible giggler too. Her name was Emily and she and one of our ugly sisters, Andy, were to be friends of mine for many years. But, in performance, it was all we could do to finish our duet of 'I Can Show You The World', when she often as not had spinach in her teeth or was helpless with laughter at my terrible dancing.

Every year, nine hundred of the naughtiest and most troubled kids in the Peak District are given free tickets for a special 'gala' first night of the Buxton panto. It was a baptism of fire. A constant noise came towards us from the auditorium for the *entire* performance. Shouting so loud it was impossible to hear the actor standing only five feet from you. When Baron Hardup began throwing sweets into the audience, the immediate response was a barrage of missiles flying back in our direction – of every denomination: maltesers, crisp packets, magic wands, rucksacks and even shoes. It went on until the curtain fell. I laughed so hard I thought I might unpop my belly button.

I also remember an awful drama when it emerged that the drummer from the orchestra had been getting rather too close to one of our dancers from the local dance school. These girls were between thirteen and fifteen and blood was spilled when the girl's parents got wind of events.

But chiefly I remember the Nureyev Suite…

THE NUREYEV SUITE

As with most of my touring jobs, I'd booked my digs in advance from a list the theatre had posted to me ahead of rehearsals. It was always pot luck what kind of room, and what kind of home, you ended up in. No 'trip advisor' then, but I could look after myself and had few needs (if I could use the kitchen and the laundry facilities and had a door to my room that closed, I was happy), so I was guided purely by price and distance from the theatre.

When I arrived, I originally thought I'd lucked out: I could see the theatre from the front door, but, as the week of rehearsals went by, I realised I had entered the Twilight Zone.

The small, two-bedroom flat I was sharing with a single mother and her silent teenage son was a mess, but, I'd seen worse. My first night there I was made to feel welcome. A Chinese takeaway was shared with me and a rented movie was watched as we got to know each other a little.

When I woke up in the morning, though, the silent teenager was standing over my bed. I'd been put in his room and he needed to get ready for school. His mother assured me it was fine. It was just for a few weeks, he was perfectly happy on the sofa and they needed the money, so he was under strict instructions not to complain.

He didn't complain. He did, however, go through my belongings, stealing and hiding things while I was out at rehearsals.

On my second night, the son was staying with a friend and I was again asked if I wanted to share the take-out food the mum had just had delivered, along with a couple of bottles of red wine. This I happily did, offering to put some money in for the wine. I was told very firmly that I was a guest and not to be silly. She then filled me in on her recent break-up from the boy's violent father. She cried, a lot, and finally passed out on the couch.

In the morning I was confronted by a note outside my door letting me know exactly how much money I owed her for the food and wine and telling me to please be a bit quieter around the house as her son was studying for exams. I smelled a slight 'bonkers landlady' issue and decided it would be best to leave at the end of that week.

I asked the theatre staff if they knew of anywhere that might be available last minute and I was given the telephone number of the town photographer, who sometimes took in actors as guests. I popped to a telephone box in my lunch break and called. He was very friendly, gave me his address and told me he would expect me at the end of the week. What a relief.

That evening when I got back to the flat, I let the landlady know straight-away that I would pay her for the week, but, perhaps, as it was Christmas, the son might want his room back and anyway, I could do with finding somewhere a bit more self-contained. She immediately burst into tears, uncontrollable tears, and begged me not to leave. She made me *promise* not to leave; held my hands so hard she left nail marks in the skin as she told me again and again about her violent ex, who she was scared might come back any night. I was her 'friend' she said, and I mustn't leave. I had no choice but to tell her I'd stay.

Another long evening of red wine and listening to impenetrably complicated private sagas from this woman's life ensued until, finally, I was allowed to wish her goodnight, escape to my room and close the door.

I had to get out. This was before mobile phones don't forget. I had no one's address from the company. It was well after midnight, and absolutely bloody freezing outside.

I could hear her, laughing manically at whatever television programme she was watching. The front door was not an option. I'd have to pass her in the front room to get to it and simply couldn't face another scene or any more tears or spittle in my face.

My bedroom had a small window. It was a big drop down to the small, snow-filled garden outside it, but it was my only option. I packed whatever belongings the boy hadn't stolen or hidden from me into my suitcases and threw them out of the window. I followed shortly afterwards and ran for all I was worth.

All I could think to do was to see if the town photographer might still be up and if he might take me in a few days earlier than agreed. I dragged my cases up the steep and snow-covered streets of Buxton until I found the address. I rang the bell and crossed my fingers. Lights came on. The door opened and there, in a silk kimono, was one of the hairiest men I've ever seen. I told him who I was, apologised profusely for waking him and asked if there was any way at all I could move in that night. He paused, looked me up and down, then said, 'Oh, yes, you can have the Nureyev Suite.'

The Nureyev Suite turned out to be a bedroom in the loft of his beautiful home, entirely fitted out in burgundy. Everything was burgundy. And I mean everything: the shag pile carpet, the four-poster bed, the bed linen, the sink and shower unit in the corner of the room, the curtains and the towels. I have no idea what Rudolf Nureyev's link to the colour burgundy was and I never asked. I was just grateful to have escaped from the madness at the other end of town. Mr Photographer and his partner were fantastic hosts. I was left to myself in the Nureyev Suite and was very comfortable there until the end of the job, which marked the end of a big year for young Millson.

Sadly, after a few weeks away from Cathy and taking some much-needed space, I knew it was also the end of a long relationship. Onwards.

1997

The IRA ceased fire, Hong Kong went back to China, Tony Blair became Prime Minister, Mike Tyson nibbled an ear, Teletubbies said, 'Eh-oh', people flocked to the cinema to see Kate Winslet standing at the front of that big boat (they could have been watching *Good Will Hunting*), J. K. Rowling's first little book, *Harry Potter and the Philosopher's Stone*, was published, *Be Here Now* by Oasis was the big album, the kids were listening to 'MMMBop' by Hanson or 'Wannabe' by the Spice Girls, and, everyone was dying: Princess Diana and Dodi Fayed in Paris, Michael Hutchence in a Sydney hotel room, John Denver in an air crash, Jimmy Stewart at his home, Notorious B.I.G. in an LA shooting and – 'Oh my God! They killed Kenny' in *South Park*.

On tour with
Salad Days

Miss Saigon
Theatre Royal Drury Lane

'How do you follow a pantomime in Buxton?' I hear you ask. Well, you live alone with absolutely no money in a bedsit in Deptford with a hole in the roof above the kitchen that you can literally see the stars through, and you get no auditions for months. That's how.

THE KINDNESS OF STRANGERS

Unemployment benefit was again incredibly difficult to secure when out of work as an actor, so I searched for a job which would allow time to get to auditions. I was intent on somehow being around a theatre, and soon found myself wearing the horrendous, shiny uniform of a front-of-house usher at the Theatre Royal Drury Lane. Here I stayed for many months, tearing tickets, selling programmes and ice creams and watching at least ninety performances of *Miss Saigon.*

The wage was absolutely pitiful. For working all eight shows a week I would take home £110 after being taxed at source. My tiny flat was in south-east London so I had to pay for transport into the West End by bus or train as well as the rent, which was as cheap as could be found in London but still not cheap enough. Food was my last consideration. I was living on a diet of milkshakes and baked potatoes and was not in the best of health.

It was also whilst working at Drury Lane and getting late trains or buses back to my bedsit in Deptford that I got mugged not once, but twice, and on the second occasion, stabbed in my shoulder, straight *after* I'd given the gentleman my very slim wallet.

But I enjoyed my time among that odd family, working the front of house. A really friendly and fun bunch on the whole, whom I looked forward to seeing every day. They made the mind-numbingly boring and surprisingly exhausting work bearable. They were also incredibly kind.

A couple of months into my time there, towards the end of a front-of-house meeting which we sat through daily before the shift started, a large cardboard box was brought out from under a table and handed over to me. It was full of various tinned foods, pasta, soup packets, fruit, vegetables, chocolates and silly kids' treats. They'd got wind of how hard up I was and had noticed how little I was eating on matinée days, so had kept the box open in a secret place all week for people to drop donations into, like a harvest festival collection box. I was absolutely stunned. Knocked sideways by such kindness. I hadn't told anyone quite how hard up I was. No one, not even my parents, I was too embarrassed and too proud.

I didn't manage to find out who had organised it but have never, ever forgotten this random act of kindness. No people like show people, huh? Even front of house.

The Awful Truth
BBC TV (sort of)

I was still auditioning whenever possible but could no longer afford to subscribe to *PCR*, so was relying on whatever meetings my lovely, but not A-list, agent was occasionally arranging for me.

Somewhere in amongst the Drury Lane days, I got a part in a strange fifteen-minute pilot episode of a drama documentary programme for the BBC, trying to expose how evil estate agents could be. I was given a tape recording of the real estate agent I was playing, talking about how he ripped his clients off in secretly recorded interviews. I was to learn the transcript *exactly* as it had been recorded, with every cough, every 'um' and every 'er' included. The man sounded like a complete tosspot. I loved playing him.

I was dressed in a suit and taken out in a car with a crew of two, the director, who was also the camera operator, and a grumpy sound man. We would stop at random locations and pop out so they could film me wandering along chewing gum and talking directly to camera.

It was never shown, as far as I'm aware, but it was a great experience and a much-needed drop of money.

Salad Days by Julian Slade and Dorothy Reynolds
Number One Tour

Salad Days felt like a huge step for me. I'm not sure that it actually was: a touring version of a recent West End production of this dotty old English musical, with a famous director, my first job above Equity minimum wage, a brief escape from my money worries, and a really good credit on my little CV, even though it was another musical. What was with all this singing?

I was excited to meet the director, Ned Sherrin, at the audition. Here was a man who had directed all the greats, including a recent production of *Jeffrey Bernard is Unwell* starring Peter O'Toole at The Old Vic, which I'd watched open mouthed with joy from the cheap seats.

I sang my audition song (to this day I only really have the one audition song, 'I Remember' by Sondheim). Ned then asked me to read a bit of the script. The part I was up for was a not-so-bright young thing called Nigel. Ned asked me if I could read him a little like 'Tim Nice But Dim', a posh, buck-toothed and very dim character from Harry Enfield's TV sketch show. I didn't own a television but knew who he meant. I put my mouth into a position that felt like I had enormous buck teeth, thought 'posh', and read again. They fell off their stools laughing. I was in. They offered me the job in the room. As I was leaving, I asked if there was much dancing as I had two left feet. They looked at each other, shrugged and told me, 'No, darling, hardly any dancing at all.' Sometimes, people lie.

You'll have to take my word for it but in *Salad Days,* I danced a tango, I Cossack-danced, I did a six-bar tap solo and was part of at least three other frantic chorus numbers, which were full of what can only be described as unfeasibly energetic, crazy English dancing.

The tap solo was one of the hardest things I have ever learnt. I had to break it down into tiny, tiny segments and repeat it hundreds of times to get it into my muscle memory. I also had to play a couple of bars of two-handed piano every night – as I had never played a piano, this was equally painful to learn, finger position by finger position, agonisingly repeated until the right noise came out.

The dance routine to the ironically titled, 'Look At Me I'm Dancing', nearly had me in traction. There were days during early rehearsals when I'd wake up alone in my Deptford bedsit unable to move my legs out of the bed. They seemed to have been injected with cement. It was a herculean effort to get to the bathroom, let alone all the way to rehearsals on the Holloway Road. Somehow, my body got used to it, but that 'Look At Me' number remained exhausting to the end of the job.

SHERRIN THE LOVE

Rehearsals were a real learning experience for me, not only on the dance floor. I learnt a lot about the games that are played in commercial theatre. We had a 'star' director, whose award-winning name on our posters was reassuring to the public and helped to sell tickets, but it almost seemed as if Mr Sherrin was only paid to cast the show and then to attach his name to the poster. For three weeks he would arrive on time at 10 a.m., set up camp at a table in the corner of the room with his newspapers, his notebooks, and with a CD Walkman plugged into his ears. There he would work away, planning the weekly arts show he wrote and presented for Radio 4. We were the second cast of his production of *Salad Days* and it's entirely possible that he may have contributed more to the original, but with us it was pure lip service, while our lovely old choreographer directed every beat of every scene.

I found this unacceptable. Sometimes, when we struck a problem in a scene or a song that was hard to solve, I would look over at Ned engrossed in his own world and ask loudly, 'Ned! *NED!* What do *you* think we should do?' He would look up like a startled herring and say that whatever our choreographer thought was fine by him, and dive back into his papers. He only ever stood up to direct when the producers came to visit. On those occasions, he would position his chair centre front and look very attentive.

He was, however, excellent value on tea breaks and lunch breaks. Always happy to tell theatre stories from bygone days or to gossip about stars, alive and dead. He had an encyclopaedic knowledge of the theatre, which I was all ears for. He also sometimes made our toilets at those rehearsal rooms unusable. No one in the history of the universe could make such a stench. Sorry to lower the tone but it's important I get the sheer glamour of my early career across to you.

BIGGINS!
We began rehearsals with none other than Christopher Biggins playing the wonderful role of all the uncles. I felt my showbiz credentials were finally complete ... Biggins!

I spent a long afternoon in the first week rehearsing a comedy musical number that involved just him and me as a couple of bowler-hatted civil servants. This was an extra little character part I'd volunteered for yet again. The (for once) simple choreography seemed a little beyond Mr Biggins, however, and he got more and more angry with himself through the afternoon.

The following day, he didn't turn up for rehearsals and no one could get hold of him. Finally, a message came in from his agent that he'd 'bumped his head' at home and wouldn't be taking part in the production anymore. I wondered if the dancing throughout the rest of the show along with a huge amount of lines to learn was too much and he'd simply bolted. We were left with just two weeks to rehearse someone else in and, by luck, Edward Baker Duly, who had understudied the role in the West End, was available and arrived for our last few rehearsals word perfect and ready to go.

'SUMMER, AND SUNSHINE, AND FALLING IN LOVE'
So sings the lead character, Jane, in the show's most beautiful song, 'The Time of Our Lives', and life was doing its best to imitate art. *Salad Days* is a musical all about

having fun, until being faced with the sweet agonies of adulthood, and that summer was a kind of zenith for my carefree life before responsibilities and cares arrived in their various forms.

It was my last great lungful of undiluted, responsibility-free air. Actually, that isn't quite right. In a strange way, if you discount childhood, it was actually my *first*. Certainly my first summer as an adult without someone else to think of. I'd been a serial monogamist with someone else's feelings to consider since the age of fifteen. I'd only had a handful of girlfriends but the relationships had each lasted a few years. My father had been in and out of remission with cancer but at this time was doing well, and we Millsons were using our default optimism and a fair amount of denial to keep any fears at bay. I was young, healthy, confident and single. Not that I was interested in doing anything about that last status. I was far more concerned with the endless daft excursions, the swimming in lakes, the punting on rivers, the games of tennis and the constant picnics that the mostly wonderful and friendly cast were always arranging. The sun really did shine an awful lot that summer as we toured the country in that ridiculous but sweet show. I was living life to the full and laughter was my drug of choice.

I had a couple of best pals in the company. There was Angela, who we called 'Mother' as she not only knew best but was chief organiser of all extra-curricular activities, and the other was Caroline. Caroline played opposite me in the show as Fiona, an equally 'Nice But Dim' character. She was very forgiving of my frankly dangerous footwork as I danced opposite her every night and was great fun to be on stage with. We talked and laughed a lot. By the end of the job, we were pretty much inseparable but not connected romantically. I had no idea that she was to be my future wife, that we would go on to be married for twelve years, that we would have two beautiful children and one very ugly divorce together.

My only romantic connection during this period was with a beautiful Canadian dancer I'd met in London. I would see her occasionally when home between tour dates. She was a fair bit older than I was and was quite an event in my life. She taught me a great deal, not only about sex but also about Martha Graham and crop farming in Saskatchewan!

When her British visa ran out, she proposed marriage to me. She said she was totally serious. I was even put on the phone to her father to discuss the 40,000-acre farm in Saskatchewan that I would stand to inherit. Tempting though that may be, and addicted to her as I was, I never saw that farm. I walked away. But it was strange. The idea of marriage had been planted. Deep in my subconscious an alarm had been set and a clock was ticking.

The idea of responsibility didn't frighten me. Far from it. I'd grown up with parents who were happily devoted to not only my brother and to me but also to each other. Much of what I'm speaking of now I can only see because time has lifted that veil from the past, but it seems clear to me that I was desperate to become a version of my father before he was taken from us.

I LOVE JAZZ

Roughly halfway through the tour, we had to lose the wonderful Edward Baker Duly from our company as he had a prior commitment on another job. He was replaced with almost no rehearsal by a man by the name of Robert Longden. Robert had co-written one of the biggest flops in the West End's history, *Moby Dick – The Musical,* but on stage, in my opinion, he posed a quadruple threat. It seemed he couldn't sing, dance, act or remember any of his words. For weeks on end it felt as if we would sit or stand on stage as he effectively murdered what had previously been some of the show's most charming numbers, gamely spouting utter gibberish for minutes at a time, almost as if he was speaking in tongues.

People had paid good money to see the show and I was bemused as to how it was allowed to carry on. I had the lines which followed one of his more extraordinary numbers and started to improvise myself. 'I love jazz,' I would say through my imaginary buck teeth as soon as the song was over.

I burnt some bridges when our producer came to see the show at the Cambridge Arts Theatre. It was predictably awful; Robert Longden had given a car crash of a performance and we had all carried him through. But there was our producer, smiling and standing next to him at the bar afterwards. I was dumbfounded. Despite being held back by wiser people than me, I approached him and, to quote my dad, 'cut him a bit of a new arsehole'. Young whippersnapper though I was, I had standards and was sick of having to stand on stage and be associated with such shite night after night. The producer couldn't deny it was unacceptable but also had no intention of doing anything about it. We were on our own.

NO PEEKING
As a little footnote to this job, Caroline and I subsequently

became good friends with the composer, Julian Slade. He had particularly enjoyed our performances as Nigel and Fiona and we stayed in touch after the job was over by letters and occasional phone calls. Only in his late sixties, he wasn't in the best of health and seemed older. He wanted us to take him to the theatre. He said he felt out of touch and wanted to see whatever shows everyone was talking about. He'd pay for the tickets and dinner if one or both of us would accompany him. This was fantastic news. He was delightful and strange in equal measure and we had several great nights out at the theatre, always in the front row due to his fading eyesight. I don't think I'll ever forget his squeaks of shock as we sat in the front row to watch glass bottles getting pushed up arses during Mark Ravenhill's brilliant play, *Shopping and Fucking*.

Julian loved to sketch and draw and was a decent artist. He asked me if I'd sit for him. I said I'd be delighted and arrived at his garden flat in Chelsea for our first session. The tiny basement flat was completely monopolised by a full-size grand piano, for which I can only imagine a wall was removed to install. Victorian chaises longues and clutter of every description were squeezed in wherever they could be squeezed. It was a genteel pigsty and smelt like a used bin bag, but I have always adored older people's company and taking time out to be with them, so I was perfectly happy. I did, however, feign a tummy bug when he offered to cook. He sat me down opposite him and began to sketch.

Sitting for an artist is an interesting experience. You quickly get used to being observed but unless your eyes are closed for the picture you cannot help but observe things yourself. I noticed the dandruff all over his shoulders, the dust on every surface was suddenly visible and his cats had clearly taken over as I started to notice little piles of cat shit scattered hither and thither.

Silence is also something you get used to quickly when sitting for an artist. Julian would gaze at me for very long periods of time between strokes of pencil against paper. The silence only served to amplify something else I hadn't previously noticed about our darling Julian, and that was his flatulence. He seemed totally unaware of the damp little farts, which escaped him every few minutes. Most consistently when he moved to fetch water or move a cat.

After an hour or two, I was released. I was under strict instructions not to look at his efforts so far. Not until the picture was finished. I sat a couple more times over the next month, never getting to see the work in progress. Halfway through my final visit, he left to go to the toilet calling, 'No peeking!' I couldn't resist, I had to see what our time together had produced. I turned the big sketch pad over and saw my name at the bottom of the paper and, above it, a few pencil scratches, gentle random lines made by a pencil, and nothing more. There was no drawing; he had been miming as he gazed at the young man opposite him for a few hours each week.

The Beaux Stratagem by George Farquhar
Cannizaro Open Air Theatre

A few months of solid unemployment followed. I made the move north of the river to live with Caroline and her brother in a little basement flat in Albert Street, Camden. The fact that I was an out-of-work actor living on the very street where the real life *Withnail and I* had lived didn't escape me. I searched out various jobs to pay the rent. Humiliating but lightly linked to my profession. I was part of a three-person troupe performing a lunatic half-hour version of *A Midsummer Night's Dream* on midsummer's eve to a bunch of very rich and very drunk people at a country house. We rehearsed this in my tiny bedsit. *Fun.*

I also dressed as a human tennis court. A green Velcro full-body suit, with several yellow Velcro tennis balls attached to my body and head. In the full heat of July, for three days, I had to walk up and down the lines of people queuing to get in to see the tennis at Wimbledon, spouting 'poems' about tennis. This was a publicity stunt for the Nike team at Wimbledon. I was a source of great amusement to what seemed like the richest idiots in the world, as they threw their strawberries and Pimm's-soaked cucumber slices at me. *Not fun.*

I also travelled alone to Dublin to see some of the Dublin Fringe Festival, on an incredibly tight budget. I'd found a special offer in a newspaper, London to Dublin by coach and ferry for ten pounds, and I was booked in to stay at the Dublin YMCA. I can't remember much about the trip except for that horrendously overcrowded dormitory bedroom at the YMCA, rain, trying to like the taste of Guinness, and a long conversation with Alan Cumming in a pub one night.

Soon after returning, 'Joey's Jobs' managed to secure me an audition for a production of another great classical comedy, *The Beaux Stratagem*. It was to be what I called 'Posh Fringe'. There was a slim wage of a hundred pounds a week or so plus travel but it was a great play, a relatively well-known director, and a well-established annual open-air theatre festival at Cannizaro Park in Wimbledon.

I was over the moon when I was offered the brilliant role of Archer. I'd always fancied a bash at open-air theatre and, after *The Rivals,* was raring to have another crack at a leading role in a similar play. More importantly, it would be another solid credit, another campaign fought.

EARNING MY STRIPES

The military analogy has always held strong in my mind for some reason. I've thought of all my auditions and jobs as 'earning my stripes', clocking up mileage in active service. I still do. Weeks in rehearsal rooms. Hours in front of paying audiences, minutes in front of cameras. It didn't matter which rehearsal rooms or even which role; it didn't matter which theatre or how big or important the audience; and it certainly didn't matter which camera I was in front of. I *knew* I had a lot to learn. But to practise your craft you have to actually, well, *practise your craft.*

It's a cruel art form to find yourself addicted to. *Any* other creative practice – music, art, writing, photography, even dance – can be practised alone. It would be possible in any other activity to hone your skills at home. To grow. Not so with acting. Yes, there are books to read and, trust me, I'd read every book I could beg, steal or borrow. I'd learned of fantastic *theories* and *ideas* from books. But to absorb them, I would need to *try* them. Either in rehearsal or in performance.

I'd learnt huge amounts from watching theatre too, as much from terrible performances and productions as I did from great ones. But I always knew it was worth nothing until I was out there, *up* there, testing it. Thus it was that, for these early years, I cared more about the *quantity* of credits far more than the *quality.*

DIRECT ADDRESS

I suppose what I'm doing now in writing this, is finally taking an inventory of all the early campaigns I fought. As I look back at the younger me acting his tights off in the rain as Archer in *The Beaux Stratagem,* I get a real sense of *him* there and *me* here, at exactly the same moment as sensing *him* here and *me* there.

If the military analogy holds up, then he is a bright-eyed young private and I am some kind of battle-scarred captain. We are staring at each other now across the decades, saluting and trying not to laugh.

It wasn't a great production but, boy, oh boy, did I enjoy it. Another short rehearsal period where I could smell potential laughs but, having learnt from *The Rivals,* kept my mouth shut, kept my powder dry and waited until we had an audience to test exactly how I wanted to play much of it.

Archer had a lot of speeches direct to the audience and a great many one-line asides to them too. I can't explain why but this has always felt like the most natural thing in the world to me. I'm always so delighted to 'meet' my audience every night. I can't imagine how scary it must be to try to pretend there is a 'fourth wall' there as some actors do. The audience are always the final member of the cast, the *best* member of the cast, and they *always* have the last word when it comes to the questions 'Does it work?', or 'Is it funny?'

I would ad lib a little, or eyeball the audience occasionally if the terrible weather, or tripping actors, or spittle in my face prompted me to do so. It worked and is absolutely appropriate for plays of this period. Laughs were many and loud. My 'show legs' and 'leading role legs' were getting stronger. As was my voice. I remember Caroline (who was now officially my girlfriend) coming to meet me after the show. She told me that, as she crossed the half mile of hotel grounds that led to the theatre, she could hear my voice booming out above all the others. That made my day. That barrel chest of mine was coming in useful.

It was a short run but an important job for me, not least because it got me a new and wonderful agent, Jan Evans. Jan had been to see another client of hers in the show and politely enquired via that client whether I was happy with my current representation and if I might be interested in coming in for a chat. I think she genuinely saw something in me that night and was devoted to me, and I to her, for many years. A brilliant agent, loved in the profession. It was an absolute 'no-brainer' that I should move to her.

SACKING YOUR AGENT: LESSON ONE

Don't do it in person! I really liked my first agent, Janet, so wanted to do what I imagined was 'the right thing' and tell her in person. I arranged to pop along to her office in Richmond. I didn't plan what I was going to say. I would just 'be honest'.

Well, that was a fucking terrible idea.

There's an incredibly limited vocabulary for leaving your agent and it bears an uncanny resemblance to the vocabulary used when leaving your girlfriend or wife. Sooner or later, the conversation arrives at this:

ACTOR: I'm, erm, I'm leaving you, I'm afraid.
AGENT: What?
ACTOR: Look, I absolutely adore you but I just feel it's time to, well, move on.

AGENT: Haven't you been happy with me/us?

ACTOR: No. Well, I mean, *yes,* of course I have. It's just… It's not you, it's me. I need to shake things up a bit and well…

AGENT: Who is it?

ACTOR: What?

AGENT: Who? Who are you leaving me/us for?

ACTOR: Well, I'm, I'm not totally sure yet.

Pause

ACTOR: I mean, there is somebody but…

AGENT: *Who?*

ACTOR: It's (fill in the blank with slightly better agent).

AGENT: Get out.

There are variations of course. I've heard of painless separations but have yet to experience one myself. But lesson learnt; I was never going to be in the room for that conversation again.

A Night Out by Harold Pinter
Hampton Wick Theatre

An odd couple of months followed. I worked unpaid as an assistant director for my friend, Stuart Mullins, who was directing what turned out to be a bit of a 'fringe hit' production of *A Night Out* by Harold Pinter, at a pub theatre somewhere in Hampton Wick. It was a stage premiere of a lesser-known early radio play by Pinter.

It was fascinating to sit on the other side of the rehearsal process, but I was a little over-zealous when Stuart had to be absent for a day during the final week and left me with the simple instruction of just making sure everyone knew their lines. Pinter would have enjoyed my enforced exactitude but I apologise to anyone I shouted at!

I had to wait for some kind of notice period to end before I was officially off my first agent's books and, almost as if to make some kind of point, she suddenly came through with the first auditions for television work she'd ever got me. Both meetings were with the same casting director, both were for Channel 4, both were sitcoms. I got them both and within the space of two weeks, I'd filmed them both.

Dressing For Breakfast
Channel 4 Television

The details of this, my first ever television appearance, are hazy, but I remember my few minutes on set well. I was really excited to start my television career. To earn my first tiny stripe. My small scene was shot at night on location somewhere in London. I was to play a man who strolls out of a hotel with his girlfriend and gets straight into a cab, which had pulled up for the leading lady of the show. The scene went something like this:

STAR OF THE SHOW: Hey! That's my cab!
ME PLAYING UNNAMED MAN: Sorry, all's fair in
    love and taxis.

A bit more dialogue from the star about her terrible day.

We relent, I mumble an apology and give her the cab.

End scene.

I was introduced by name to the leading lady for our quick camera rehearsal and we blocked it through. I'll never know why but she was in a foul mood, or possibly exhausted, and was surprisingly rude to me. I was standing less than a foot away from her, exactly where the director had told me to stand but she wasn't happy. 'Is he going to stand there?... If he says it like that I can't really say my line how I want to... Couldn't he just wait until I've done the thing with my coat...?' etc etc.

'Excuse me,' I said loudly, 'we've just been introduced. I'm standing right here, my name is Joe.'

Shocked silence. (That filter was missing once again.) Had it not been the end of a long night shoot, I think she might have had me sacked. When the programme aired, my scene was there and came out quite well, but they didn't put my name in the credits.

In Exile
Channel 4 Television

This was a very different experience. I had a decent guest role with a few good scenes in one episode of what seemed like a great new comedy series, and it was to be filmed in front of a live studio audience.

We rehearsed for a week in a big shed somewhere on the edge of Teddington studios. This felt very like theatre rehearsals but with *a lot* more tape on the floor marking all the endless camera positions and moves. The director was much more concerned with the bits of tape than with the actors but our producer Mark Williams, himself a fantastic actor and comedian who I loved watching in *The Fast Show*, was great with us and seemed to love what I was doing.

TYPECAST AGAIN

In Exile was a comedy about an exiled African General and his son adjusting to middle-class life in suburban North London. I was to play the son's new English friend, Raphael, who was a dancer, and gay. The last detail being an alarming surprise for some characters when revealed. As Raphael, I was to sport the strangest hairstyle I've ever been given, an oceanic wave of a quiff. I was dressed in tight black leather trousers and a little vest. Joe Orton's ghost was smiling.

There was a lot of ego flying around the rehearsal room from the two lead actors, Patrice Naiambana and Fraser James, who I had most of my scenes with. But the build-up to filming in front of a live audience was really exciting. We rehearsed Wednesday to Friday, and then went in front of cameras and audience on the Saturday evening.

Filming in front of a studio audience can be confusing: who are you doing the actual performance for? The cameras? The audience? Or both? I seem to remember focusing on one person in the audience – well, on the studio floor anyway: our producer Mark Williams.

I remember feeling strangely calm and certain on the night of the recording. I'd even had a couple of tiny new ideas in my dressing room, which I bravely saved until the red light was on and we were recording in front of the audience. Hearing Mark's delighted laugh ring out when, just before my exit, I leaned in for an unrehearsed kiss on the lips of Patrice Naiambana's homophobic General, was a wonderful moment.

David Copperfield by Charles Dickens, adapted for the stage by Matthew Francis
Greenwich Theatre/Sheffield Crucible

The drama school I'd attended was called The Rose Bruford College of Speech and Drama or, as we knew it, The Rose Bruford College of Bleach and Trauma. I loved the place: great teachers and an ethos of high standards and low egos. It's now known simply as 'Rose Bruford College' and being made a 'fellow' there recently was one of the greatest honours and surprises of my life.

When I attended, the college was split over two large campuses. We spent our first year studying at the beautiful house and grounds in Lamorbey Park in Sidcup, where voice classes could be taken by the side of the lake and all was beauty and inspiration. By contrast, the second and third years were spent almost entirely in an enormous abandoned Victorian school building in Deptford, South London.

Just down the road from the fairly grim Deptford campus on Creek Road was the tourist mecca of Greenwich, one of the most beautiful parts of London. I spent so many hours of those years wandering or learning lines in Greenwich Park, eating chips as the Thames sailed by me at the *Cutty Sark*, and more often than not walking again and again to gaze at the posters, production photographs and cast lists outside the Greenwich Theatre on Crooms Hill.

HOW TO STALK A BUILDING
Greenwich Theatre was not only the nearest theatre to me at drama school, it was the best. It was one of the last remaining professional repertory theatres in London.

There were the giants in central London, The National Theatre, The Royal Court, The Donmar etc. But after those, there were theatres like Greenwich and Hampstead, trying to survive on limited funding from the London Arts Board, the Greater London Council and occasional West End transfers.

While I was at Rose Bruford, Greenwich Theatre was under the stewardship of the brilliant Matthew Francis. All the productions I saw seemed incredibly grown up, cool and unattainably 'proper'. It was a field of dreams and I was drawn to the building like a magnet. I saw as many productions as I could afford and, when my money ran out, had the canny idea of getting a job there as an usher.

The tiny wage was insignificant. What mattered was that for many evenings of many of my terms, I got to breathe in the atmosphere of that building and see every production for free, sometimes a dozen times. I remember a spectacular *Dr Faustus*, a hilarious *Entertaining Mr Sloane*, and an incredibly awful *Macbeth,* with some dude I'd barely heard of called Mark Rylance playing Macbeth as a mumbling American cult leader. Jane Horrocks as Lady Macbeth urinated for real all over the stage every night during her 'out damned spot' speech. One could always tell when she'd been at the asparagus.

As soon as I'd graduated from college, I began writing to Matthew Francis. Every time a new season of plays was announced, I'd read them, choose a realistically sized part from each and write my fan/begging letter. My persistence eventually paid off and I received an invitation to audition for the role of Rodolpho in his forthcoming production of Arthur Miller's *A View from the Bridge.*

I read well, I think, we got on fantastically, and my agent

was told the job was mine. Soon afterwards, however, I discovered I'd have to 're-audition' for the role. Matthew Francis had suddenly had his entire next year's funding for the theatre cut by the Greater London Council, and was going to have to pull out of rehearsals to attend to crisis fundraising and management duties. I felt outraged on behalf of 'my' theatre. It was with a real feeling of Blitz spirit and camaraderie that I happily came to read for Rachel Kavanagh, who had just been promoted from assistant director to director, and who Matthew felt ought to be allowed to meet all her cast before contracts were signed.

Rachel wasn't so keen and I quickly went from 'just cast' to 'uncast'. I felt no despair, only an inflamed desire to get on that stage one day. I didn't have too many months to wait...

Matthew Francis didn't have much luck convincing his local funding bodies that his hugely successful, much-loved and well-attended theatre was worth the tiny funding it was used to receiving, so decided to go out with a bang. He announced that his swansong production as Artistic Director, and indeed, as far as anyone knew, the last ever in-house professional repertory production to be produced at Greenwich Theatre, was to be his own adaptation of Charles Dickens's masterpiece ... wait for it ... *David Copperfield...*

I broke open the stationery cupboard once again.

Whether my recent close call with *A View from the Bridge* had anything to do with it or not I'll never know, but I found myself back in an audition room with Matthew Francis. I think we were both pleased to meet again. I was to read for the part of Steerforth. My time up in Liverpool, reading that novel cover to cover twice and singing my way through a kind of cartoon version of the character, paid off. I felt incredibly passionate about the story and still had so much to learn about the part. I think Matthew was slightly taken aback at quite how keen I was when he mentioned that there would be various other smaller parts to play. I scored ten out of ten for passion if nothing else.

STEERFORTH RIDES AGAIN

David Copperfield is one of those novels it's impossible to praise highly enough. Its scope is massive but it is such an enjoyable book to read. Dickens could deal with the big stuff in life better than anyone, the most bleak and nihilistic moments always only a few paragraphs away from laugh-out-loud comedy. Nobody does it better, and nobody other than Shakespeare can draw so many characters so well. *Copperfield* is Dickens's most autobiographical of novels. He himself called it his 'favourite son'. How strange that life should be leading me into this novel's heart again so soon, and via the same character.

James Steerforth is a beautiful mystery. He arrives in young David Copperfield's life like a glittering firework of charm, wit, wealth, beauty and impossible grace. His addictive personality, malevolent streak and violent boredom take a while to become visible to David, by which time it is too late. The damage has been done, and hearts and lives have been broken. Steerforth performs a great act of selflessness but it is to be his last. He drowns in an angry storm trying to save the life of a good man. Lightning and the full force of nature finally extinguish him.

I had been devoted to him as a character in that daft musical but here was an opportunity to really do him justice. Matthew's adaptation of the novel for the stage was staggeringly good. It felt like artistic joy and a tiny measure of glory was there for the taking. All I had to do was actually *do* it.

KEEP YOUR OWN INSTRUMENT

So many big lessons were learnt on this job. The first sprang out of this overreaching ambition of mine to paint a perfect portrait of Steerforth. I did too much homework, a little too much daydreaming about him and found myself going home from early rehearsals feeling really disappointed in myself. Matthew had a million things to think about whilst directing this monster of a show in four weeks but somehow took time to nurse me through this with some wonderful conversations. Lessons I have never forgotten.

The first penny fell when we were rehearsing an early scene between the young David and the young Steerforth. Set in their school, a nervous David is taken under the popular Steerforth's wing. It was the first appearance of Steerforth in the play and I was entering with my fully loaded bag of Steerforth knowledge oozing from every pore. He was complicated, he was deep, he was bright, he was dangerous, he was dark; but he was also darkly humorous. Of course, it was a mess. I didn't feel alive or truthful. I couldn't find my way out.

Matthew said that plays were like music: different characters felt like different instruments in different scenes. 'Right now, in this scene, David is like a small, delicate oboe, sad and reflective in amongst all the raucous schoolchildren, who are like loud percussion. Then Steerforth enters and he is a French horn. Clear, bright and beautiful. Yes, later on he gets his oboe scene. He may even become a cello. But right now, you must be all major key and clarity.

At the moment you are coming on like an entire one-man band. You must "*keep your instrument*".'

It felt like a great window opening. I saw my job a little clearer. How an actor can only really do one thing at a time. Or, as my dad used to say about so many things in life, 'How do you eat an elephant?... One bite at a time.'

I went back through my script and baptised the emotional sections of the play from bright to dark. I simplified the objectives and actions I had scribbled into the margins of the script from things like, 'Impress an impressionable new sponge with my infinite depth' or some such guff to, 'Spread the joy' or other short, fun actions. Rehearsals were transformed. It's a learning curve I'm still enjoying.

BRUCE AND VERN

We were a cast of thirteen playing around seventy characters between us. Steerforth was a wonderful, wonderful role but he had fairly big breaks between scenes. I was kept insanely busy playing nine other parts, all with costume changes and different voices and physicalities to pop in and out of. It was exhausting, hard, hard work. I was in heaven.

Only one actor beat me to the 'most parts played' prize and that was Brian Poyser. Brian was at this time in his mid to late sixties and made me feel like a total failure. He effortlessly gave a heartbreaking, show-stealing performance in his main role of Mr Dick but also beat me through every quick change into each of his *thirteen* other roles!

Brian and I were paired as a sort of father and son bailiff outfit, who arrived intermittently through the play every time David or Mr Micawber went bankrupt. We were given no scripted dialogue but instantly became a perfect double act. As performances went on, the silent duo began to communicate quietly as we lifted tables and moved chairs. With no discussion, it quickly emerged that he was 'Bruce', and I was 'Vern'. We were also inexplicably from the Midlands. Bruce would boss my silent Vern around and hit me sporadically. Vern took it all on the chin and would just stare lovingly at Bruce. After many weeks I was sometimes heard to mutter, 'I love you, Bruce.'

Brian was a hugely important friend in my life. Certainly, his was the strongest friendship I'd thus far made in an acting company. Age was utterly irrelevant. We were both Peter Pan. We adored each other, respected each other's work, and made each other laugh a great deal. Brian and I were to be very close friends right up to his death in 2009. I can see his imp-like face and his nose wrinkling mid-giggle even now.

Brian was the first of several surrogate father figures I have drawn friendship and strength from over the years. In fact, it was Brian that I chose to have standing by at my father's funeral a few years later, to step in for me if I couldn't get through the passage I'd chosen to read. Here though, back in 1997, my wonderful father was still very much around, but work and geography and his intermittent fights with cancer meant I didn't see him nearly enough.

UP AND AT 'EM
As I sat in the noisy dressing room before the first preview, I secretly took stock, and smiled. The actors I was playing with, the sheer quality of execution all round, in design, music and most of all in Matthew Francis's direction, were superb. I was where I wanted to be.

Our first preview performance ran at nearly four hours!

The next day we came in and Francis handed us all individual handwritten lists of exactly what cuts he'd made and how we were each individually affected throughout the entire show. Thirteen actors playing nearly eighty parts. We all went away to study our crib sheets alone. With barely any extra rehearsal, the show ran smoothly that evening at just over three hours. An incredible achievement.

Here again, a real press night approached. Every paper would be sending their head honcho to this one, and my new agent (along with everyone else's agents) would be bringing casting directors throughout the run. It was a hugely important step up for me. Luckily, by the time we went in front of the press we had become a real team, fighting together to push this beautiful monster up and over the hill every night. It was a great production: five-star reviews in nearly all the papers, sold out for the entire run. But despite all this, Greenwich Theatre went totally dark after our last night.

1998

The Good Friday Agreement was signed in Northern Ireland but, a couple of months later, a car bomb exploded in Omagh killing twenty-nine; Bill Clinton was named *Time Magazine*'s man of the year then, soon after, found himself telling the world, 'I did not have sexual relations with that woman...'; Frank Sinatra died, Private Ryan was getting saved and Shakespeare was In Love at the cinema, all the kids wanted Furbies, DVDs made their first appearance, Shania Twain told you, 'You're Still the One', 'N Sync 'Wanted You Back' and Celine Dion's 'heart went on'... and on and on and on.

Gasping – Watford Palace Theatre

SHEFFIELD MON AMOUR

Once *Copperfield* closed at Greenwich we learned that it was to transfer for a month's run in February at the Crucible Theatre, Sheffield. There was a month or so to wait until then and Caroline had got a job singing in an opera at Le Châtelet Opera House in Paris, with a small apartment in the Bastille area as part of the contract. I jumped at the opportunity to live in that beautiful city with her for a few weeks.

Paris can amplify love like nowhere else. It was a happy time. The ticking of my internal husband and father clock was too loud to ignore. One trip up a freezing Eiffel Tower was all it took. I arrived at the Sheffield Crucible direct from Paris, engaged to be married. I was twenty-three.

Copperfield was equally as rewarding at Sheffield; a very different space to play, with entrances through the auditorium now woven into the show. There was a lot of laughter on stage and off. Matthew Francis had joined the acting company as our former Micawber wasn't free for the run in Sheffield. I also can't forget accompanying Brian on a terrifying drive through snow across the infamous 'Snake Pass' to an audition he had in Bolton, and a great set of digs in the loft room of a house full of vegetarian lesbians.

The run finished and I was back to London, looking for work.

Misper
Glyndebourne Opera Youth Project. Some Church Hall, Somewhere in New Cross, London

Almost as soon as I got back to London, a friend of Caroline's from the opera world roped me into an unpaid charity production of a children's opera in a church some-where in New Cross, part of the Glyndebourne Opera House outreach programme. All I knew was one of the adult performers had dropped out at the last minute and I had to learn three songs, several scenes of dialogue, and arrive at a dress rehearsal ready to go.

It was a big event for the area – a hundred or so of the most underprivileged children in South East London had been rehearsing this thing in their spare time for months on end. The experience was surreal, just plopping in at the dress rehearsal.

My character was an older teenager and the leader of one of the gangs in the story, so all my scenes and songs were performed with my gang of ten or so genuinely tough kids from local estates. I felt extremely daft at times leading this gang as we sang such wonderful lyrics as, 'hanging around, nuffink to do, give us peanuts, don't, don't, don't give a monkey's for you' etc. But it was fun, bonkers actually, and another campaign fought. Another tiny stripe won.

Gasping by Ben Elton
Palace Theatre, Watford

I was in need of money to survive again so I thought I'd see what an employment agency might be able to find for me. I have to say, they didn't seem too hopeful. My qualifications were, and I quote, 'not good for anything except poncing about on a stage'. If I ever wanted to begin in any other world, I'd be going in at the ground level or, in my case, lower. I was eventually given a job as a filing clerk in the enormous basement rooms under St Thomas' Hospital, London.

I had never conceived of how many hard copies of patients' files hospitals had to keep. Hundreds and hundreds of thousands of brown cardboard files, containing scraps of paper and doctors' notes about everyone who had ever come under that hospital's care. A fresh shopping cart full of files would be wheeled up to me every hour or two, which had to be emptied and each file systematically trudged back to its correct place in the filing system. Though important work, it was driving me loopy with boredom. And the lack of daylight wasn't for me. After only a few days, I begged the employment agency to see if there was anything else, possibly above ground. There was, just for a week or so. If I so desired, I could be an assistant porter around the hospital as a regular porter was off sick.

I jumped at the chance and spent a happy week delivering things hither and thither and transporting by wheelchair or trolley every kind of patient, living and dead, to every part of the hospital. I even had to help put one recently deceased lady into a bag for the mortuary. The week flew by but, I was soon back in the filing dungeon. I started praying for an audition and, finally, I got two.

The first was for the upcoming season at the still fairly new Globe Theatre. It was a bit last minute, and quite an old-fashioned audition. They were considering me for the role of Orlando in *As You Like It* but, at the first audition, I had to perform a pre-prepared Shakespeare speech to a panel of the season's directors, these being Richard Olivier, Lucy Bailey and the Artistic Director of the Globe, Mark Rylance. I only had a day's notice so there was no time to learn a new speech. I arrived the next day having re-learnt the speech from *Much Ado About Nothing* that I had used to audition for drama school six years previously.

I hadn't really thought things through. The small talk with the three directors was fine but, when they asked me to perform my speech, I was suddenly struck by the fact that the last time I'd watched *Much Ado About Nothing* it had starred Mark Rylance as Benedick. He'd been magnificent, and famously so. What kind of arrogant prick gave a Benedick speech in front of him?

'What have you prepared?' Mark himself asked.

I blushed. Then I told him that I'd totally cocked up and brought Benedick. Which now made me feel a bit of a dick. This made him laugh and he got up from his seat and stood with me, asking which speech I'd prepared. He was so kind and encouraging. I told him it was the 'I do much wonder...' speech, we talked a little about where Benedick was in the play at that point, then he asked me to perform it, very simply, straight to him.

He listened attentively, reacted, asked me questions mid-line like a pal in a pub I was telling the story to. I reacted in turn and it became a scene, a game, with my Benedick getting more and more self-righteous as it progressed. As soon as I'd finished, he asked me to start again straight away, performing it for the whole room. I did just that and enjoyed myself enormously. Smiles from Richard and Lucy. I could tell I hadn't impressed enough to get the gig, but as I was leaving the room Mark said, 'You know, Benedick is a part you absolutely have to play one day.' I left the room walking on air. It took another eight years, but he was right.

The other meeting felt a little more within my reach. I knew all about the Palace Theatre, Watford, one of the last remaining professional repertory theatres on the edges of London. Those were words that made me really excited when placed in close proximity to each other: Professional. Repertory. Theatre. The part I was to audition for was a great supporting role in *Gasping*, a comedy by Ben Elton. The director seemed lovely and I remember him looking delighted when I spoke about 'transitive verbs' when we were discussing what my character might be up to in one part of the scene we were reading. I was in.

We had just under four weeks to get a very wordy, fast-flowing, multi-scene comedy up and running. Ben Elton had done considerable rewrites to update all the topical jokes, so this was in effect a new play.

TOO MUCH TAI CHI

Paul Jepson is a good director but I wonder if he might have been a little over-ambitious with what he wanted from those rehearsals. As I remember, he had recently finished a long course at some wonderful European physical theatre/clown school and he really wanted to share with us all of the, no doubt, wonderful experiences he had had. We did a great deal of jumping and rolling around and I recall a leaping game, where I was encouraged to actually 'try to fly'. He was also, as I'd gleaned in the audition, keen on 'actioning the script', discussing what each actor was intending to play on each line and attaching transitive verbs to our scripts as we went. Now this is *right* up my street personally, although I only tend to use it when I need it; when I feel I'm getting vague in my performance. But I'm not sure how I feel about insisting all actors having to use the same process. On this particular occasion there were some other important things missing. By the end of the third week, we hadn't really gone through the play up on our feet and it became clear that the eldest member of our company (an American actor who hadn't been on stage for many years) and our lead actor, who had an incredible amount of dialogue, were far from knowing their lines. I'd spotted early on that the basics weren't being covered in the rehearsal room and had done a great deal of work at home to ensure I was off book.

I'd already moved on from the mindset I'd been in on *The Rivals* where everything had to be perfect. I was responsible only for my part in proceedings, and thoroughly enjoying creating my character, a kind of super-yuppie with lines such as, 'In order to succeed, you have to break, or bend. Personally, I'm a bender.'

Due to nerves and the nature of our rehearsals, we had a few very interesting first performances, actors calling 'YES?' into the wings of the theatre to get fed lines by the poor stage management more frequently than I'd ever witnessed. Once lines were learnt, though, the play flew. I experienced a very similar joy in my work as with *Loot*. An important role but not a leading role, so all the pleasure of performance with only a fraction of the responsibility. Centre midfield again. My research into the science of making an audience laugh whilst serving a play was allowed to continue. The Palace Theatre, Watford is also a very lovely theatre to play; a beautiful addition to my collection.

THE RESPECT OF YOUR PEERS

Ben Elton was a hero of my youth. My brother and I were huge fans of everything The Comic Strip produced on television and knew every line of *The Young Ones* by heart. So, when at our press night Ben took me aside, eyeballed me and told me very seriously that I was 'a funny guy, really funny, I've never seen that part get so many laughs,' I was on cloud nine. It's not vain to cherish such rewards sometimes. Unless you are in that tiny fraction of a fraction of a fraction of actors who spend their lives winning awards, or 'acting trophies' as I call them, then these moments, when somebody you have respected and learned from turns towards you as a peer and respects *your* work, are golden and rightfully treasured. It's nice to be told you are moving in the right direction by someone who knows the way.

Black Vodka
Test Commercial

Some very strange cash jobs filled the next gap, again lightly linked to acting. Caroline and I both somehow got involved with corporate role-play work, travelling as far as Belfast sometimes to stay in hotels and play guinea-pig, awkward clients for salesmen and insurers from various companies for hours on end. I played a car salesman in a corporate video for Mercedes-Benz, and did some role-play work for the CID as they practised the unpleasant end of heavy interview techniques (interrogation) on us. We were told our stories in minute detail, which we then had to memorise, and we were kept in separate cells between interviews and were only to reveal what we knew if we really felt we had to. I tell you now, if I ever get in serious trouble with the police, I'll be spilling the beans.

I then booked and filmed what still remains my only ever commercial.

A LITTLE NOTE ABOUT MY WONDERFUL LIFE AS A COMMERCIALS ACTOR
This was, as I say, the only commercial I've ever filmed

but I want to make it clear that, during the first four years or so of my career, I auditioned for hundreds more with absolutely zero success.

My strike rate for getting acting jobs for television, film or theatre must have some kind of average. I would guess that perhaps one in twelve of my auditions is successful. I think it would be accurate to imagine as you read this that for every job I write about in this book, there must have been at least ten or more for which I was unceremoniously rejected. My strike rate today is much the same.

ADVERTS CAN BE A LOAD OF BOLLOCKS

Before I digress into the psychologically scarring effects of getting rejected on a regular basis for over a quarter of a century, let's get back to commercials. I just couldn't get them. At all. Apart from this one for Black Vodka, I only ever got close to one other and that was only due to my testicles upstaging me in the audition. Read on, do.

I dragged myself to yet another advert casting set up by my agent. It was for a fizzy drink of some kind and I was warned that I may be asked to take my shirt off in the room, as the advert required the actor to go topless. I sighed but agreed to turn up and try my best. I'd been in similar situations before. Advert castings are attended by as many models as actors, and my early head shots must have been just handsome enough to get me into waiting rooms alongside really good-looking models. This was usually fine as what happened in the room was often as much about acting as modelling. The dread came when they wanted to sometimes see our bodies. Then the toned and honed models were at a very distinct advantage.

In my twenties, I had what I can only refer to as the body

of a retired chess player. I'd never lifted a weight in my life. I was fit, from years of football and skateboarding but had never seen the inside of a gym. There was absolutely no muscle definition to be seen. I was shaped like a long-armed barrel.

I sat in the waiting room with what looked like half a dozen Calvin Klein models, reading the few pages of script about some man swimming in boiling lava and being saved by a fizzy drink, when the receptionist asked if we could all take our shirts and trousers off and be ready in our underwear to save time. Nobody batted an eyelid and simply started stripping to boxer shorts and t-shirts all around me. I could see six-pack stomachs and shaven chests everywhere. I felt sick. With my shirt off, it was only the position of my nipples and my belly button that gave any clue as to which was my chest and which was my stomach.

Finally, it was my turn. As I entered the room, I was asked to stand in only my underwear on a painted cross on the floor and give my name and agent's details into the camera. I had worn what I thought were my very best underpants – a pair of jersey boxer shorts that seemed to always look clean and were vaguely modern. Then it was time to improvise the advert with the casting director calling out instructions as I went:

'OK, you're in boiling lava, you're dying, pleading for help, when ... suddenly ... you're handed a can of FizzPiss.' (I wish I could remember what the drink was.) 'Now you are loving it in that lava! So swim, dance, go mad... Dance! Enjoy it... That's it...

'Great, thank you, next!'

I'd gone for it. I was handy with a bit of mime and happy

to 'go mad' in my own sub-Jim-Carrey way. I'd made some fairly funny faces, even put my head between my legs at one point and stuck my tongue out at the camera. Who knows, maybe this time I'd triumph over those posers.

By the time I got back to my flat, the light was flashing on my answer phone (before mobile phones entered our lives, that flashing red light always seemed to promise the hope of a job offer). It was indeed a message from my agent saying to call her straight away. Apparently, they'd 'loved' what I'd done and wanted me to go back in a couple of days to do exactly the same again in front of a few more people.

I returned later that week and was shown into the room; there were at least ten people crammed in behind the camera. There was also a strange atmosphere, as if I'd just interrupted a private joke. But I thought nothing of it, and happily stripped to my underwear and stood on the cross to perform my lava dance, which I'd been working on and was now sure they would go for. Everybody was watching intently but seemed disappointed. A few were giggling, or, more precisely, trying not to giggle. I felt exposed and weird. As soon as I got home I called my agent and told her how odd it all was. She said she would investigate.

What she told me a few hours later was one of those things you just never expect to hear. She said the casting director was very sorry. He felt awful, but, when they'd watched the audition tapes of the original auditions, somebody had noticed something about my lava dance. Apparently, as I'd bent over to put my head between my legs and stick my tongue out at the camera my testicles were visibly sticking out from my clearly not-so-wonderful-as-I-thought boxer shorts. He further explained that, by some fluke of camera angles, they were positioned exactly where my eyes should have been. It had caused a sensation in their office. Paused, rewound and watched in slow motion by all. They had called me back in just so everyone could meet Mr Ball Face in the flesh. He assured my agent the tapes would be destroyed, but I wonder...

How times have changed. It seemed I just had to accept this. I wasn't even given the job as compensation. Thank God this was before the days of YouTube or Mr Ball Face could have gone viral.

A LONG WAY FROM KANSAS

Perhaps the one commercial I did get was sent to make up for this experience. Sadly, it was only what is known as a test commercial; the money for filming it was poor but if the advert was bought for syndication by the makers of the 'product', I would make a decent sum. The product in question was *Black Vodka*, or, *Blavod*. The advert was sadly never seen but it was an incredibly enjoyable day's work.

The theme was a young couple in love doing things young couples in love do: eat breakfast, take bubble baths, eat picnics, have pillow fights, get married. The twist was that everything that would normally be white was seen in the advert as black: the whites of my eggs at breakfast were magically black, the bubbles in the bath we took together were black, the cream on our strawberries at the picnic was black, the feathers flying during the pillow fight were all black and, of course, she wore a beautiful black wedding dress. We somehow shot it all in one long day in and around Primrose Hill.

The young lady playing opposite me was a model, not an actress and, as far as I was concerned, a supermodel. I had no idea how to even talk to somebody who looked like that. It was as if she'd just stepped out from the pages of a glossy magazine. To this farm boy from Berkshire, it was like meeting an alien. She was the most insanely beautiful woman I had ever seen at close quarters. I couldn't talk to her for the first couple of hours. It seemed an unbelievable piece of casting that a woman like her would ever be with someone who looked like me. I didn't think of myself as bad-looking exactly but I knew my place, and it wasn't in glossy magazines or alongside women like that. As the crazy day went on, however, I discovered she was in actual fact just a human being after all, and fun to work with.

I was devoted to my fiancée, Caroline, but I enjoyed imagining, just for a few seconds at a time, that this really was my beautiful girlfriend with endless legs and a perfect bottom, wearing only a t-shirt and knickers as she made my breakfast. Near the end of the day when we were asked to just keep on kissing and giggling as they framed a long shot of our picnic from a hundred yards away, I remember thinking, 'I love my job.'

The Real Inspector Hound / Black Comedy
by Tom Stoppard and Peter Shaffer
Donmar Warehouse Productions / Comedy Theatre

It seems to me that theatre is the only part of the entertainment industry where it's definitely possible to gain advancement through merit. Much of my television and film work has come from the 'throw enough shit at the wall, some of it will stick' school of career advancement, but, it is possible to see real links through much of my history in the theatre.

You really do never know who is in the audience watching at any performance and when they might remember you. It transpired that Anne McNulty, casting director at the Donmar Warehouse and probably one of the most respected and loved theatre casting directors in England, had been along to see *David Copperfield* at Greenwich the previous year. I had no idea she had seen the show. But she had taken note of my performance and had apparently been singing my praises occasionally ever since. Over the next few years she became a kind of fairy godmother for me. Many was the time I would find myself in jobs and directors would tell me, 'Anne said we ought to meet you,' and these were often productions she had no personal investment in. I know she has done the same for other actors. There aren't many casting directors who think about actors in such a pastoral way. Despite her being incredibly busy with massive responsibilities, I was always able to meet Anne in Soho for a cup of tea and a chat. I cherished her blunt, optimistic and salient advice whenever I had choices to make.

Back in June 1998, however, I was absolutely thunderstruck to even have an audition for a Donmar Warehouse production. The Donmar was unique. Everything it touched during these years seemed to turn to gold. It was impossibly cool; it was hard enough to get tickets to *see* a show there, let alone be *in* one.

The Real Inspector Hound and *Black Comedy* had already moved into the West End and together were an absolute and total smash hit. I'd read the reviews and seen the adverts on the Underground and in newspapers telling the world that this was the funniest piece of theatre anyone had seen for a long time. Indeed, it had been such a hit that the sold-out six-month run at the Comedy Theatre (now renamed the Harold Pinter Theatre) was being extended by an extra eight weeks. Two of the original cast, Nicholas Rowe and Sara Crowe, were unable to continue as they had prior engagements, so there were two roles to be recast in a hurry. Sara Crowe was replaced by the brilliant Amanda Harris, and, thanks to Anne, I was thrown in the mix to take over from Nicholas – and, somehow, I got it.

So, at twenty-four years old, I made my West End debut playing an 89-year-old, deaf, German millionaire called Bamburger, complete with wig, ageing make-up and even a little nose putty. This was my role in *Black Comedy* by Peter Shaffer. I was also playing Simon Gascoyne, the handsome leading man of the creaky play within the play that is at the centre of *The Real Inspector Hound* by Tom Stoppard. I'd had secret desires to be in *The Mousetrap* for years, so this was ticking multiple boxes.

It was an inspired pairing of two brilliant and hilarious one-act plays, both written and set in the 1960s. They had nothing in common except for how funny and clever they were but made perfect partners for a crazy evening at the theatre. Greg Doran's production made a virtue of the 'weekly rep' qualities, by deliberately making sure each member of the cast played a totally contrasting role in each play, which added to the audience's delight.

SUPER SUB

Amanda and I were to rehearse for a couple of weeks with the understudies. Then, in the week before we took over, we had just one full dress rehearsal with the actual cast. I also signed on to understudy a brilliant young actor by the name of David Tennant, playing the lead roles in both productions. Even though the show was sold out with queues down the street every night for returns, I was encouraged during that last week of rehearsals to come along, stand at the back and watch if I wanted to. I went every single night.

I stood, open-mouthed, watching the cast raise the roof with laughter. I'm not sure I've ever seen a play that makes an audience laugh as much as *Black Comedy*. It was deafening at points and I saw one audience member carried out with chest pains. I was thrilled to think I'd be up there with them in only a week but absolutely terrified I would ruin it all. They had been playing together for a long time and had a kind of sixth sense for each other's timing and movements. I dreaded dropping a single laugh.

David Tennant's role that I had to learn as his understudy in *The Real Inspector Hound* was huge, with endless Stoppardian rants of eccentric logic. His role in *Black Comedy* was also large but *physically* it was monumental.

Black Comedy uses reverse lighting. The play opens in pitch darkness with the actors behaving as if they can see perfectly well. But soon there is a power cut, the stage is flooded with bright, bright light and the actors move and behave as if they are in total darkness. It's a simple but brilliant conceit, hilarious to watch and perfect for farce. David's ever-increasing collage of cock-ups, physical tangles, pratfalls and mishaps was like a one-man ballet of mayhem.

To go back to my footballing analogies, this felt like being plucked from the Sunday leagues to come on as a substitute for Manchester United in the last twenty minutes of the FA Cup Final. It didn't help that the actor I was taking over from, Nic Rowe, was brilliant. I adored him in the show; something about him really tickled me.

My solution was simple. I decided I would begin by giving an exact replica of his performance. I put myself in the shoes of the actors I was to be on stage with the next week and concluded that this would be the most reassuring thing for them. After a few weeks, once we'd all got used to each other, I could perhaps begin to put my own stamp on things. As I watched the show, I paid forensic attention to the way Nic played every scene and replayed it again and again in my mind as I cycled home. I can be a fairly decent mimic when I put my mind to it and enjoyed adopting all his physical mannerisms and vocal traits.

Another scary element to the whole equation was the fact that, as Bamburger in *Black Comedy,* I had to fall down a trap door every night. I had a rehearsal day with the stunt director, who was at least seventy years old, and I was told he had created stunts for Laurel and Hardy! The trap door was tiny, with a ten-foot drop down onto crash mats below. I loved stunts and physical challenges and was not afraid of the drop so much as how I had to do it. The audience had to believe I was walking in the pitch dark before I dropped, so it was essential I didn't shatter the illusion by looking at the hole in the floor before I dropped like a stone into it. Even a slight glance would be picked up on by the audience and reduce the shock and surprise that added to one of the biggest laughs of the night.

I learnt to believably get myself to a position where I was standing on the upstage side of the trap door, but sideways on to it, facing into the wings. I could use my peripheral vision to check I was roughly in the middle of the square, then, in two clear, separate movements, turn to face front, resist the urge to look down, say my last line and step cleanly off into the unknown. It was extremely hard to do. The urge to sneak a peek was enormous and the trap was so small that my nose would brush past the front of it as I plummeted down. Eventually I learnt to keep my eyes open as I dropped and finally developed the perfect startled expression to stare at the audience with as I went. As I rolled off the crash mat every night under the stage, I could hear the round of applause and rolling laugh that this bit of business always earnt.

WEST END CHERRY

Well, Monday night came around, as Monday nights tend to do, and it went surprisingly well. I didn't fuck anything up, not even my false nose on the front of the trapdoor. There was a sort of first-night party in the circle bar afterwards just for Amanda and me, where I got to meet Tom Stoppard and Peter Shaffer. I don't get star struck often but writers can make me feel a bit dribbly. Peter wrote *Amadeus* and *Equus* for heaven's sake, and Tom's plays dazzled me. I didn't know then what an important man Tom Stoppard was to become in my later life, how much he was to help my career, or that one day I would end up sharing a very bizarre cab ride through a snow blizzard in Boston with a rather amorous Peter Shaffer! Keep reading dear reader, keep reading. Keep writing then, Millson. OK, deal.

FLIES IN THE OINTMENT

The first couple of weeks went really rather well. I felt settled and part of the company and it was a rollercoaster of big laughs every night. I sat next to Geoffrey Freshwater in the dressing room, and a friend's Border Collie called

Marlowe, who I looked after from time to time (and loved a ridiculous amount), would sit under the dressing room table during the show and chew everyone's socks. I seemed to be accepted as one of the gang. One member of the cast, Nichola McAuliffe as Mrs Drudge, was always trying to make me laugh during our scenes by turning upstage and muttering 'hurry up' or, 'get out of my light', or simply, 'fuck off' under her breath at me as I was doing my bits. Hilarious stuff.

Things went a little sour later in the run.

The first awful experience was when, waiting in the wings one night at the top of the show, David Tennant said to me, 'Hey, Nic Rowe's in tonight, Joe, we're all going for a drink after if you want to come.'

'Yeah, great. See you after,' I said.

Then, suddenly, my skin went cold and sweat broke out all over me as if I was in the middle of a high fever. I simply had not considered this possibility. I'd been getting along famously doing an impersonation of another actor's performance. I hadn't asked him, I didn't know him – and he was about to *watch me do it!*

I'm not sure precisely what my fear was. I think I was worried that my performance was suddenly not flattery, but *theft.* Why hadn't I found my own take on things? I could have started to work on new ideas, but his worked so well. What would he *think?* I was falling into an anxiety tailspin and there was no way out.

Suddenly, I heard my cue and I felt myself walking, robot-like, onto the stage.

Once out there, I froze. Completely. Eventually someone gave me my cue line again and I quietly began speaking. Trying not to sound like my usual exaggerated version of

Nic Rowe, I ended up sounding like, well, nothing very much. I was saying the lines without any expression. I couldn't light my cigarette or look my fellow actors in the eye. I was blushing so deeply my face felt like it was on fire. Eventually, the laughter that other actors were still getting pulled the play back onto the rails, and I slowly climbed back on board. But I was half an actor, giving only half a performance all night.

I was dragged to the bar afterwards. I really did want to meet Nic, mainly to tell him how brilliant *he* had been in the show. Nic is now a friend. I don't see him often but we always enjoy each other's company, and the thing that made me love him on first meeting was not that he was kind about my performance; oh no, he was honest. Truthful. 'What happened out there?' he said. 'Everyone told me you were brilliant in this but you looked like a rabbit in headlights, it was rubbish.' So much easier to deal with than lies. He did, however, think my trapdoor fall was a bit better than his. I'll take that.

The second awful experience was of a very different flavour. I was happily wandering back to my dressing room after my last scene in *Real Inspector Hound* one night, to start my change from handsome English chappie to ancient German fella, when I saw that, standing in front of my dressing room door, was Nichola McAuliffe.

'Hello, Nichola,' I said innocently, wondering if she'd come for a play with Marlowe the dog. 'Don't you fucking "hello" me,' was her opening. What then followed is hard to exaggerate. She raged at me, shouting such a rapid torrent of verbal abuse that I simply couldn't understand, although I did manage to pick out the colourful language scattered here and there. She had to go back on stage to perform the last scene of the first half but finished with, 'Come and see me in my dressing room at the interval!'

I had no idea what I'd done but, whatever it was, it surely must have been terrible to elicit such a response. I could only imagine I had somehow *ruined* her performance without realising. Had I somehow cut a whole scene of hers or killed some of her laughs? I was dumbfounded. It had seemed like a perfectly usual, fun show.

I stood shaking for a couple of minutes, then my feelings shifted from undiagnosed guilt and shame to anger. There really wasn't anything I could have done on stage that would merit that reaction. New young thing that I was, I knew my basic human rights, so went straight to the company manager's room, not to tell tales but just to inform him of the situation. He checked with stage management and nothing whatsoever had gone down in the book as being out of the ordinary so far with the evening's performance. He asked me if I wanted him to come with me to Nichola's dressing room but I said I'd be fine on my own.

This is how I remember what unfolded. I went downstairs to her dressing room and, trembling slightly, knocked on the door. 'Come in,' came her bright reply. 'Close the door and sit down.' I dutifully closed the door but told her I'd rather stand.

'Would you like a cup of tea, Joseph?'

I politely declined and asked her to please tell me what I'd done to upset her.

'Well, you see, Joseph, you're very, very talented. You remind me of a young Olivier. Did I ever tell you about the time that he…'

I interrupted. 'Sorry, Nichola, what did I *do?*'

'Well, you see, comedy is a very strange business and...'

Again I had to stop her. 'No, I'm sorry, just tell me what I did to upset you.'

'Well,' she began finally, 'you've been standing at least a foot further left than you should be in our section down by the footlights and there are dozens of people in the front two rows who simply cannot see me! You must never block other actors like that.'

There was silence as I realised with horror that, for weeks, all of her upstage hissed asides to me had been filled, not with humorous camaraderie, but with anger – and over *this!*

I finally found my voice and, for once, kept my temper locked away. 'Why didn't you just tell me? I had no idea I was in a bad position for you and would have fixed it at once. You know I had barely any rehearsals and almost none with you. Why didn't you just ask me, or, rehearse with me before the show one night?'

'Well, it's done now. Are you sure you wouldn't like a spot of tea?'

I again politely declined and walked, open-mouthed, back to my dressing room. I dreaded my scenes with her for the rest of the run.

FATHER MINE

This production was one of the last stage performances my father saw me give. I remember him and Mum organising a trip to London to come and see the show. How they both adored it and how they tried to make a family night of it with my brother, his girlfriend, Caroline and her mum and brother all in the party. Caroline's family never had great chemistry with mine; we were always a little bit 'common' for them it seemed.

There was no possible way Mum and Dad could afford it but Dad insisted on paying for all the tickets, and then a trip to a posh restaurant they had heard about called Ottolenghi's. The final bill must have been shocking, but Mum let him make his gesture. It was a salute to the future, a celebration of his son's achievement and a very Arthur Millson kind of 'fuck you' to his money worries, his fear of death, and certainly to anyone who might dare to look down at him.

Sometimes I feel like we're one and the same person. How I wish he'd been around for more of this story.

The Talented Mr Ripley
by Patricia Highsmith / Phyllis Nagy
Watford Palace Theatre

A few weeks before the end of the run in the West End, I had an audition for another play at Watford Palace, this time for the Artistic Director, Giles Croft, who would be directing a new adaptation of Patricia Highsmith's brilliant thriller, *The Talented Mr Ripley*. I had got to know Giles a little during the run of *Gasping* and liked him very much. He had seen me in that show a few times and the audition went well. I was offered the role of Dickie Greenleaf, which was to be played rather brilliantly by Jude Law only a year after our stage production, in the 1999 movie directed by Anthony Minghella.

Inspector Hound / Black Comedy had also been my first decent wage; not silly money but, with two or three weeks before rehearsals began at Watford, I booked a last minute, very cheap package holiday to Greece for Caroline and me. With *my own money!*

This was a huge deal for me on so many levels. I had struggled financially one way or another since leaving home as a teenager. It was thrilling; I had only flown in a plane once before. It was also my first experience of a truly foreign landscape. I was agog at the arid, rocky terrain of mainland Greece and its pearl-blue seas for the entire week, much to the amusement of my well-travelled fiancée.

We were quite the smug young couple of actors as Caroline also had a job to come back to at Perth Repertory Theatre in Scotland. It was a great holiday, complete with memorable episodes of sunburn and alcohol poisoning. On our return, we dashed straight from Heathrow Airport to King's Cross Station, where I put Caroline onto the sleeper train to Perth. I then went straight to my bed to sleep with my new script and all its possibilities.

WRITERS IN PAIN

It was wonderful to be back at Watford so soon. It felt like 'my' theatre and I liked to imagine I was there on an old-fashioned, long-term repertory contract.

Though *Ripley* was well known as a novel this was its world premiere as a piece of theatre. The adaptation had been written by Phyllis Nagy, a brilliant American writer who had recently been Writer in Residence at the Royal Court Theatre. She was incredibly passionate about her play and was at every rehearsal, where she spent most of her time at the back of the room, shaking her head and breathing in sharply through her teeth. Which doesn't inspire too much confidence.

I liked Phyllis a lot and I think she enjoyed my work,

but she couldn't bear what some of the cast were doing and seemed to be at odds with our extremely nice director, Giles Croft. I sensed that had this been a rehearsal room in New York, certain people might have been sacked and recast. But this was Hertfordshire, darling.

I sat with an irate Phyllis after rehearsals a few weeks in and asked her why she was so upset. She explained that so much of it didn't 'sound right'; that *this* was wrong, *that* was wrong and it was killing her to watch. I asked her why, in that case, she wasn't directing it too then and she said she wished she was, and that she always would in the future. Young as I was, I tried to reassure her that it seemed to be going better than she thought and that the writing, which was terrific, and the story would hold. I was also bold enough to say to her that surely theatre was a collaborative art form, which comes with huge compromises and frustrations at times but also wonderful, unexpected results at others. If a writer wishes to have total control over their artistic output, then writing only novels or poetry could satisfy them. A play is a dead thing without its actors and audience. Like Braille without a finger to read it. I don't think I used these exact words at the time but I remember the conversation and how this was the first professional playwright I had really got to know. Theirs seemed such a tough profession. Way tougher than mine. I was intrigued. Phyllis was polite enough to listen to me, but I'm not sure if I did anything to ease the itchiness of those rehearsals for her.

MAGENTA'S FEATHER DUSTER

Our director, Giles, had other problems to deal with, including the most senior actress in our company, Patricia

Quinn. Now Patricia hadn't done a play for a while. Quite a while. She had spent many years attending fan conventions and performing tribute performances all relating to her greatest hit which was, admittedly, incredibly cool. Patricia was the original Magenta in both the stage production and the movie of *The Rocky Horror Show,* and didn't we know it.

As Magenta in *Rocky Horror,* she was always seen with a feather duster and, appropriate or not, she was holding it in rehearsals for all her scenes as Tom Ripley's alcoholic mother. It went on for weeks. Giles, who had perhaps never seen *The Rocky Horror Show,* would politely ask her to 'maybe lose the feather duster?' and he would simply be ignored. With bigger fish to fry he let it go, until the final week when he politely insisted.

'Patricia, it's really odd for her to have a feather duster. I'm sure she's never done a day's dusting in her life, she has servants for such things. Shall we just drop the duster now?'

'But, darling,' came the reply, 'I'm an *icon*. I have to have the feather duster.'

The feather duster stayed, and it could be argued that it added more to the show than its owner. I've never had much patience for lazy actors and Patricia seemed to be from another planet. She'd been made a 'Lady' when she married Sir Robert Stephens and I think it may have gone to her head. We were expected to act as her tea-makers, line-feeders, and all-round lesser mortals.

Nobody seemed too keen to put her in her place and I was happy getting on with my own work, until after a terrible dress rehearsal where Lady Stephens knew few of her lines and had played the entire performance as Magenta from

The Rocky Horror Show. We all went back to a swelteringly hot rehearsal room for notes. Patricia entered, and halfway through one of Giles's notes she said, to nobody in particular, 'Somebody close the windows, I'm freezing.' No one hurried to close any windows as we were all hot. I got up from my chair, went to one of the prop cupboards in the rehearsal room, grabbed a rug and gave it to her. She glowered at me for the next five minutes without blinking, while we all tried to concentrate on our vital notes session.

'Have. Some. Respect!' she finally hissed at me.

'Earn it,' I calmly replied.

The younger members of the company were some of the loveliest people I'd worked with and I enjoyed working in an American accent again, and trying to be specific with it. Dickie Greenleaf, according to the script, had grown up in Martha's Vineyard. So a Martha's Vineyard accent was what I researched and delivered.

The play opened well, received far better reviews than we expected and I enjoyed playing my part. Matthew Francis's 'keep your own instrument' lesson was invaluable as this character had to maintain a free and upbeat spirit no matter what was happening to him. It was an oddly delicate task.

Watford Palace was again gorgeous to play but, in contrast to the laughter-filled run of *Gasping,* the theatre seemed to have developed something of an echo. Despite great reviews, we emptied the place. People were frequently heard getting up and leaving mid-scene. Joe Orton called this, 'The Bump And Trot Brigade'.

Sometimes members of the audiences would spell out their reasons for leaving. One night, we were in the middle of one of Tom Ripley's dream sequences in the second half where he and Dickie were lovers. We'd just started to kiss when a man stood up in the front row, came up to the front of the stage and, only feet from our faces, shouted, 'Disgusting!' before walking out.

My lovely new agent, Jan, was keen to get me back on to the television and I was not about to argue. I went in for every job she could throw me at with absolutely no success, but I felt I was getting better at the auditions. Towards the end of the run of the play, I auditioned for yet another huge job I was never going to get: a new lead character in what was then one of the most popular television dramas in the country, ITV's *Peak Practice*.

As if...

Peak Practice
Carlton Television / ITV

'Do you watch the show?' I was asked by one of the producers of *Peak Practice* at my unexpected second audition.

'Yes! What? *Watch* the show? I *love* it. Well, you know, my mum loves it, and I watch it with her sometimes. I don't have a television,' I improvised.

'What does she like about it?' the producer continued.

'Well, she loves animals, so, you know, it's right up her street.'

The fact that *Peak Practice* wasn't anything to do with animals or vets but actually about doctors working on humans in a rural medical practice was news to me, and I made the producer's day, it seemed, as he was still laughing when I left the audition.

I'd given it my all and knew I had nothing to lose, and I

genuinely hoped for nothing except perhaps to have made a big enough impression to be considered for a guest role in an episode somewhere down the line.

This was still pre-mobile phone days but I'd recently purchased a pager, which lived permanently in my pocket and would vibrate whenever somebody left a message on the number.

A few days after the audition, I was on the train from Euston out to Watford to head in for a performance of *Ripley* when my pocket buzzed and the message read, 'Please call as soon as you possibly can. Jan.' My agent generally left messages on my home answer phone for me, so it was with sudden pangs of optimism that I waited for the train to pull in at Watford so I could use a pay phone there to call her. Could I possibly be in the running? Maybe they wanted to see me again? Or maybe it was just that I'd forgotten to pay my subscription to *Spotlight*.

There are some moments you really do never forget and this one is burned onto my memory. I can see myself now, putting money into the pay phone outside the ticket office of Watford Junction Railway Station, tapping those numbers and holding my breath.

The news was unbelievable. The part was mine and I'd start filming in a few weeks.

Surreal is the only word for how it felt to walk from that call box to the theatre and perform the play that night. It's not disingenuous to say that I'd never imagined myself becoming a television actor. Jobs of this level, that paid this kind of money, were for other people. It wasn't my abilities I doubted; I had a healthy enough dose of confidence in those, or at least in my potential as an actor. It was more the industry itself that I was suspicious of, and perhaps I still carried some inner working-class inferiority. This was a deep feeling of moving out of my depth, away from my tribe. Nobody from my family had swum in the waters of either wealth or fame and though this new job was not going to drown me in either, I was in for a decent splash.

The words 'talent' and 'luck' are used a great deal in conversations about this business. I don't know what the word 'talent' really means and I don't understand my relationship to the concept of 'luck'. The 'earning my stripes' philosophy that I'd developed in my early career may well have been some kind of insurance against such frightening and elusive concepts. Luck and talent were ephemeral; they couldn't be proved or relied upon, but, performances I had given and reviews I'd received could.

Well, some version of luck *was* on my side with this one. I'd walked into that audition on just the right day and given just the right unaffected performance after they had endured months of internal arguments over what kind of new actor would best serve the show.

PRIME TIME

It's hard to grasp now how big a show *Peak Practice* was for ITV in 1998. When I joined the cast, the average viewing figures were around the twelve million mark. This was high then but would be utterly extraordinary now.

Peak Practice had a very small cast of regular characters; it generally only ever had three leading actors at a time, the original three having been Kevin Whately, Amanda Burton and Simon Shepherd. The chemistry had to be just right as the fans were loyal and each actor carried a lot of the story. The actors I was to join were Gary Mavers, who had been there a few years, and the wonderful Haydn

Gwynne, who was still relatively new to the show herself.

My opening contract for that first series was more money than I tend to get for television work today. It was also my luck to get this job at what was the very end of a golden age for leading actors in British television. I was not only to receive my fairly extraordinary wage (with no 'options' so it could and did increase substantially each series), but also a very generous living allowance with which to rent a beautiful cottage in Derbyshire, first-class rail travel to and from London as often as required, solo use of a large Winnebago with driver at all locations and a personal driver from my digs to the set whilst in Derbyshire!

These days, I'm lucky to get a parking space in a field for my own car, a chair with four legs, a rabbit-hutch-sized, shared, 'three-way' dressing room, a Travelodge on the edge of town and lukewarm water for my tea.

NERVOUS YOUNG ACTOR vs COCKY GIT

There were only a few days between the end of the run of *The Talented Mr Ripley* and travelling up to Derbyshire to start work on *Peak Practice*. This was a big gig and I was nervous, especially when a friend who worked in the publicity department of Carlton Television telephoned me and gave me a long lecture on how my life was about to change forever. I developed a pronounced eye twitch where my lower right eyelid would vibrate at a hundred miles an hour. Not ideal for close ups!

I see now that part of the nervousness was because I had so little to hang my hat on as an actor. The material I read at the audition was from old episodes of the show. They didn't have a character to speak of for me yet. They were storyboarding and writing around the clock. I had lunches with producers and head writers where I presented an incredibly confident front. They really wanted me to go into that cast and 'shake things up'. I told them in no uncertain terms that I was the man for the job and was afraid of nothing.

Twitch, twitch...

A few days before I travelled up to Derbyshire, I was sent my first episode. I was so thrilled to have so many scenes that I didn't notice, or at least didn't acknowledge my disappointment, that there was very little happening on the page. Dr Sam Morgan was just a young, eager new doctor who kind of looked and sounded a lot like Joe Millson. This added to the nerves. It meant I had nothing to hide behind, character-wise. When I finally got in front of those cameras, which would be recording my work so that it could be shown in the front rooms of over twelve million homes, I would be looking and sounding like me. Me! I wasn't even a fan of looking in mirrors. The eyelid started twitching like it was attached to an electric toothbrush.

This was many years before David Mamet had written his wonderful book *True and False,* which so eloquently explains how there is no such thing as 'character', just lines upon a page. A book which extols the joys and virtues of finding simple, playable actions for each scene, turning up on time, hitting your mark and just doing your job.

No, yet again I would learn things the hard way, the slow way but, perhaps, the lasting way.

NO PRESSURE

I'd noticed something else in the script, which did nothing to alleviate the epileptic eyelid. My character started many of his scenes by pulling up in his car; he was also often to be seen getting into his car and driving off. I did not drive. I had never had the time or the money for such extravagance and living in London since my late teenage years hadn't missed it.

I deliberately kept quiet about this until contracts were signed and sealed. To be fair to me, they'd forgotten to ask. I knew it would be an issue but didn't want to give anyone a reason to give this job to another actor. A few days before my first day, I got in touch with production claiming to have only just realised it was an issue and apologising for any problems it might cause. There was a minor explosion of angst as they realised they would have to hire a low-loader truck to mount my character's action vehicle on for all my driving shots, a big expense they didn't need. They told me that I had to pass my test, and soon, or I might be let go. I'm not sure how true this was but, at the time, I believed it totally and for a whole month spent every evening after wrap taking night-time driving lessons so that I could take my test as soon as possible. The desire to keep the job was a powerful motivating force; I passed my driving test first time with nearly a one hundred per cent score.

The remainder of the year flew by in a blur. The hours were long and the days were many. I was thrown in at the deep end, learning the skills and building the muscles that only long-term work in television can give you, but which have been essential to my screen work ever since. These include learning not only to endure waking at 5 or 6 a.m. every day of the week but to relish it. A dialogue is entered into with yourself. A negotiation: 'OK body, OK brain, how do you want to play this? We have to be absolutely ready to go, firing on all cylinders by 8 a.m. sharp when the cameras roll. What do you need? Silence? Food? Early morning jogs in the Peak District mist before work? Loud music and dancing? Jokes, gossip and banter on the make-up truck? How much food to give energy but to avoid an 11 a.m. crash? Eggs or Weetabix?' These really are the questions that make a huge difference on a long-running, freezing-cold location shoot such as *Peak Practice*.

In case you are wondering, I tended to lean towards the loud music on waking, exercise, banter and jokes school of preparation. I also learnt the life-saving skill of the 'cat nap'. Eventually, I was able to use a twenty-minute break between shot set-ups to get at least ten minutes' delicious sleep and be ready to go the second I was shaken awake.

Line-learning muscles in my brain were also rapidly expanding until eventually, happily, I was able to absorb several pages of dialogue at 10 o'clock the night before shooting. This bears discussion, I feel. Learning lines for theatre seems to happen in a deep groove in the brain, slowly etched away at over weeks of rehearsal. Actors are often heard to say how, with theatre work, they don't recall learning the lines; that lines go in by a kind of osmosis. Scripts are held in hands, scenes walked through again and again, week after week and, before you know it, the pages are left in bags in the corner of the room and the scenes begin to fly. It's a long runway and a slow take-off. Lines learnt for theatre live in a corner of the brain, a drawer in the cerebral office, which can then remain accessible for months, even years.

Learning dialogue for extended filming work and especially television is entirely different. It's a kind of disposable expertise. There is *no* rehearsal before the day (except for rare exceptions). No runway; immediate take-off; a helicopter launch. Even if you are in the rare position of having a shooting script weeks before shooting, it's often counter-productive to do too much homework on the actual dialogue. You've no idea which order the scenes will be shot in so don't know which scenes to prepare first. Substantial rewrites will inevitably be handed to you, often only the night before shooting, or even on the day. So eventually, it becomes necessary to embrace the situation.

Once my theatre-trained brain really accepted the fact that it was OK if I made a mistake in front of a camera, that we could always 'go again', there was a virtue to the rapid-line-learning system. I found I had to really listen to the other actors to know where I was in the scenes. *Never* a bad thing. Also, any delicate searching for the exact line of dialogue (so long as it is found relatively quickly) is picked up by the all-seeing camera as something real: the camera sees a human being in front of its lens choosing what to say. Thinking. Used correctly it adds to the naturalism. It's a fine line though; it's a very different thing from not learning your lines. That's not what I'm talking about. No, I stayed up until 1 a.m. before a 5.30 a.m. start dozens of times to ensure I knew my dialogue, but even then I was often working from a shallow trench.

Here's a funny thing though: I still find that, should a scene take a long time to shoot, instead of getting more familiar with the dialogue, after three or four hours if we haven't finished the scene and moved on, the lines start to drift away from me – as if they were only ever on a short-term loan from my poor, battered brain. It's most peculiar, and fascinates me still. With theatre work, generally speaking I get better, more confident the longer the work goes on. But, with filming it's often advisable to use my first few takes as they are often the best.

I was learning that a massive key to filming work is self-discipline. It's essential. No one is going to hold your hand; 8 a.m. always comes and you'd better be ready with some decisions made as to how you're going to attack the scene, or it will feel like you are naked on a knife-thrower's wheel. Oddly, the firmer your choices are, the easier it is to then go in a completely different direction if a director asks you to. It's easier to jump from one solid rock to another than onto a rock from out of the sand.

COME BACK!!!!

Now then, this is the point in this story of mine where, if I were reading it, I might start to lose interest. I've always loved any writing by actors about their early careers; I devoured actors' biographies and autobiographies from drama school onwards. I wasn't always too keen on the long essays on childhood but I adored the early struggles and scrapes on their roads to some kind of success. I couldn't get enough of the romantic struggle of the artist trying to survive but, often, once the actor started to really succeed, I would lose interest. As their lives became easier and their success greater, I would stop worrying about them, rooting for them, and many is the actor's biography whose final chapters remained unread. If you are anything like me, may I take this opportunity to entreat you, dear reader, to perhaps keep reading? Though this was a remarkable turn of fortunes for young Joseph Millson, and a brief period of light fame, comfort and success, trust me, it didn't last. Plenty of struggles, disasters and face-falls lie ahead, both professionally and personally.

But I will admit it, I was having a fine old time. I had work to do, lots of it; I was engaged to be married and feeling very grown up about that; I had my first car, a deliberately cheap, old and eminently crashable blue Ford Fiesta, which I *loved*. I was flying. Nothing compares to the feeling of freedom a tank-full of petrol in your own car gives you when you've been relying on public transport or other people's cars your entire life. I was getting to know the M1 motorway incredibly well, driving up and down from Derbyshire to Camden every week, or to Bedfordshire where my mum and dad were running a country pub.

ANTS IN PANTS?

In front of the camera, I was feeling more relaxed, nerves were receding, the eyelid had finally stopped twitching, but something was stopping me from feeling truly happy in my work. I've already mentioned how there was not too much of interest in the character of Dr Sam Morgan, but it was more than that. As our Christmas break from filming approached and my first long shoot was drawing to a close, I couldn't stop the feeling that I simply wasn't enjoying the actual 'acting' part of it all. Learning the technical tricks and jargon of a film set was still fascinating me and I was developing a wonderful relationship with the crew, who were all skilled and experienced. But, that bit between 'action' and 'cut' had begun to leave me cold, numb and dissatisfied.

There were two parts to my self-induced grumpy quagmire. Firstly, I couldn't work out who I was doing 'it' *for*. With theatre it was always clear. In a rehearsal room there was a director, watching and shaping proceedings.

Then the performance moved into the natural arena of a theatre, where the transaction of giving and receiving between actor and audience is always crystal clear.

On set, even with a large crew it seemed that nobody there was actually just watching or listening. During takes, there would be absolute silence and many eyes would gaze at the monitors in video village. But everyone had a job to do, something very *other* than watch the story. Make-up might be watching for hair continuity and shiny skin etc, sound would be watching for shadows from the boom or listening for aeroplanes or pesky overlapping dialogue, the director of photography and his team would be worrying about the light etc etc. Even the director herself would often be preoccupied with valid concerns about how this shot would cut with others, crossing the line or how on earth to get everything shot in the time allotted. For want of a better word, what was missing was an 'appreciator'. And I don't mean somebody stroking my back and telling me how marvellous I am after every take, I just mean somebody to give it all to – to do it for.

I was, of course, aware that months later there would eventually be several million 'appreciators' watching in sitting rooms all over the country, but it was too abstract an idea to actually fill the void I felt on set. I came up with a strange idea that helped me briefly. I started to imagine a large, attentive theatre audience was squished inside the camera, like sardines in a tin, and they were all somehow managing to share a view through the lens pointed towards us; hundreds of eyes looking through a single keyhole. But as this patently wasn't true, it couldn't help for long.

The second part of my grumpy quagmire turned out to eventually hold a solution to the first. It has helped me ever since when things get tricky, on screen or on stage. Even when I was happily imagining my theatre crowd squinting through the camera, I was still frequently unhappy in my scenes. As a doctor in a medical drama, I was there to facilitate the extraordinary and awful traumas being suffered by the individual guest actors playing patients in each episode. Time after time, I stoically watched wonderful actors as they wept, twitched and shouted their way through the scenes. I would fill in with my dialogue between their acting solos. My lines seemed to go round on a loop, episode to episode: 'Is there something you're not telling me?' or, 'She/He/They need(s) you to be strong for him/her/them now' or, 'Hop up on the couch and let me take a look' etc. I was nakedly jealous of all the 'acting' the guest actors got to do. I was one of the leads in the show, I was going to be seen on television by a lot of people week after week – a fact that still astounded me – and I wanted to show the world what I could do. I was so very eager to please and to impress. Day after day I invested totally in every scene, felt every patient's pain with them, gave every scene my all. But it felt like I was pissing in the wind.

WAY HAY!

As Christmas approached, my first episodes began to air, Tuesday nights at 9 p.m. The combination of fear and pride as my name came up in the opening credits was a strong cocktail and I was unable to judge whether my performance was quite good or really awful. There was so very little to the character and his story in those early episodes, I just couldn't tell. I suspect the latter.

During a break from filming for a few weeks over

Christmas, I went to stay with my mum and dad at their pub in Bedfordshire. It was here that real life caught up with me, took me by the hand and tried to turn my face towards an undeniable truth: my father was not well. Not well at all. Denial is not just a river in Egypt, however, and we Millsons continued to avoid the subject throughout Christmas.

It was, in fact, sitting in a post-Christmas dinner slouch watching television with my mum and dad that the solution to my first-world acting problems emerged.

Along with most of the country, we were watching yet another re-run of the ever-brilliant *Morecambe and Wise Show*. I was laughing loudly with my Dad at gags we knew almost by heart, when I had my little epiphany. Eric Morecambe was a natural clown, like Tommy Cooper. He simply *was* funny. But unlike Cooper, I think Morecambe would have been nothing without his fantastic 'straight man', Ernie Wise. I began to see Ernie Wise's job in parallel to mine, a thankless task while Eric got all the laughs – or, for me, while guest actors got all the 'acting'. But Ernie Wise seemed to *love* his job; he seemed to be filled with joy. He and Eric were perfectly symbiotic, one couldn't exist without the other. I remembered how much I had loved my 'centre midfield' theatre jobs in the past and suddenly realised there was no reason whatsoever not to apply the same philosophy to my work on camera. Surely all I had to do was find out exactly what *my* job was, in every scene, and do that. Nothing more. Nothing less. Enjoy feeding the other actor in every scene. And, verily, it came to pass that I also realised, like a very obvious but somehow revolutionary thunderbolt, that here was the solution to my first problem. I suddenly knew who I was 'doing it for' in front of the camera: *the other actor.* They would always be there, and even if they had no idea, I decided I was going to give every actor I worked with from here on in my total concentration, attention and love. That was the plan anyway…

1999

'I see dead people,' said Haley Joel Osment to Bruce Willis in the year's smash hit movie, *The Sixth Sense*, and he wasn't alone: 14,000 dead in a Turkish earthquake, civil war began in Albania, the Columbine school shooting in America shocked the world, as did TV presenter Jill Dando's mysterious doorstep murder, hard drinkers everywhere mourned the loss of Oliver Reed and a complete solar eclipse was seen all over Europe; in response to the strangeness of the new millennium approaching, cinema got silly and tried hard to make us laugh with *American Pie, The South Park Movie* and *Austin Powers: The Spy Who Shagged Me*, Ricky Martin was 'Livin' La Vida Loca' and Britney Spears sang 'Hit Me Baby One More Time'.

Twitch ... twitch

Peak Practice (again)

FILM SCHOOL

'*Peakies*', as I came to call it, was an incredible gift on so many levels, but for an actor it was priceless. I filmed forty-nine episodes of the show, from five series over two and a half years. That amounts to thousands of hours on set, in front of a film camera, earning those stripes and clocking up those miles. Single camera, slow, detailed work with the most experienced crews in the country.

It really was my film school, with the teeny added excitement/pressure of a few million people watching my mistakes. I worked with so many brilliant and experienced actors, actors I'd been watching on TV or in films for years. With my new, happier, 'Ernie Wise' mind-set, I was more open and able to learn from them. I'll never forget the enormous compliment I was given by one of my heroes, George Costigan, who had come in to film an episode. He was in a terrible rage as we began to shoot one of our scenes. I asked him if he was all right and he said the scene he'd just shot before coming to me with some other actors was terrible and lifeless and had made him incredibly frustrated. Then he added, 'You're all right, Joe, you like a bit of an "act up", but those other fuckers just can't be arsed.' He had no idea what that meant to me.

I broke so many cherries as a screen actor, including my first proper bed scene. In one episode Dr Sam found himself getting a little too close to a patient played by the beautiful Angeline Ball, who I'd drooled over in *The Commitments*. Any nerves I had were wiped away when the day arrived by her sense of humour, her 'let's crack on with it' attitude and her firmly placing my hands on her

127

boobs during the first take. Since that day trust, respect and a sense of humour have been my preferred tool-kit for love scenes.

The directors I worked with, episode after episode, were some of the most experienced in the game. 'Old school' though most of them were, they dropped pearls of wisdom in my ears whenever I chose to listen, and all of this was shot on film: super-sixteen-millimetre film, which is a slower and more care-filled process than with digital cameras. I feel blessed to have learnt my camera technique this way.

But better than all of this for a country boy from deep, dark Berkshire was the amazing Peak District countryside I was living and working in. Every day was a location day for the first couple of series, before some interior locations were finally moved into a makeshift studio. I am and always have been a nature boy and the freezing fresh air of the Peak District was life-affirming. It was healing too. I was manically busy with work and filling most of any precious spare time with plans for my forthcoming wedding in May. But I was almost religious about taking a regular private walk or jog near the cottage I was staying in. Almost every day I would commit to it, rain or shine. No phone, no music and no company, I could meditate just a little and call my thoughts my own.

Halfway along the walk one day, I somehow found a secret, sacred spot. On an impulse, I scrambled through a thicket of bushes that covered a steep slope and there I found the most incredible private view of the Derwent Valley. Here I would stop, every morning, and sit propped between a tree and a rock, gazing out at the endless tree-filled valley below, and have conversations with myself about the things I didn't dare discuss with anyone else. Little things like, is my beautiful father going to die soon? Do I really want to marry this woman? Stuff like that.

But then I'd see it was time to go to work, or time to learn some lines and get some sleep, and would dive back into the fast-flowing stream of my life.

Blankety Blank
ITV

Life was changing. The money had started to become an actual reality in my bank account; the Ford Fiesta had morphed into a ridiculously powerful second-hand Mercedes-Benz which now floated me up and down the M1 every week. I was lightly famous. My face was on very large billboards around London; I appeared on morning chat shows and on the cover of shiny television magazines. In supermarkets at certain hours of the day, I was mistaken for various other more famous people. I started to recognise that look in people's eyes when they think they know you, but can't quite decide where from. I even said, 'Hell, yes!' when I was asked to appear as a guest on the classic game show *Blankety Blank,* hosted by Lily Savage.

My neighbour on my left through the recording was the cricketer, Phil Tufnell. I didn't follow cricket and knew nothing about him so, when after the short rehearsal he asked me if I fancied 'grabbing a quick drink before we record the show', I gamely agreed. For anyone else who is as ignorant as I was, Mr Tufnell is a delightful and hilarious man but was also a celebrated hell-raiser who was famous for his drinking binges whilst on tour.

One hour and several pints of lager later, we returned

to record the show. I was a complete mess and was by turns crying with laughter, clinging to the furniture, or reading the little signs that Phil Tufnell had written and was holding up under the table to make me laugh when the camera was on me. These would say things like, 'You look silly' or, 'You're on *Blankety Blank*' or simply, 'TITS'. It was hard to tell if Paul O'Grady as Lily Savage was really amused or really pissed off. Unbelievably, the contestant who reached the big final question, which could win him the holiday of a lifetime, picked me as the celebrity to 'play' with. He could have gone for Phil, or one of Boyzone, or someone from *Coronation Street*. But, no. He had to pick me. He was asked a question with a missing 'blank' word and he and I alone had to write down the same word for him to win big...

'When I go to the seaside, I like to have an ice cream. My favourite flavour is BLANK ripple,' said Lily.

Drunk as I was, I knew we were fine. I diligently wrote down 'raspberry'. When they asked us to show what we had written, the contestant had written 'strawberry'!

'Strawberry fucking ripple! STRAWBERRY ripple!' cried Lily Savage. 'Who's ever heard of strawberry ripple?'

TURNING TABLES

By April, I'd been filming *Peak Practice* for six months or so and my wedding in May was fast approaching. When the job was first offered to me back in October of 1998, I was already engaged and the wedding date had been set. My agent and I had made it very clear that I would need a two-week break from around 20th May for the wedding and a honeymoon. We were assured that, although this would be midway through the shooting of series eight, they would ensure it was a light workload for me in that block and get me to the church and the honeymoon on time. Caroline and I had even scheduled the big day to be on a Sunday to make sure any friends working in theatre would be able to attend.

The first sign that there might be trouble ahead came a couple of months before the wedding. I was asked by the producers if I would mind my two-week break being shrunk to just one week, as they might need me for some work in that block. I was frustrated but understood the needs of the show, and managed to cancel the ten-day honeymoon that had been arranged and book a replacement honeymoon for seven days. I reminded them once more of the date of the wedding and begged them not to change things anymore from now on. 'Of course, of course,' came the reply.

Each episode of *Peak Practice* took roughly two weeks to shoot and there would always be a read-through of the episode a week or so before that block of work started. This would happen in a large portacabin-style room with lots of long trestle tables, and would be attended by *all* cast, producers, directors and heads of department. It was also usually when schedules for the shoot were handed out for the first time, detailing which scenes were being shot on which day.

Just about a week before my wedding, I sat at one of these read-throughs, merrily munching on a free sandwich. I was looking forward to a light episode with hardly any scenes, as everybody knew this was the episode I was mostly having off to go and get married. As per usual, this was the very first time I had laid eyes on the script and we were all effectively sight-reading.

As the scenes rolled by, I quickly came to realise, I wasn't merely in it more than I expected, it was a HUGE episode for me, with long stunt sequences in white-water rapids and underwater shoots saving another doctor from drowning. This would normally have been exciting news, but not now. Not this month. It was all I could do to keep reading out loud to the end with everyone else, and not dash for the table with all the schedules on it there and then.

The read-through ended and I grabbed a schedule. As everybody stood up and milled around, laughing and drinking wine from paper cups, I returned to my place at the table with a dry mouth. It was worse than I could possibly have imagined. Caroline and I were to be married on Sunday, 23rd May, in Berkshire. According to the schedule I was down to still be filming *in a river* in *Derbyshire* until 8 p.m. on Saturday, 22nd May. I then only had three days off before being very busily scheduled right to the end of the block. Three days! Two weeks had become one week and was now three days! Why had no one spoken to me? They'd known about my wedding for six months! The honeymoon was paid for. Non-refundable. *Important!*

I found the first assistant director, who I knew was responsible for the schedule on this episode. He said he'd been told about my wedding day but knew nothing about me needing a week off. My anger was beginning to coil; I didn't know exactly who it was that had screwed up. I tried to call my agent, but it was the evening and I couldn't get hold of her, and nobody in production seemed to care or accept that there had been any oversight.

It was somewhere around this moment that I turned over every table in the room, including the ones with the sandwiches and wine on, got in my car and drove home.

I feel a sting as I write this, which is difficult to name. It's partly shame, partly embarrassment, partly sadness and partly a ghost of the righteous anger I felt that night.

My occasional flashes of temper can make me shudder when I look back on them, but on this occasion I find it easy to cut my younger self some slack. Twenty-four years old and under intense pressure, I was working incredibly hard; it was not unusual for me to work fifteen or sixteen continuous days when we had two units on the go at once with different rest days. I was already feeling guilty that I wasn't seeing enough of my fiancée in the lead-up to our wedding and couldn't help more with preparations. Caroline was almost single-handedly dealing with it all, and had also recently held firm through a very real bout of cold feet I'd experienced about getting married at all. I'd nearly cancelled the wedding, and still she was hanging on in there. I couldn't face having to tell her yet again that our honeymoon was scuppered. I was also still sitting on the ever-ready time bomb of my dad's cancer, my dad, who was also my best friend and who had agreed to be the best man at my wedding.

It was my first realisation of how small a cog in the television machine the actor is. The programme is a product that has to be made, and delivered, on time. Millions of pounds are at stake, and my principles and my needs were invisible. Any promises made to me were inconsequential to the ITV machine.

Well, the day before my wedding was spent filming underwater stunt sequences, not in a film studio's underwater tank but in the cold and stagnant pond of a stately home somewhere in Derbyshire. Here, Gary Mavers and I would hold not only our breaths but also heavy stage weights in each hand, to help us sink down again and again to the bottom of the twelve-foot deep pond. We'd wait at the bottom, still holding the weights, until the drifting silt from the riverbed cleared enough to shoot. I would then open my eyes as wide as I could and drag the 'unconscious' Gary to the surface.

I arrived at the Compleat Angler hotel in Maidenhead well after midnight. My dad and Stuart Mullins had waited up for me but everyone else was asleep. I remember us gate-crashing another wedding party's disco and me collapsing with exhaustion into profound sleep on a sofa in the hotel lobby.

THE MARRIED MAN

The next day arrived, as next days tend to do, and off to my wedding I went. I was happy to be there, but feeling decidedly queasy. No food could I keep down. Still, it was a beautiful day and I felt I was totally in love with Caroline. From this distance, I wonder if even then I was also in love with the story; with the job titles, *Husband* and, hopefully one day, *Father*.

My own father, who was also my nervous best man, took me into the pub beside the church just before the big moment and bought me a whisky. I knew he and my mum hadn't exactly fallen in love with Caroline and found it uncomfortable being around her and her posh family, but they had been only positive and hugely supportive of our wedding plans.

As we sat at the bar in our matching three-piece morning suits, drinking our whiskies, Dad took his car keys from his pocket, slid them along the bar to me, looked me in the eye and told me very calmly and clearly, 'You can *go...*

If you want to, right now, and it will all be fine. We'll sort it out and everything will be OK.' He made sure I knew he was serious, and asked me to think about it. I looked him in the eye and paused. We were, for that moment, more like brothers than father and son. It was an escape hatch that on the surface I didn't want or see the need for, but, somewhere deep inside of me, I understood. I was determined to make my own choices, my own mistakes, and slid the keys back along the bar.

None of the beautiful wedding food did I eat, I was feeling too sick. Many thought it was nerves. In fact, the pond water I'd been forced to take in through both my mouth and open eyes during the preceding day's filming had given me some kind of bug. Thank you, ITV. By the last day of our very short but wonderful three-day honeymoon in Florence, I was still feeling strange and starting to experience blurred vision. As soon as I was home, I went to see my doctor and was hurriedly prescribed strong antibiotics to combat what he suspected was a minor case of Weil's disease – a delightfully dangerous infection that can only be contracted from the waterborne urine of cattle or rats. Again, thank you, ITV.

Monogamy by Craig Baxter
Pursued By A Bear Theatre Company,
Latchmere Theatre

Another small diversion, dear reader, if you'll forgive me, to fill you in on something that had been growing and developing over the preceding eighteen months or so. (No, not my ego!) This is already becoming a sprawling tome of tales, although I have been trying to stick to my career as an actor only, as much as I can. However, other avenues were being explored.

Ever since I'd assisted Stuart Mullins on his production of *A Night Out*, we'd been developing plans to run a theatre company together. We were a good team and both wanted to work on new plays, and we knew how difficult it was for new writers to get commissions and actual productions of their plays. To set us apart from the crowd, we decided on a unique template: we would find our writer and commit to that writer for as long as it took to workshop and fully produce three of their plays. We wanted to give him or her a home and a sense of support. Our mission as we began to search and beg for funding was as follows:

Play One would be an extant play, which had been submitted to us by the writer when he or she was originally under consideration. This would be workshopped, given all the help it needed and, as soon as possible, produced with a professional cast.

Play Two would be a direct, specific commission from us, an exercise for the writer in writing to a strict commission brief and, for us, a way to ensure we had a play that was affordable and fitted with whatever the funding bodies seemed to want to see produced. Again, this would be workshopped, given full rehearsed readings and drama-turgy before we produced the final (usually third) draft.

Play Three would be a 'blind' commission. This meant that we would give the writer a date for delivery of his or her play, but the rest was up to them. It could be about whatever they wanted, and require whatever they desired. There were no limits and we would do everything humanly possible to support and realise their dreams.

We wanted to give writers freedom to grow and,

importantly, freedom to *fail*. Not every play had to be a hit, but we would be there supporting them until all three had been produced, and then away they would go. And on to the next writer we would go.

Those were our noble intentions. We had incredible commitment and energy, a great name, 'Pursued By A Bear', but back in early 1998, when we officially formed the company, what we didn't have was money. None. Nada. Zilch.

LET'S JUST DO IT

That first year, we read hundreds of plays by some wonderful writers and eventually settled on Craig Baxter, a former zoologist from Cambridge, as our inaugural writer in residence. Craig's first play with us was called *The Animals*, a brilliant one-act play and a blacker than black comedy about some anti-vivisectionist campaigners taking things too far. All through late '97 and early '98, we workshopped the play and fundraised for the production. Eventually, we somehow pulled together just enough money to mount a full production of the play, which we took to the Dublin Fringe Festival 1998 where it got some great reviews.

It was important to me that the company was not a vanity project. My role was officially that of 'associate director'. I didn't want to act in the productions, I just wanted to help get them on. I was a ball of energy, good at smooth-talking helpful people and I *loved* my other role as assistant director in the rehearsal room.

Back at the end of 1998, however, after the thrill of mounting play one, I was suddenly very busy with *Peak Practice*. I felt sad that I was unlikely to be as involved in play two when Stuart and I came up with an idea. What if I broke my rule and was in the second play? Play two was always planned to be a 'write to order' exercise for Craig. He could write a dynamic play for a small cast with me in mind for a leading character. It really was silly not to cash in. Whatever publicity I was getting for the TV show could only be hugely helpful for a brand new, penniless theatre company.

The big problem was time. The show had just gone from filming only six or seven months of the year to ten months of the year. Fantastic for the bank balance but not so great for either the private life or pursuing other projects. After the trials of trying to book my time off for the wedding and honeymoon, I knew better than to ask for time off to appear in an as yet unwritten play at god-knows-which theatre. There was, however, a tiny window of possibility. Between the end of series eight and the beginning of shooting series nine, there was a break from filming of almost three weeks. But it was already early June, which meant this break in filming was only three months away at the end of August.

We were nothing if not ambitious. One way or another, we decided we were going to go for it. I knew it wouldn't be the best way to start a marriage if my only three weeks away from filming were crammed full of endless rehearsals and performances away from Caroline so, much to her delight, we gave Craig the specific commission to write a short play for two actors, one male, one female that could most definitely be played at least once by us – and to write it FAST!

It was also plainly obvious that we didn't have time to raise money for this production in the same way we had for *The Animals*. I had money, not limitless money, but I had money. I was effectively buying a bespoke play. I could actually think of no better way of spending my money than in commissioning, producing and performing a new play with my wife, with my best pal directing and for *our* theatre company.

As I was only going to have a three-week break, we knew this was to be a short 'try out' run of the play, but finding a theatre in London that was available at such relatively short notice, and for just a one-week run, was not easy. Eventually, we managed to book a week at a well-regarded fringe theatre space called The Grace Theatre (now known as Theatre 503) and, though it wasn't going to be easy, we were sure we could rehearse a play in the other two weeks my schedule offered as free. Rehearsals would be held at our company's regular London rehearsal space in Southwark.

Amazingly, Craig came up with the goods, and how. In just over a month he had sent us the first draft of the really moving and funny play, *Monogamy*. It was Craig's homage to Harold Pinter's *Betrayal*. The story of a relationship was told backwards, beginning with a drunken reunion long after the split and then pinging gradually forwards to the unlikely falling in love at the start of their story. Hindsight makes it a moving and painful experience to read or watch, as the audience knows the ending from the start, can see the mistakes being made and the potential happiness being wasted.

REHEARSING IN GARAGES

I don't think it will be a massive surprise if I tell you now that things didn't go as planned. With alarming predictability, the filming schedule started to get behind in the lead-up to my three-week break. We lost two days of rehearsal. Then we lost another. Then, the entire first week of my break was definitely cancelled and the next looked fragile. I might no longer be able to rehearse in London at all. The actual performance week was safe it appeared, but this was a complicated, virtuoso piece for two actors and required real rehearsal.

It says a lot about the way Stuart and I approached the running of our company that cancelling the production never even crossed our minds. We were determined, not just to do it, but to do it well. The publicity, such as it was, was in motion and a designer was building our set. We would simply rehearse it that first week around my filming schedule in Derbyshire, whenever we could and wherever we could.

August arrived and Stuart came up to stay in our little cottage with us. I was still filming crazy hours and trying to learn the play in any spare minutes I had. Thankfully, it looked as though we were going to get our one week's rehearsal in London just before the play opened, but we absolutely had to start rehearsing the week before, even though I was filming most daylight hours. We'd just work into the night. Whatever it took to get the play into shape.

We had no luck finding a rehearsal space in rural Derbyshire that was near our cottage, affordable, and available to hire at precisely any hour of the day or night that we could possibly use it. Then, as we were all set to move all the furniture out of our front room and stick electrical tape onto the carpet to mark out the set, the wonderful couple who owned the cottage came to our rescue.

Right opposite our kitchen door was their family garage. A large double garage that housed Keith's beloved Jaguar.

He agreed to move it out for the week and, if we put everything back exactly as it was when we'd finished, we were free to clear the space and mark out our set on the concrete floor. So, amongst lawnmowers and bicycles, garden furniture and toolboxes, we began our work. We made a sign from a piece of scrap wood, which read, 'Pursued By A Bear Rehearsal Rooms', and nailed it above the door. It's still there now.

STEP OUTSIDE

Stuart was as eager to stretch his wings as a director as I was as an actor. We rehearsed incredibly thoroughly, sometimes into the small hours of the night, with games and character work, all on the freezing concrete floor of the garage. By the time we moved into a proper rehearsal room in London, we knew our characters well but had a long way to go with shaping a complicated play.

Stuart was even tougher with us in London, which I'm usually fine with. I like to work hard, but there was an afternoon when wires became very crossed. It had been a fun but sometimes stressful process. Stuart and I had trained at the same drama school and had worked together already as actors and as co-directors. We were devotees at this time of 'actioning' scripts; baptising each beat of each scene, sometimes every line, with a transitive verb so that if asked, 'What are you playing there?', an answer was available and discussions could begin. It's an excellent safeguard against vagueness or playing states and can keep performances outwardly directed towards the other actor. But with only a few days to go, it was starting to feel a little dogmatic and academic. We needed to get the actual play into shape, into our bones. Added to this was the fact that

Caroline wasn't trained in this way. She had trained as a singer first and then briefly as an actor. I'd only worked with her in a musical before. The way Stuart and I were talking must sometimes have seemed like double Dutch.

She bravely found her feet most of the time but I remember us reaching a real cul-de-sac of confusion for her at one point and I knew she was both exhausted and frustrated. I suggested we take a tea break. Stuart said no, absolutely not, 'we keep going'. I repeated that it really would be a good idea for us all to take just a few minutes and a little air outside our basement rehearsal room underneath a Baptist chapel.

'No, let's keep going,' Stuart insisted. It was, all of a sudden, a point of principle with him that we only stopped for breaks when he said so.

I was most confused. My co-star in a two-hander play, who just happened to also be my wife, was close to tears; my best friend and co-director of the company we ran together was suddenly acting like a sergeant major and I was the one paying for it all.

I saw red. I asked Stuart to 'step outside' away from Caroline, fully intending to set him straight and to knock some sense into him if needed. What actually happened was that, as soon as I was in the open air and away from Caroline, I burst into tears of pure stress and hugged Stuart to me like a long-lost brother.

Through sheer force of will and some really, really, *really* long rehearsals, we got the play into shape. Our short week's run in the tiny Grace Theatre was exciting. I'd never had a part written for me before and Craig seemed to have an uncanny sense of where my strengths lay. My character, Paul, was a perfect storm of 90s' Britpop, lager-fuelled cockiness, trying to negotiate his way through love. There were some fantastically funny lines. The theatre was packed out with genuine punters and lots of useful theatre people. We got terrific reviews including a four-star review in *The Guardian,* which was hugely helpful for the company.

This was one of the only performances I'd ever given that my dad didn't see. He 'wasn't having a great week', as I remember. No part of me didn't believe that this was temporary, that he'd feel better soon and be there for the next one. Well, maybe one part of me: the little voice I kept gagged and bound under a big pile of optimism and work.

The run ended and again the life-train moved right along. Caroline started rehearsing almost immediately for a long national tour of the musical *Blood Brothers* and I was back up to the sheep-filled fields of Derbyshire to start on the next series of *Peak Practice.* Physically depleted but artistically refreshed. I wonder if I even stopped in to see Mum and Dad on my drive back up North. What I'd give to drop in on the two of them together now.

2000

The world did not end, mobile telephones graduated from yuppie luxury to essential accessory, the London Eye was hoisted into position, the Tate Modern opened its doors; on its doorstep the new Millennium Bridge was opened – and promptly closed again due to safety fears, Ken Livingstone became London's first ever elected Mayor, Mad Cow Disease swept over Britain and much of Europe; in the Netherlands, a new reality TV game show called *Big Brother* had its pilot series; on the radio, Craig David was getting a lot done in '7 Days', if people talked about *All Saints* they meant the pop group not the clothes shop; at the cinema, Tom Hanks was *Cast Away*, *Billy Elliot* danced away, and Jim Carrey gurned away in *How The Grinch Stole Christmas*.

Monogamy – Riverside Studios

Peak Practice (again)
Swiftly followed by *Monogamy* (again)
Pursued By A Bear Theatre Company,
Riverside Studios London

PRODUCER HAT

I'd been filming non-stop right through the autumn and on into the spring. Long, hard hours of enjoyable work. I loved the crew and the discipline of it all, but performing *Monogamy* in a theatre, even for a week in the previous year, had reignited an addiction to live performance, which had to be fed. My every spare moment from set during December and January was spent working with Stuart to secure a transfer for our production of *Monogamy*. We had been talking to several London theatres about this as a possibility and the Riverside Studios in Hammersmith eventually came through with genuine interest, a slot that fitted with my break in filming and at a reasonable rent.

I say reasonable rent… That was only in comparison with other London theatres, which were asking for unbelievable sums of money. Even with careful planning, the remounting of *Monogamy* at the Riverside Studios, with a set rebuild for the bigger space and a proper print and publicity budget, ran into tens of thousands of pounds. Pursued By A Bear was still a way away from receiving project funding from the Arts Council or any other funding body, so this was to be entirely funded by my television career.

As a 'K-list' TV celebrity, I received occasional approaches from *Hello* magazine or *OK! Magazine* for awful interviews or photo shoots. I had always said no. Caroline and I had even turned down a sizeable sum of money when they'd wanted to cover our wedding. To help claw back some costs from the show, however, I decided to try to turn the tables and use these magazines and my slim celebrity status. I contacted *OK!* and told them I thought I had a good thing for them: my wife and I were in a play together, straight after our wedding. It was called *Monogamy*, and there would be a fantastic press night party, full of celebrities to photograph. Surely that was worth some money? Eventually *OK!* signed on, but only to the tune of five thousand pounds, and only if we provided them with a list of invited celebrities who they deemed worthy and, again, only if at least eighty per cent of them actually turned up.

My producer cap firmly in hand, I begged favours from every friend of a friend I could muster to give the magazine a half-decent list. We had an amazingly showbiz venue for the party already secured for free thanks to the fact that Caroline's cousin was married to the co-owner of the über trendy *Pharmacy* restaurant in Notting Hill. So, the plan was that with a fair wind the press night party would help recoup some of the production costs, at the same time as promoting the play and the company.

The press night arrived, we had been able to re-rehearse and Craig to partly rewrite the play. It was definitely a more polished product and the press night performance went brilliantly; the laughs were loud and the applause was long. The publicity had been good too: we had somehow managed to make the play appear on the London theatre radar, however briefly.

My plans for recouping some money on the first night didn't go quite so well. We had put out an 'all celebrities alert' to our friends, friends of friends and friends of friends of friends, to please come to our opening night party. I had spent much of the day of our press night at the party venue, making sure everything was set up perfectly. The aloof manager was very experienced with such evenings and asked me how much money I was going to put behind the bar. I hadn't thought of this. But of course people would be expecting at least their first drink for free. Feeling generous, I agreed to put down a thousand pounds. After that, they were on their own.

We raced to the venue after the show and were immediately met by the none-too-friendly *OK!* magazine team, who were very disappointed in the celebrity turn-out so far and threatened to break our contract unless the celeb list rose quickly. Hurried phone calls were made to as many from our list as I could contact, and I assured the magazine cretins that they would all be along soon.

I finally managed to find a moment to get to the bar to claim a celebratory drink for Caroline and myself. The barman handed me my two small glasses of champagne and asked for twenty pounds. I explained that I was with the *Monogamy* party and, indeed, it was I who had put the money behind the bar. He looked particularly unimpressed and said, 'That money ran out about half an hour ago.'

'Half an hour ago?' I squeaked. The party hadn't even been going an hour and most of the people we needed for the celeb quota hadn't turned up yet! Many of whom I didn't really know and I couldn't expect to drag them there and not provide them with at least one free drink. It transpired that, thus far, it had been a totally open bar and most of our guests had decided to have a crack at the cocktails. I put another large chunk of change behind the bar but said there were to be no cocktails and no more champagne.

By the end of the night, the celebrity quota was just about met and the magazine said they would pay up. But we had spent so much on booze and food that the whole thing only just broke even. So nothing lost but also nothing gained, except some really cheesy publicity.

We ran for a month at the Riverside Studios and were virtually sold out for the entire run. The reviews were excellent again and word of mouth seemed to genuinely be bringing audiences in. It was a massive achievement when, after all our receipts were counted at the end of the run, we had actually tipped into profit – by just over four pounds. But still, in theatre that's a big win.

IN YOUR FACE

I had taken great pride (and no little expense) in printing programme scripts of the play to be available for just a few pounds. I wanted people to read our writers' work as well as see their plays. I loved the way the Royal Court Theatre offered programme scripts and wanted to follow suit.

My character, Paul, had several monologues, which he spoke directly to the audience. I loved this, always have. With my imperfect eyesight it had never been too scary to face the blurry crowd directly. One night, however, I couldn't help but notice a lady in the front row who had barely lifted her face from the script all evening. After a couple of my speeches, I began to 'use' her, to the delight of the rest of the audience. I stood right in front of her and would try to get her attention, but to no avail. She was keeping her head down and her eyes on that script. I impersonated her, shouted lines right at her. Nothing. Eventually, this culminated in what I thought might be a hilarious idea. I pretended to forget my lines for a second and reached to grab her script to find out what my next line of dialogue was. It was only as I took the script from her hands that the face of my mother-in-law suddenly came into sharp focus. I had no idea she was in the audience that night. She'd been hiding her head in embarrassment ever since an early scene in the play, when her daughter had to re-enact smelling someone else's vagina on me. Which is fair enough when you think about it.

Was It Something I Said?
BBC TV

Somewhere during the run of *Monogamy,* I took part in a very posh rehearsed reading of a new sitcom for the BBC, where I got to play opposite Julia Sawalha. We rehearsed for two or three days then did a very polished, script-in-hand performance to a room full of the high and the mighty from the BBC. The show never came to anything and is still buried in the great graveyard of unmade scripts.

Chums!
LWT Television

STRIPPING VICARS

It was at around this time that I had the nerve-wracking but funny experience of appearing as a guest on a live TV sketch show. The show was called *SMTV Live!* It was presented by the now omnipresent Ant and Dec along-side Cat Deeley. A popular part of the show every week was *Chums*. This was their brilliantly made pastiche of the worldwide smash sitcom, *Friends*. Every week, they would send up the American sitcom with fantastic guest appearances from celebrities including the Spice Girls, Britney Spears, Victoria Wood, Mariah Carey and even Tom Jones. I don't want to start dropping names and trying to act all big and clever with celebrity stories but my episode of *Chums* starred *me* alongside *Sooty and Sweep!*

The show went out live on Saturday mornings and I was only booked the night before. A desperate call from a lovely ex-girlfriend of mine called Bronwen, who was now a floor manager for ITV. A far better-known celebrity had pulled out at the last minute and she wondered if I would jump in to save their skin.

I arrived, saw Bronwen for about two minutes, then was launched into the chaos of a live children's TV show. The programme was already on air, I was thrown into a room and put into a vicar's costume. The costume was admittedly a big clue but I politely asked if anyone could tell me anything more, or perhaps give me a script for the *Chums* sketch. No such thing was available. Ant and Dec and Cat read their lines live from autocues or from idiot boards held up for them. I was told that I was playing some kind of vicar who was going to marry one of the lads to Cat Deeley. Someone also mentioned that I may have to do a striptease. 'Righto…' This was all going to be live in front of millions of people within the next half an hour or so. I already had nervous giggles threatening to take hold.

I found Bronwen somewhere and begged for a sneak peek at the 'script', such as it was. During a commercial break, she snuck me over to the set and showed me the prompt boards which we were to read from. I actually had quite a lot to say as the vicar but the 'lines' were written in such small writing, I was never going to be able to see them from the stage. I was short-sighted and had come without contact lenses or glasses. It was at this moment that I was introduced to the utterly charming Ant and Dec and Cat. They dragged me up onto the set and we mucked about with Sooty and Sweep for a few minutes before they had to dash off to their places for the next segment of the show. Bronwen told me I probably had about fifteen minutes before I was on, so I sat there in my vicar costume by the side of the cameras and learnt my lines from the prompt boards, while pop stars sang and children got covered in gunge all around me.

Before I knew it, I found myself standing behind the door to the set, waiting for it to be opened by either Ant or Dec, and we were 'on'. It's a very special madness, live television. Interviews on sofas are scary enough but a five-minute sketch with mad presenters and two puppets with huge egos, each armed with a surprisingly powerful water pistol, was something else!

I wish I'd been an actor in the days when the BBC used to put out live dramas every week. That must have sorted the wheat from the chaff pretty quickly.

Peak Fookin Practice

GOOD OL' BOY

I went straight back to work, finishing what was left of series ten of *Peak Practice*. It was time to negotiate the new contract for the next series of the show, my fifth, but I knew in my bones it was time to leave. The money was fantastic but I already had more than I needed. I'd even been able to get a mortgage on a flat for Caroline and myself in Camden. Unbelievable good fortune but, despite my experiments in pretending to be an Ernie Wise straight man, the work on *Peak Practice* was nullifying my sense of creativity. I was exhausted and keen to get some time off soon to spend with my parents. Dad hadn't been in great shape and I wasn't seeing enough of him.

The producers were very keen for me to stay. I don't think it was any particular attachment to me but they'd lost a succession of regular cast members over the last few years. By the end of series ten, mine was suddenly the longest-standing character still in the show and they wanted to keep fans happy. I agreed to film six more episodes of series eleven later in the year.

So, the early mornings and the late finishes kept on coming. My character's storyline was finally beginning to hot up. The hours were insane, but I was happy. I was a machine, going full steam ahead. I was invincible.

Then my father died.

I was in the thick of a really heavy block of filming when I was told Dad had suddenly moved into a hospice. I drove the terrible triangle between home in London, work in Derbyshire and the hospice in Bedfordshire many times at all hours. Memories of those last days and hours with and around my father are cruelly clear.

I was home for a rare day in our flat in Camden when the phone rang. I heard my mother's voice tell me he was 'gone', and my spine lost its scaffolding.

The sensible thing could well have been to call production to see if there was any shuffling of schedules that could be done to give me a break. But I had less than two weeks left on that block of filming before I would have a genuine break. I knew that if any days were cancelled for me now, it would be chaos for production and only ever a postponing of the work. The days would have to be made up elsewhere. I just wanted to get it done and get out. Mum understood and I drove in the middle of the night back up to Derbyshire.

I didn't want anyone to know. I could handle working and was glad of the distraction. The more work the better. What was imperative in the first days was that nobody knew and nobody gave me any sympathy. I got through the first couple of days with my head down, but then one morning on the make-up truck, my lovely make-up artist, John, asked, 'How's your dad doing, Joe?'

I heard myself saying, 'He's fine, now.'

The 'now' was a giveaway and, in the silence that followed, everyone in the room caught up. Faces of sympathy turned from every corner of the truck to look at me and it was more than I could bear. There are times when pity and sympathy are harder to bear than cruelty or hate. I still insisted on getting the work done but they were good enough to squeeze as much of my filming into as few days as possible, so that I could get away sooner to my family and the funeral.

LUMPGATE

One night, towards the end of that very week, I woke from a thin sleep. It was the middle of the night and, I shuffled through the darkness into the bathroom to use the toilet. I felt an itch on the side of my nose and reached up to scratch it. I hit something with my finger. Something solid and not part of me was in the way. Things can often seem surreal or dream-like in the middle of the night and I thought this was some strange nocturnal mix-up. I felt for my nose again, realised something was amiss and turned on the light.

What I saw couldn't be real. My right eye was swollen as if I'd been stung by a wasp or punched by a heavyweight boxer. Below this was what appeared to be a golf-ball-sized lump growing out from under my eye just to the side of my nose. It was perhaps 3 a.m. and I was supposed to be getting picked up for filming soon after 6 a.m. I was on my own, nobody would be awake or grateful if I called them, and I really had no idea what I'd be telling them. So, I went back to sleep.

When my alarm went off at 5.30, it was all still there and bizarrely solid to touch. I called the second assistant director as soon as I thought he might be awake and tried to explain that I may not be able to put my face in front of a camera today. I think he thought I was winding him up and he told me to come in as soon as possible.

Nobody could quite believe it, or explain it. I was scheduled to be in every scene filmed that day and almost as busy on the following days. This is where film and television gets interesting for the money men. It's not as if someone can fill in for a leading actor. Their face is their face. A doctor was summoned immediately to set. He was none the wiser and at first suspected a bad reaction to some kind of insect bite. He suspected it would clear up in a day or two but, to cover his back, insisted I see a specialist skin doctor as soon as possible. For the time being though, much to the producer's utter horror, work had to be postponed and insurance had to be claimed. Someone said it would cost at least fifty thousand pounds to cancel each day!

I was required to do camera 'tests' for the insurers to look at as evidence that I was 'unshootable'. Make-up department did their level best to minimise the lump and the swelling. With the entire crew and cast hanging around,

I was stuck on a swivel chair, lit for a few minutes by the director of photography and filmed slowly swivelling in front of the camera on the chair. A special clapper board was made up for the event and held under my chin as I spun with, JOSEPH MILLSON – LUMP – WITH MAKE-UP written on it. After a clean-up, the whole process was repeated for the far more terrifying sequel: JOSEPH MILLSON – LUMP – WITHOUT MAKE-UP! This would all have been fairly humiliating at the best of times, but I was also still in shock and grief from the loss of my father and trying hard to avoid any extra attention.

The human body is a clever thing though, and some kind of inner guardian angel was watching over my sanity. I was refusing to stop. To take a break. To process. It really was as if my body had said, 'I see, you refuse to stop working, do you? We'll see about that. Now then, what do you do for a living? Acting, is it? For the camera, you say? Which bit of me do you use most? The face? OK, big guy, try acting with *this!*'

I was sent home for what everybody hoped would be just forty-eight hours' rest and then a speedy return to Derbyshire. After two days, the eye swelling had almost totally gone, but the lump was, if anything, bigger! I knew I was starting to rattle the wallet of someone high up at ITV when I was told a car was coming at once to take me to a doctor of dermatology on Harley Street. I was rushed up to the plush office of a very nice doctor who stared at the friend on my face without blinking for a long time. He poked and prodded and talked to me (and it) at length. He asked if I had any cysts that I knew of. I had indeed, one on my jaw, and one to the side of my nose, which I presumed had been swallowed up by the monster bump.

He eventually diagnosed an infected cyst; cause of infection never to be known. He then explained to me that he was under strict instructions to get rid of this thing as soon as humanly possible, by 'any means necessary'. He had been asked to clear his schedule that day so that he could operate immediately if needed. This was alarming enough, but he then told me the trouble with cysts like mine was that they calcify at an alarming rate, meaning they solidify under the skin into something as hard as the cartilage in your nose. He could remove my cyst at once but the problem was that it was growing *inwards* as much as it was growing outwards. A cystectomy at that stage would leave me with a pock mark the diameter of a golf ball, possibly for life.

Not a great piece of news for a brave young actor setting out on his quest for world domination.

Thankfully, Harley Street doctor or not, he was not being paid enough to wilfully disfigure me. He had another idea, which the money people wouldn't like as I would need a couple more weeks away from set, but which might possibly save my face. It was a prescription which combined cutting edge drugs shipped in from the US combined with ancient cures passed down from very old times.

I was to take an extreme version of a drug developed for treating severe acne. This would 'dry me out from the inside', confusing the calcification process. The drug was not licensed in the UK and I had to sign a long waiver form agreeing not to sue if and when I suffered strong side effects. The side effects listed as 'probable', not as 'possible', included suicidal depression, cracked and bleeding lips, nose bleeds and even eye bleeds! 'Delightful, where do I sign?' I was also to apply a cotton bud dipped in boiling hot water to the very bottom corner of the lump three times a day. This would over time 'soften' the skin. I was told it would eventually make the skin paper-thin allowing a hole to be made in it to 'drain excess fluid'. Sexy, right?

All went pretty much as described. All of it. The depression may have been hard to distinguish from the crushing grief I was finally allowing to creep out of me, but the eye bleeds were easier to spot, as was the pus that leaked from my lump at regular intervals, especially when I smiled.

After a couple of weeks, I was just about ready to go in front of the cameras again. The last few scenes of Sam Morgan's big storyline were shot almost entirely from my good side, or in shadow. I have never seen those episodes. Let's keep it that way.

Sam's Game
Channel 4, Pilot Episode

Not long before the time of 'Lumpgate', I'd been offered and had accepted a leading role in a pilot episode for a new sitcom for Channel 4, which would star Davina McCall, who would be having her first and possibly last crack at acting, Ed Byrne, better known as a great stand-up comic, and *me*.

This was to be another live studio audience affair and I was really excited but I was, of course, booked before I grew a second nose. Things had calmed down considerably by the time of rehearsal and recording, but I was sporting a small sack of skin where the lump had been. Yes, read that again if you like – a *sack* of skin – and I was cast as the hunky next-door neighbour. My confidence was not at an all-time high. However, the make-up team were brilliant, the cast friendly and we all gave it our best shot.

The recording went well, the audience laughed loudly; perhaps too loudly, it wasn't *that* funny. Davina basically played herself and it kind of worked. The character I was playing was a vain and self-loving neighbour who was hilariously unaware of how much he sounded like a dickhead. I wanted to really push this but the producer was worried I wouldn't be 'likeable'. I rather thought that was the point but accepted her way and gave them 'dickhead-lite'. I wish I had trusted and followed my instincts.

I got on very well with Ed Byrne and loved filming in front of a live audience again. I now had camera experience to add to my theatre experience and it seemed a perfect mix. My lump was almost hidden to shoot after a good coat of make-up. The writing wasn't great but the potential was there for a halfway decent *Friends* rip off and we all had high hopes a full series would soon get the go ahead.

Peak Practice (one last time)

A four-day holiday followed in New York. We tried to have fun. We did. We saw *The Fantasticks* at its original home and had a brilliant night watching Alan Cumming in *Cabaret* at Studio 54. He grabbed Caroline out of the audience for a dance on stage at the start of Act 2. She never believed me that I hadn't set it up.

It was my first ever visit to America. I'd been yearning to go there since I was a teenager. The trip was so short that it didn't really touch the sides of my appetite to discover the country. I'd no idea how soon I was going to see much, much more of it. But I loved New York. I've felt an almost spooky familiarity there every time I have been.

For us, though, it really was 'the city that never sleeps'.

We had been ripped off by our travel agent and ended up with an awful room in an enormous hotel. We were sleeping so close to the lift shaft we could hear the conversations inside it. There was barely any window at all (and what there was had a view of a brick wall), and no air conditioning, which in the middle of a New York summer was no joke.

My agent had arranged for me to meet an American agent in New York. I was all the wrong types of nervous about this and, on the morning of the meeting, I awoke with almost a full regrowth on the side of my nose. In the land of perfect white teeth and perfect skin, I decided it would be better to cancel the meeting. We spent the day bobbing about on boats around the Statue of Liberty instead, then going up to the top of the World Trade Center. Caroline loved heights but I am a life-long sufferer from vertigo. However, I wanted to give it a go for her and up we went.

It was a perfect summer's day. Even at that height there was barely a breeze; all was unbelievably quiet and calm. I stayed away from anywhere where I could possibly see over the edge, but I took a moment for myself, and sat down against a wall. All was peace. It was an extraordinary place to get perspective and try to say a few words to my dad, who seemed to be sitting there by my side.

Just one year later, as I and the rest of the world watched those towers fall, I couldn't believe that platform of peace had tumbled into dust and taken so many souls with it.

WHO ATE ALL THE PIES?

Back to Derbyshire I went to shoot my last five episodes of *Peak Practice*. I was enjoying the work very much. Then, one morning, a typed letter was left on my trailer signed by all the producers, which politely asked me to see if there was any way I could manage to 'comfortably lose a little weight'. I was both outraged and amused. I thought it was probably a wind-up and found a moment as soon as I could to pop into the producer's office. They were embarrassed but insistent that it was a concern.

'I'm not fat. And even if I was fat, so what? This isn't a modelling shoot,' I protested. They agreed entirely and weren't going to press the point if I wasn't of the same opinion but also wondered if I'd seen the show lately. I had to admit I hadn't. They showed me a couple of scenes from an episode that had aired perhaps six months previously. Then they showed me some rushes from scenes we had shot that very week. There, in front of me on the screen, was what looked like my chubby cousin – or me photographed mid anaphylactic shock. I was mortified but crying with laughter as they made the footage go into slow motion so that I could see my new double chin wobble.

I realised that a) I'd been neglecting to watch the show and, while watching yourself on screen as an actor is never too much fun, it is important to do it frequently for quality-control; b) I'd been comfort eating since Dad had died. Not just the wonderful school dinners provided whilst filming but everywhere else too; and c) I had stopped exercising. It was time to wake up and start getting fit and ready for whatever lay ahead.

I started running again, stopping sometimes to have a moment looking at my favourite view of the Derwent Valley, and I also began a regime with on-set catering which I have stuck to pretty consistently ever since: no cooked breakfasts and no puddings until the last day of the shoot. That's the rule. Not exactly torture, is it?

By the end of October 2000 it was all over. *Peak Practice* had been a huge part of my life and I will always be grateful for it. Many of the crew had become like family and they all came with their partners to my leaving party, where I sang 'My Way' through tears on the karaoke machine as if my little life depended on it.

BACK TO THE FUTURE

As is often the way when actors leave a long run in a TV show, when it came to getting a new job, I couldn't get arrested. Towards the end of the year, my agent was told that the sitcom pilot, *Sam's Game,* had been commissioned for a full series by Channel 4. It would be filming in the spring and they wanted to know if I was free. We tried to act casual and said, 'Yeah, we could probably squeeze that in.' Weeks later, when my agent started to push for more details, things got a little odd. They wondered if I would be willing to come in and 'workshop the character' as they weren't sure they had got him quite right in the pilot. I answered a resounding, 'Yes, absolutely, whenever you want.'

We waited, and waited some more. Radio silence. Then I heard from Ed Byrne that they'd cast someone else in my role. Showbiz, ladies and gentleman. Showbiz.

Caroline got a job singing in the chorus at Le Châtelet Opera House in Paris throughout December. I moved there with her for the month and relished the beauty and *otherness* of that magical city. It was good to rest, but quiet and stillness were not what I was looking for then. I needed movement.

I was about to get some.

2001

The attacks on the twin towers in New York on September 11th overshadowed so many other details from this year, even an earthquake in India, which killed 20,000 people; the first *Shrek* film tried to cheer us up, as did Deputy Prime Minister John Prescott when he punched an egg-throwing protester; Apple introduced the iPod, Microsoft introduced the Xbox, Wikipedia went online for the first time, Jack Lemmon and Nigel Hawthorne passed on to the great green room in the sky, Russell Crowe acted his socks off to convince us that he had *A Beautiful Mind* and Ewan McGregor and Nicole Kidman *sang* their socks off at the *Moulin Rouge*.

Mill On The Floss –
Shared Experience

Mill on the Floss by George Eliot
Adapted by Helen Edmundson
Shared Experience Theatre Company
National Tour, West End, Washington DC & China

TINY DANCER

Another detour, dear reader, if you will allow, to help you understand how exciting the next adventure in acting was for me.

I have always been a bit of a frustrated dancer. That isn't quite right. I have always loved watching dance and movement-based theatre and, from a very early age, I was engaged in what could be described as a detailed dialogue with my own body, testing its limits and training its intelligence. From tree-climbing and my own childhood version of some kind of woodland free running, to years of dedicated football playing, to over thirty years of skateboarding. The last of these has played a massive part in shaping my psyche.

Skateboarding has no rules, and no limits other than those set by imagination, pain thresholds and patience. At the remote farm where I lived from eleven years old to seventeen, I had my own homemade, ramshackle, floodlit, twelve-foot-wide indoor mini ramp in a barn, and an even more ramshackle larger ramp outside. I could and would skate 365 days of the year, often until the small hours of the morning. Self-discipline was all. On my own or in company, I would push my body to its limits, try, fall, get up, try again, fall harder, try harder and, as often as not, eventually conquer.

There was a primary, driving relationship between my body and my brain, which was made during these years, which is still at the heart of any joy in my work and, if we want to get deep, it is probably at the heart of all of the most joyful moments in my life.

LIGHTING FIRES IN MY HEART
As a teenager, I saw and was massively influenced by two theatre companies that I watched. At sixteen, the students on the performing arts course I was attending were all taken to see a company called The Kosh, who were touring a production called *Dinner Dance* to a local theatre. The whole thing seemed an unattainable work of beauty to me. I wasn't even inclined to acting for a living at that point but I was absolutely thunderstruck by the show. They were everything at once; they danced, or perhaps I should say moved, in the most beautiful, abstract and athletic way. In the next heartbeat, they were performing dialogue scenes of complete domestic realism with truth and subtlety, then they would suddenly burst into beautiful a cappella singing. They were booked to come to our college the following day to lead a workshop. I was dry-mouthed with concentration and admiration the whole day.

A second experience followed by chance, which, again, was before my desire to act had actually been recognised. I haven't thought about this day for a long time but I'm smiling now as I see myself there. I was in Victoria Park in Newbury on my own, using the awful but much-loved council skateboard ramp, when I saw on the other side of the park some kind of circus being set up. On reading little posters attached to trees nearby, I learned that, at 2 p.m. and 6 p.m. that day, there was to be a free performance of something called *Carmen* by a circus troupe called Kneehigh Theatre. I had nothing else on my teenage agenda that day, so sat down alone on my skateboard to watch a bit of free entertainment, expecting not very much at all. What I saw was one of the most anarchic, free-form pieces of crazy music theatre I have ever seen. There, by the polite rose bushes of Victoria Park, Newbury, these performers played live music really, really loudly and burned with intense, naked love and jealousy. They danced and sang for all they were worth; it was an incredible show.

It felt like I was in the story with them. Especially when I stayed on for the evening performance, with fire torches everywhere. I was so close, I could literally smell the performers and see in their eyes how lost in the story they were. It seemed like their lives depended on every passing moment.

Afterwards, I hung around and eventually plucked up the courage to ask if I could help them take down and pack away the set. They put me straight to work. I could hardly believe my ears when these creatures, who had just transported me into the passionate heart of Spain, spoke to me with Cornish accents. They were so welcoming and so interested in me. A big, tattooed actor, who had played the matador, told me how they lived and worked together all year round in Cornwall, and suddenly announced to the whole company that I was going to run away from home that night to join their family. I had no idea if he was joking or not; I hoped he wasn't. If they'd asked me seriously, I'm fairly certain I would have been sending my parents a postcard from Cornwall.

A few years later when I was at drama school, I noticed how in some classes when the work was 'physical' and something had to be mastered – be it dance or expressive movement, a skill required for the scene or the play – I could enter the same zone of blissful concentration as I had with skateboarding. I wanted that joy of *thinking with my body*. I was lucky enough to have been taught there by a truly wonderful Australian movement teacher called Lorna Marshall. She helped to keep my body's brain ticking for those three years.

FLOSSIE

It was in my final year at drama school that I had another massively influential experience watching a piece of theatre. At the tiny Tricycle Theatre in Kilburn, I saw *Mill on the Floss* performed by the internationally acclaimed Shared Experience Theatre Company. It was utterly enthralling. George Eliot's beautiful, sprawling novel compressed but also exploded into two and a half hours of total theatre.

As with The Kosh years before, the actors seemed limitless, most playing several roles. Beautifully written, script-based scenes were acted with perfectly judged, subtle performances. These would swing straight into incredible sequences of strong movement of almost balletic precision. The actors were so in tune with each other they seemed psychically linked. The lighting and sound were out of this world too; on the simple set, atmospheres were thick enough to taste and smell.

George Eliot has to take a chunk of credit of course. It is a truly beautiful story and the adaptation by Helen Edmundson was perfect. The final sequence, where the mill is flooded and Maggie drowned, left me sitting joyfully frozen in my seat for minutes after the show was over.

TV ACTOR NO MORE

With all this in mind, you'll understand how, when years later I happened to read in *Time Out* magazine that the production was to be re-mounted in 2001, I felt I had to be part of it.

This wasn't easy to achieve. I asked my agent to approach Shared Experience on my behalf, which she did. They declined. We learned that realistically my theatre CV thus far wasn't hugely impressive or reassuring to a company with standards as high as theirs. They were also not in the least bit interested or impressed by my having starred in some television show for the last couple of years.

This only made my desire to work with them stronger.

After leaving *Peak Practice,* it would have been relatively easy, before too long, to slip into another TV show of a similar ilk, but I knew I would learn nothing that way. I wanted change, challenge and growth. *Mill on the Floss* was the perfect move, if only I could convince *them.*

I wrote my own handwritten and heartfelt letters to Nancy Meckler and Polly Teale, the Artistic Directors of the company. I was able to honestly tell them what an influence the production had had on me, how frustrating I had found much of my work for the last couple of years and how I would love to be allowed to at least audition.

Audition I did, two or three times. I was pushed and tested, physically and mentally, at every meeting; they were lovely people but seemed to be able to smell bullshit. Emotions had to be *connected* with, not represented. I felt nervous but also utterly at home; even at the auditions I knew this was the absolute antithesis to the work I'd been doing for the past two years. There would be no skimming through a single moment of a single scene, and it was *physical.* I burned with a need to do this work.

Eventually, they gave in and I was offered the role of Stephen Guest along with my other roles of Uncle Glegg, a schoolmaster, and Satan! There was to be a tour of England, a short run in the West End, a month's run in America at the Kennedy Centre in Washington DC and a slim possibility of a few weeks touring in China, but this was yet to be confirmed. I was overjoyed; my itch to travel was almost as strong as my itch to throw myself around a stage like a dancer!

Unbelievably, in the same week, my old friend, Ben Crocker from the Magnificent Theatre Company, asked me if I wanted to play Hamlet, a role which I, along with every other actor on earth, had been quietly obsessed with since my first year at drama school. I'd seen at least one production of the play every year since I'd lived in London.

Ben was directing *Hamlet* at the Northcott Theatre in Exeter, in the early summer. The dates were a squeeze but if I learnt the play in advance and started the minute we got back from performing *Mill on the Floss* in America, we would have three weeks' rehearsal, which was just about enough. Just. I asked Shared Experience how likely the trip to China after America was and was told they weren't holding out too much hope as there had been problems with the arrangements but they would know soon. Much as I wanted to travel to China, I wanted to play Hamlet more. So crossing my greedy fingers, I did several little dances for joy before putting the play out of my mind so that I could concentrate on *Mill on the Floss*.

REHEARSALS

Rehearsals were a combination of everything I was hoping

for and a few sore disappointments. The first week was spent working almost entirely physically, creating a feeling of ensemble and learning to work in the company's language. The work on our bodies started every day with a tough, hour-long physical warm-up led by their wonderful but truly bonkers movement director, Liz Ranken (most of which is still my 'go-to' warm-up today). This would bleed into playground-like games played at full childhood intensity. We also did long workshops on the strange Lincolnshire accent we were to perform some of the play in, as well as singing, status, ensemble work, colour and elements.

Children express emotions physically, from their toes to their fingertips. As we creep into adulthood, we become socialised and restricted. Which is just as well as, having worked with Shared Experience, I can vouch for what a room full of adults expressing their emotions fully is like and it wouldn't go down well in aisle 2 of a supermarket. It's no accident that we still use phrases such as, 'I boiled with rage', 'I was sick with jealousy', 'I was crippled with embarrassment' etc. If Liz asked us to do some strange things like, embody 'the colour red' or 'fire' or 'champagne' or 'treacle' we knew it was all to help clear any blockages between our bodies and our minds so that, when required, we could express our emotions fully and physically.

The company's whole thumbprint is about making the invisible visible on stage; physicalising whatever is going on under the surface, fully, as children would. One simple but brilliant exercise illustrates this. As we moved on to rehearsing the scripted scenes, either of our directors could at any given moment clap their hands loudly once, which we all knew was our signal to immediately let go of the words and express fully without using words what we were experiencing beneath the dialogue. Somebody stirring a cup of tea, smiling and talking politely might suddenly be strangling the other actor, or dash under the table and shake with fear. On a second handclap, the actors would re-enter the written scene exactly where they had left off. This was very often nothing to do with what eventually ended up seen on stage by the audience but, in rehearsals, it ensured all the actors connected very strongly to every emotion in every scene. I was thrilled to be letting my body do the thinking for a change. My inner dancer was alive and kicking.

Things only got a little disappointing the nearer we got to the end of rehearsals. We'd become a real ensemble, physically primed, and through weeks and weeks of concentrating and playing together we were able to perform the expressive sections of movement in perfect synchronicity. The 'dancy' moments were going great! The tricky bits were the more static, traditional scenes. We'd spent time physicalising what was going on underneath the scenes and now the 'surface' had to be blocked and shaped like any other play.

There was a combination of factors working against us; Polly and Nancy had enjoyed huge success with the original production and, despite often telling us that this was a *new* production and that they wanted it to emerge organically from all of us, they were naturally attached to memories of exactly how some of the most amazing scenes from the previous production had looked. I had no problem with this as, the more scenes looked and felt like the show that had knocked my socks off years before, the happier I was, but some actors were occasionally frustrated.

As was Nancy Meckler, especially when she couldn't quite remember how they had solved a problem in the previous production and couldn't see the answer.

I adored Nancy; I think she may have given me the clearest piece of direction I've ever received. We'd tried a scene a dozen different ways and nothing seemed right. Her direction was getting confusing and we seemed to be drifting further and further from what made her happy.

'Nancy, I'm just a little confused,' I said. 'I'm not sure what you want. What do you want?'

With her brow furrowed, she answered in her Long Island accent, 'I want you to… I want you to… I want you to *fuck off!*', before bursting into peals of laughter.

UP, UP AND AWAY

An unexpected problem arose for me, which I'd encountered surprisingly rarely thus far in my career, namely, being upstaged by an actor you're playing many of your scenes with. I don't mean being shown up because they are so much better than you – that would actually thrill me. Sadly, I mean that, if the other actor plants themselves firmly up stage centre at almost all times, then you are forced to spend long spells with your back to the audience looking up stage. In another production I might have been able to shrug this off and simply turn out front as often as I could, but I wanted to keep that electrical connection we had worked so hard to create in rehearsals alive. Turning my back on another actor too frequently seemed to cut it dead.

It was a delicate issue to raise in a rehearsal room where a loving and trusting atmosphere had been conspicuously created. I mentioned my concern in private to both Nancy and Polly a week or so before we were to open. They could see exactly what I meant but reassured me that it would work itself out… It didn't.

Here I am again feeling a little itchy as I close in on an episode from my life that was uncomfortable, and where I didn't behave as I might today.

What started as an awkward week or two in rehearsals became an ongoing battle with a company member, which lasted five months, travelled three continents and depressed me deeply.

It was in late rehearsals, and especially on stage in front of an audience, that the wonderful ensemble acting we'd worked so hard to establish was lost as, night after night, the person in question seemed to fight us all for some kind of pole position. If an actor cried opposite her, she would cry more, whether it was accurate to the scene or not. If a character was admonishing her firmly, she would be twice as firm back, even if the scene written required her character to be downtrodden at that point of the play.

With hindsight, I can see how she may have been stuck in the kind of vortex I'd experienced on *David Copperfield*. She was perhaps in need of the advice Matthew Francis had given me, to concentrate on 'keeping her own instrument' in each scene. When this habit was allied to some genuine old-school upstaging, it was hard to just smile and brush it off. Nancy and Polly didn't seem to be able to help her and, to be honest, didn't seem deeply concerned: the picture presented to the audience was relatively intact. It was all a tad heart-breaking. I believed totally in the ensemble ideal that Shared Experience aspired to. The very name of the company for heaven's sake was about inclusion, a *shared experience* not only with the audience but ideally with each other.

ON THE ROAD AGAIN

None of this got in the way of an awful lot of joys and thrills, however. There was plenty of good stuff to concentrate on; the parts of the production that I enjoyed, I *really* enjoyed. Key memories and disasters from the UK tour include being knocked completely unconscious one night at the Liverpool Playhouse by smashing heads with another actor during the final movement sequence, and also walking straight off the front of the stage at the Cheltenham Everyman Theatre … a mid-performance clanger that might require a more detailed description to be fully appreciated.

I had a lot of fun playing one of my supporting roles, Uncle Glegg. He appeared in two or three of the scenes in Maggie's early life, always just behind his domineering wife who did all the talking. With a battered top hat, and a pronounced underbite I followed Mrs Glegg closely wherever she went, holding her favourite chair in front of me for her to sit on whenever she needed to. If she suddenly stood to take a strong walk around or across the room to make a point, I would be right behind her with her chair.

We'd been playing at the Yvonne Arnaud Theatre, Guildford for a week or two, which had a large stage, before moving to the beautiful old Everyman at Cheltenham, which had a much smaller stage with, incidentally, a very long drop of at least five feet down to the seats in the stalls.

All was going well on our first night in Cheltenham. I was enjoying my grunting performance as browbeaten Uncle Glegg, I was alive to Mrs Glegg's every need. She stood and took a strong walk around the stage. In a flash I had her chair in my hands and, holding it in front of me, I followed close behind. She took her usual route down to the front and around to the other side of the stage. I'm not sure exactly what happened next, but presume I must have taken the exact route I'd taken at our previous theatre; this was perhaps three steps further downstage than actually existed at our current venue. Like a character in a cartoon walking off a cliff, I tried to walk on air before I, along with my top hat, chair and underbite, plummeted five feet down into the stalls. Although I knackered my ankle a little, I managed not to injure any audience members in the front row. I popped the chair back up to where the scene was trying to continue then unceremoniously hauled myself back up onto the stage.

STAGE DOOR JOHNNY NO MORE

The tour was finished after six weeks or so and the set was squeezed into the tiny stage of the New Ambassadors Theatre in the West End of London; the very same theatre where I'd worked as stage door keeper only a few years before. How quickly some circles can be squared. It was with huge satisfaction that I introduced myself to the stage door keeper and carried my bags through to the rat-infested dressing rooms below.

The production was in fine form by now, the movement sections were working beautifully and, after three months of consistent work, we were a fit and finely tuned ensemble.

The reviews were unanimously glorious. It was a limited run in the West End of only six weeks so it really was a hot ticket. The queues of people waiting for returned tickets would always be stretching up the street. We received standing ovations at every curtain call; movie stars were spotted in the audience. This was not usual.

During our West End run it was confirmed that we would

after all be going to China after our trip to Washington DC, courtesy of the British Council. This was wonderful news but also sad, as I had to wave farewell to what might be my only ever shot at playing Hamlet. I tried to convince Ben that we could put it on with the eight days' rehearsal we would have after my return from China. He didn't feel this was quite enough rehearsal for the greatest play ever written and moved on to another actor.

USA

Before we knew it, we were on our way to Washington DC for a month's run in the enormous Eisenhower Theatre at the Kennedy Centre. I was so excited to get my first American work visa in my passport; my desire to live in America was getting its first real fix. It felt good to be there again and to be there not as a tourist, but working, contributing something.

Here too, the show was a hit, winning a Helen Hayes award and selling out the huge theatre. I think it was celebrated in America largely for its inventiveness; the subtleties of the text and the humour were often lost on the audience. We'd tried to soften the edges of the thick Lincolnshire accents in the early scenes but we might as well have been speaking Welsh.

My private, pathetic war with an upstaging actor was still being waged night after night. Things were getting alarmingly physical and not in a groovy physical theatre way. There was a beautiful piece of movement we'd developed in rehearsal between us, which gradually grew from a sedate row in a boat on a river to an expressive dance of sex on a piano. Sounds ridiculous? If I hadn't seen the show myself I'd agree but it was actually beautiful and very moving. However, as the tour went on, I found myself again and again physically manhandled by my 'lover' into the downstage and underneath position. The connection we had once shared as actors was lost.

Though my frustration fixated on the upstaging element of these wrestling matches, what I was really angry about was being abandoned by another actor and being barred from performing the scenes in an inclusive, shared way. The waste of potential every night was killing me. Eventually, I'm ashamed to say I snapped. One night on that huge stage, as I was held downstage and out of the light mid-expressionistic fuck, I flipped. Literally. I took hold of her and physically tried to switch our positions. I wanted her to see how it felt down there. She pushed back. We literally wrestled our way through that scene and the two scenes that followed. To the audience, I suspect this never looked much more than a kinky physical love game but, up close, it was an awful descent from the trust and respect that theatre requires and it upset me deeply.

We weren't the only ones going through tough times. A wonderful young actress was playing young Maggie; she was the living embodiment of Maggie Tulliver's inner child and the true heart of the show. One night, in front of over 1,000 people, in her very first scene she suffered some kind of mental breakdown. I didn't know her well and wish I could have been more help. I watched helplessly from the wings as, mid-scene, she sank to the floor, unable to stop crying.

At first, it looked as if she'd simply got carried away with the scene and couldn't control her emotions. One or two of us in the wings must have giggled, tutted or muttered some kind of 'pull yourself together' type statements. In a flash, Pip Donaghy, the eldest member of our company, turned on us and taught me the first of many valuable lessons I learnt from him. 'Stop that,' he said furiously. 'She's one of us, we take care of our own.'

After several minutes, she dragged herself back into the scene and we all followed Pip's lead and tried to support and help her through the show.

I have since found myself being Pip in other companies over the years. Theatre is a vulnerable place to be at the best of times and support is essential. But on that night, nothing that young actress said on stage could be understood as it all came out through painful sobs. Awful to watch. In any other job it would be so easy to stop and say, 'Please, please, let's get you home so you can sleep.' But with no understudies and over 1,000 people having paid a lot of money for that particular evening's performance, the show actually must go on.

By luck, we were resting the next day. When we returned the following week, she was present and able to work but I didn't feel she was ever happy in the show again, and going to China with it was perhaps the last thing she wanted.

'The show must go on' rule when there are no understudies is no joke. On early tours, I'd been unable to attend the funerals of both my grandfather and my uncle. It may seem a frivolous way to earn a living to some but difficult sacrifices are made that would be unacceptable in other professions.

I was determined to make the most of being in Washington. Caroline came out for a brief stay and after that I used every available hour to explore. I took long bicycle rides and canoe trips down the Potomac River.

CHINA CRISIS

I had been in Washington DC for over a month when we returned home to England for all of two days, before spinning off to the other side of the earth and an entirely different time zone again. By the time we landed in Beijing, we didn't know our teeth from our tits, and when we learned that all of our luggage had accidentally been flown to Moscow and may not be returned to us for up to a week, some people in the company were rather upset.

I didn't care; I felt overjoyed to be in a part of the world I never dreamed I'd see. I was so grateful for the experience and filled with wanderlust. We were to perform only a handful of times in Beijing before taking a train to Shanghai to do the same. We would have many days free for sightseeing, such as was permitted to Western tourists. It was a fascinating time to visit Beijing; preparations were underway everywhere for their forthcoming hosting of the Olympic Games. This included endless building work and loud explosions in the sky as the authorities experimented with controlling the weather.

ANOVVER BRUNDER

It transpired that part of the reason this trip had not been confirmed earlier by the British Council was the Chinese government's feelings about the 'revolutionary nature' of the novel, *Mill on the Floss*. Our production was booked to coincide with the first ever official Chinese translation of this 140-year-old novel, which had been on the banned list due to its feminist nature; a compliment I suspect George Eliot would have been thrilled by.

But this isn't a book about my travels; it's supposed to be about the acting stuff somewhat. So I won't mention the time I decided to absent myself from the organised tours and went on a solo trip on a crowded Chinese bus to a remote rural town a hundred miles from Shanghai, how I had a lovely time there on my own, feeling like a true alien, but could find no bus back to Shanghai for my evening performance so rode on the roof of a truck for three hours to make the show. I won't tell you how weird it was having fully armed and silent members of the Chinese army backstage with us at all times as they guarded their surtitle translation machine, which we were using. I won't bore you with the details of how hard it is to find food as a vegetarian in China, or how I had a laughing fit on my own in the Forbidden City listening to Roger Moore's almost certainly drunken narration in the headphones provided. I don't need to tell you about climbing a remote corner of the Great Wall of China with Nancy Meckler, or the mass ballroom dancing lesson I joined at 6 a.m. in a park in Shanghai, or the intense and prolonged food poisoning I experienced in Shanghai, which made getting from the hotel to the theatre a monumental achievement and destroyed the cream breaches I wore in the play. I will, however, tell you a little about how the Chinese army weren't too keen on my puppet-based installation art.

CHAIRMAN LUCY

In the early scenes of the show, one of the characters was played by a puppet – a beautiful, child-sized puppet of a pretty little girl controlled by the actors on stage with her. Lucy was a sweet and perfect child who Maggie couldn't bear to be compared with, so the beautiful, unmoving, smiling doll face of Lucy the puppet worked fantastically to highlight how she appeared to Maggie. Lucy had done all her work by the end of act one and, over the course of the tour, an unofficial and unspoken game was starting to be played. Every now and then near the end of the show, Lucy would be found backstage dressed in completely different costumes which, as the months went by, grew from novelty t-shirts, sunglasses and hats to full bondage gear. She was even sometimes found in uncompromising positions with other dolls or toys. I'll never forget seeing Buzz Lightyear doing unspeakable things to her...

The strange concrete theatre in which we were performing in Beijing had some archaic equipment lying around backstage, including a very large glass case covering an old lighting desk. I was inspired. I spent the next couple of days scrabbling around the city buying some torches, a large piece of red velvet-like material and a traditional, communist-style boy's suit. I prepared everything meticulously so that, during a small break in the second half, I was able to dress Lucy and lay her out on the red velvet in the glass case, with her arms across her chest. I taped torches in position to light her, put the glass lid back, then stood my sign, which read 'Chairman Lucy', respectfully in front of what now looked like her state coffin.

This all went down very well with the tired and slightly bored acting company but less so with the soldiers from the People's Liberation Army. They dragged me into a small room, locked the door and took turns to scream and shout Chinese obscenities in my face for half an hour. They seemed frustrated that, due to our extreme visibility in the public eye, they were unable to punish me physically for my disrespect.

Disrespect it was. A foolish and ignorant thing to do and

I apologised profusely. I am, however, still quite proud of having won the 'Best Dressed Lucy' contest.

JOB LAG

Mill on the Floss had been an intense experience. A few months of solid unemployment followed, which were gratefully received by Caroline and myself as a chance to actually spend some time together in our new home in Camden. The wages with Shared Experience were very low but some remnants of savings from *Peak Practice* were still hanging around, so, for a month or two, we had the luxury of not having to panic when the phone didn't ring. I don't think I've really known that feeling since.

Auditions did start coming in, mainly for theatre, which was fine by me; really good meetings some of them but though these often went well, I wasn't getting offered the actual jobs. The reasons you don't get offered jobs in this profession are as mysterious as the reasons you do. Everything is subjective and everything is about other people's tastes and ideas, which you can never know, or control. But it is always difficult to work on a script, to fall in love with a part, to know what you could do with it, get into the room, like the director, smell the whole thing – and then hear nothing.

Four Nights in Knaresborough by Paul Webb
The Touring Consortium, Number One Tour

NO DEODORANT FOR DESPERATION

Ironically, the next job I did get came from an audition where I'd decided I didn't want the job before I entered the room.

Four Nights in Knaresborough had been a bit of a hit a couple of years previously at the Tricycle Theatre in London and this was to be its first production since. A Number One Tour was planned, hopefully to be followed by a West End run. Nick Moran, who, though an experienced theatre actor was best known as the star of the wonderful film *Lock, Stock and Two Smoking Barrels*, had already been cast as the star name in the production.

The play is based on a fascinating moment in history. In 1171, King Henry II hires four knights to arrest Becket, the Archbishop of Canterbury. Things don't go quite to plan and Becket is killed. The four knights then flee to Knaresborough Castle in Yorkshire, where they ensconce themselves for a year to avoid the wrath of the public and the Pope. Over the course of four separate evenings in January, March, September and December, the play charts the gradual decline of the knights, both mentally and physically.

Despite being a historical drama, the language is ostentatiously modern and littered with delightful profanities. I loved the play on first reading and prepared the enormous opening speech that Morville delivers to the audience at the start. As ever, I arrived a little early for my audition, and sat on a small wooden chair in the tiny corridor outside a room where I could hear an actor reading for the same role. This is never ideal; insecurities about my own work are only ever a few inches away when meeting new people, and my imaginative ego is always on hand with some useful thoughts about how brilliant the other actor sounds in there.

My allotted time to audition came and, as per usual, went. Another ten minutes rolled by. I realised the previous audition had finished and they were just chatting, which is absolutely fine but it was a very thin door and I could tell they weren't talking about the play, just gossiping about people they knew. Again, all fine and part of the small talk that surrounds auditions, but before I knew it, half an hour had passed since the other actor had finished 'auditioning'. I wondered if perhaps they'd forgotten I was coming and thought he was their last actor, so I politely knocked on the door. Somebody answered and told me that, yes, they knew I was there and they would be with me when they were ready.

I sat for a further ten minutes listening to more gossip, which included inaccurate personal details about someone I knew, before finally seeing my smiling rival depart and being ushered in myself. I just wanted to get it done and go home. They were clearly going to offer the role to the man they'd just met. I must have had a face like thunder as I stepped into the room to shake the hand of the director, Paul Miller, who is probably the friendliest and gentlest director I've ever met. The producer offered me a glass of wine, which I'd never encountered in an audition before; I wondered for a second if it was a test to weed out alcoholic actors: the 'how greedily do they accept a drink at an audition?' test. I declined. Small talk was attempted but I'd got myself into some kind of sulk and I couldn't climb out, so I asked if I could just read the scene.

I began Morville's rant and flew into a rage with it. I hadn't rehearsed it this way but it seemed to fit. I didn't care. I knew the job wasn't mine. I didn't want to hear their polite responses so picked up my bag before the last line and finished the speech by walking out of the door and all the way home.

I was, of course, offered the job the very next day. I think it was after this event, as I sat discussing the mysterious art of auditioning with Caroline, that I coined an ever-pertinent phrase: 'there's no deodorant for desperation'. When you desperately want or need a job it seems to push people away from you, but when you don't give a fuck, they sit forwards in their chairs and pay attention. Trying to find a way to generate the impression of the latter while actually feeling the former is the holy grail of audition techniques. I think this also applies to the dating games people play.

The tour was not too long and quite well paid compared to dear old Shared Experience, which we had christened 'Shared Expense'. It was also fairly sure to transfer to the West End afterwards. I accepted happily. It was a wonderful, tricky part: a misanthropic and intelligent man trapped in his own castle with what he considered were three idiots. A very straight straight man. I knew that a commercial production like this would be a totally different experience to the one I'd just had, a more traditional way of rehearsing, and I was looking forward to the challenge of applying the Shared Experience process privately if I could. I wanted to see if I could achieve the same feeling of vivid inner life without Polly and Nancy leading the way. An exercise in self-discipline was what I was aiming at and partly what was achieved. There was just an awful lot of alcohol drunk along the way.

ROCK AND ROLL-ISH

Rehearsals were a hurried and slightly frustrating affair, not so much for me but for our delightful director, Paul Miller. Four leading actors, each with a little too much testosterone, who all knew exactly what they wanted can't have been easy. Many years later I bumped into Paul and he said, 'What you have to understand, Joe, is that I hated you all, equally.'

My chief memory from those weeks in that church hall in Southwark are abandoning rehearsals on the morning of September 11th to go and watch and re-watch the unfolding news reports of the attacks upon the twin towers in New York. We found ourselves in the front room of a complete stranger who lived opposite the rehearsal space. As everyone who remembers will be able to tell you, it was a surreal day, a feeling of the universe having been shifted upon its axis.

Later that day, as we sat silently in the churchyard outside the rehearsal rooms, on Copperfield Street no less, Nick Moran found himself in an altercation with a disgruntled cyclist, who was very pissed off that we had moved his bicycle from against a bench where he had left it. He grumpily put his bike back where he wanted it to be, called Nick something unpleasant and went into an office nearby. It says a lot about the feeling in the air that day that none of us batted an eyelid when Nick put the bicycle flat on the floor and jumped up and down on its wheels, until they pointed in three different directions.

I cropped my hair very short, and grew a beard for the role. I bore an uncanny resemblance to a muddy tennis ball but was thrilled to be away from hunky-leading-man territory, be it in George Eliot's world or ITV's.

We opened the show fittingly enough in Canterbury at the Marlowe Theatre. It was in Canterbury Cathedral in the winter of 1170 that the four knights we were portraying had 'scattered' Thomas à Becket's brains over the altar steps to please their beloved King. I've always loved history. It was by far my favourite subject at school and this story fascinated me. The play was brilliant, well researched but far from precious. I took a peculiar delight in visiting the site of the actual murder and imagining it all.

The good people of Canterbury, however, seemed underwhelmed by our offerings, and unhappy about the strong language littered through the play. Towards the end of our run at the Marlowe, we had our sign language-interpreted performance scheduled. At this time most theatres managed to offer at least one night where a sign language interpreter could stand alongside the actors and communicate the dialogue being spoken to those with severe hearing impairments in the audience. It just happened to be on one of these nights, and during a long scene between just Nick and myself, that a very unhappy member of the audience decided he wanted to make his opinions known.

Mid-scene, we heard the always recognisable gruntings and rumblings of a pissed-off audience member; these usually start as a kind of frenetic bark, which they are clearly unable to hold on to any longer, such as, 'Rubbish!' or, 'Get off!' etc. This is generally followed by a deliberately loud and 'huff-puffy' exit from the theatre. Not on this occasion. This man was determined to make us feel his pain. We tried to carry on but had to occasionally stop to ascertain how much of a problem we had. Tricky at the best of times but, when you're also trying to work with and for a wonderful sign language interpreter who doesn't know the script as well as you do, it becomes delicate to say the least.

The barks had become a tirade. We were all now absolutely clear that this was not why he came to the theatre; that language of this sort was uncalled for. We were waiting for the ushers to remove him when Nick was struck by a moment of inspiration. Without saying a word, he made it clear to me and to the sign language lady that we were to stop trying to compete with this man and let him say his piece. We duly listened to another minute or two of righteous anger and, when he seemed to have tired himself out, Nick walked over to the sign language lady up on her podium and appeared to be trying to find out from her the correct bit of sign language for something he wanted to say. He then walked back to centre stage, looked at his fingers for a moment, faced front, and gave the man the V sign. It brought the house down and we and the audience clapped the man out of the building.

I loved Nick for this and it was the beginning of a long friendship. I travelled with him to many of the venues in his exhausted 1970s camper van, which he'd christened (and labelled) *Excalibur*! The interior was decorated with faux leather and flock wallpaper. It wasn't the fastest of vehicles; journeys that might reasonably be expected to take four hours from London would take seven. We arrived at Darlington Civic Theatre so late for our first performance there that we parked illegally directly outside the stage door, where our first costumes of full suits of armour were waiting for us, and went immediately to stage without seeing a toilet, let alone our dressing rooms.

This was a very 'party hearty' tour. We would positively 'go drinking' after almost every performance. Wherever we were, be it Cambridge, Wolverhampton, Plymouth, Darlington or Bromley, we would somehow find the only bars that would let us drink all night. The other 'knights', Tim Dantay and Robert Cavanah, were equally on a mission; it was a little like being in a minor rock band.

Hangovers (or sometimes drunken states) were carried onto stage at many a matinée.

I had grown up in a pub run by my parents until I was eleven years old, which had resulted in me choosing to be teetotal until my early twenties, so it was out of character for me to be drinking so much, and an interesting direction to be taking. I suspect it was partly a release valve for my undiluted grief. There was also a slightly tight-collared feeling for me in my marriage though we were demonstrably 'happy' and had begun to flirt with trying for a baby. This was something Caroline had reservations about at first, but I had none. 'There is never a "right time",' I would say blithely. My inner desire to become a father, ostensibly to become *my* father, was a strong song that I couldn't stop singing.

The work wasn't suffering too much from the late-night imbibing of vodka and absinthe. In fact, I was taking an absurd delight in my role, particularly the very beginning of the play where I had a two-page monologue direct to the audience: a brilliantly written, political speech, full of fire and misanthropic humour, which allowed me to really let loose at any latecomers, talkers or sweet-wrapping rustlers.

I was racing home from the tour every Sunday and commuting to the nearer venues. On one such Sunday morning as I stood in the kitchen, bleary-eyed and fuzzy-headed, Caroline came in from the bathroom clutching a piece of white plastic with a blue line across its centre. Life was, in that instant, forever changed. We were thrilled; I was ecstatic. But somewhere behind my wide smile was a heart that was broken not to be sharing the adventure with my dad.

VEGETARIAN CRAB STICKS

While we're on the subject of mothers and fathers, this was also the tour that allowed me to meet one of my grand-fathers for the very first time. I wasn't even fully aware I *had* a living grandfather on my mother's side until I was an adult. He had left my mum's life when she was only small and my absolutely wonderful grandmother (known to us simply as 'Gra') had brought her up on her own in a time when things were considerably harder for single mothers. Both Mum and Dad came from some version of a broken home. My dad's mum died when he was a teenager. They worked hard at keeping our nuclear family a strong and happy unit but didn't seem to want to talk about where they came from much. To the extent that, somewhere in my childhood, I'd decided that mum's dad must have died. I was somewhere in my twenties when I realised my error.

I was intrigued. It turned out he was living in Cornwall, still with the lady he had left Gra to be with. I wanted to meet him but had never really felt an urgent need to organise the event. However, after Dad died, things felt different. For me and especially for Mum. When I told her my tour details and that one of my venues, Plymouth, was not a million miles from him, we made a plan for her to come down to Plymouth, see the show and travel with me the next day to meet him.

I can't imagine how nerve-wracking and emotional it must have been to meet her father again after so many decades, but remember her hand shaking in mine as we approached his little house.

The door opened and there stood a missing piece of my genetic jigsaw. He was tall, like me and my brother (no one else in our family seemed especially tall), and more than that, his face was so very like my face. When he opened up a broad smile it was uncanny. It's an odd thing but, unless you're adopted, the way you look and where those looks come from is something you never stop to think about. But this man standing before me reminded me of me enormously.

The next surprise came when he spoke: a rich Geordie accent poured out of him. I knew a wing of my family was from Durham but hadn't twigged how closely related I was to that part of the world. If I'd ever been lucky enough to meet my dad's mother, Jessie, I would have heard her strong Glaswegian accent.

He was charming, friendly and welcoming, as was his partner. Whatever his past, this was the man we met that day and he was, from that day forward, a lot more involved in our lives. I'll never forget what he said in his Geordie accent as he led us through to the kitchen for a snack…

'Now, I know you're a vegetarian, Joseph, so we've got you crabsticks!'

That wasn't the only excitement during our week in Plymouth at the Theatre Royal. One night, Robert Cavanah felt too sick to perform, and I experienced for the first time the horror of playing in front of an audience with an understudy who was completely unprepared and too belligerent to use a script. This was undoubtedly more horrific for we actors standing open-mouthed beside him than for the useless lump himself. We would wait goggle-eyed for anything resembling our usually snappy script to emerge from the lumbering hulk of an actor, who, I'd suddenly remembered, had spent much of our rehearsal period snoring audibly from behind a curtain.

Things like that can be excused or even funny in amateur

dramatics, but when several hundred people, all complete strangers, have parted with hard cash to take a risk on a new play, it's shameful. There was also *no* excuse. We'd been on the road for weeks. He'd had plenty of rehearsal time. It was also not about nerves. He seemed extraordinarily bullish and confident that much of what he was doing was *improving* upon the work he had been watching up until now!

I took a long walk on my own by the sea that night, my soul's frame unable to contain all that was swimming inside it: the shameful three hours I'd just lived through on stage; the all-consuming knowledge of impending fatherhood; meeting my grandfather; the lack of my own father and an unbearable mixture of hope and fear about my future, as a man and as an actor. Heavy stuff. But all manageable after some strong sea air and a heftily salt-and-vinegared portion of chip shop chips.

The tour continued to be a vivid experience, both at the theatres and away from them. We took *Excalibur* on a tour of all the locations in Cumbria used in *Withnail and I,* and I found myself jumping naked into the freezing stream where, in the film, Richard E. Grant tries to shoot fish.

Robert Cavanah and I had a fight after we squabbled about something on stage. Robert is shorter than I am but built like the proverbial brick shit-house and was strong enough to lift me up against a wall by my collar. The rest of the band – sorry, cast – broke it up and it was all fine a day later.

We took a cast trip at 2 a.m. with a few tins of beer to the actual castle in Knaresborough where the play is set, and ran around the ruins quoting bits of the play. Half an hour later from out of nowhere, two policemen arrived wondering what the fuck we were doing. Four grown men prancing around a castle ruins in the middle of the night. When I came down off the wall to give an explanation, I don't think I could have sounded much more like Withnail:

'You see, we are *actors*, officer, and we're touring a play about the four knights who killed Thomas à Becket and this was the very castle where they ran away to. Indeed it was *my* character's castle, Hugh de Morville. We're performing not many miles from here and just couldn't resist. We may have had one or two beverages, officer, but I can assure you we are *actors* and this is *research!*'

The policemen told us to pack up and move on and might have muttered something about fairies as they walked away.

Not entirely surprisingly, the hoped-for West End run of the play didn't materialise. We hadn't received glowing reviews on tour and our producers didn't quite have the money. Or perhaps they didn't have confidence in their unruly cast.

I went merrily back to our flat in Camden and helped paint our tiny spare bedroom a sunny, gender-neutral yellow ready for our unborn baby to sleep in. We were six months away from its arrival, but I was bouncing off the walls with excitement.

2002

Eminem was 'cleanin' out his closet', the euro became the official currency in twelve European countries, terrorists targeted nightclubbers in Bali to devastating effect, Queen Liz celebrated her Golden Jubilee but also had to attend her mother's funeral, John Thaw, Spike Milligan and Dudley Moore died, Pierce Brosnan waved goodbye to Bond with *Die Another Day* and *My Big Fat Greek Wedding* was the surprise hit film of the year, trains crashed in Potters Bar, Ford stopped making motor cars in Dagenham and a genuine earthquake hit Dudley!

The Clearing – Shared Experience

The Clearing by Helen Edmundson
Shared Experience Theatre Company
National Tour – Tricycle Theatre, Kilburn

The lovely people from Shared Experience had got in touch before Christmas about a possible part for me in their next production – a play written by Helen Edmundson, who had adapted *Mill on the Floss* so brilliantly.

The Clearing is, in my opinion, one of the most under-rated plays of modern theatre. It's as well written and expressive as Arthur Miller's *The Crucible* but has never achieved the same reputation.

Set in Ireland during Oliver Cromwell's campaign of terror against the Irish, it focused on the time of his 'to hell or Connaught' campaign, a genocide rarely mentioned in school history lessons. *The Clearing* was to be directed by Polly Teale.

Shared Experience had a strong feminist leaning as a theatre company and most of their productions over the last few years had centred around female central characters. Robert Preston in *The Clearing* was a rare male leading role, an English soldier posted to the furthest outposts of Cromwell's campaign in Ireland on the promise of land. He goes on the most incredible journey, from an open-hearted and compassionate man, who is simply doing his job, to a leather-bound 'ironfist' soldier of hate.

I nearly wasn't able to play the part. Shared Experience don't use understudies. Our baby was due to be born during the last couple of weeks of the run and the company was unable to guarantee that I could attend the birth. I was insistent that I would be present when my first child was born. I would never miss a show for anything less but when that call came in, I'd be running.

I understood their predicament; they couldn't easily risk losing a show's revenue. Eventually, I was extremely grateful and flattered to find out they were going to go the extra mile and hire a good actor for a small sum, to be semi-rehearsed and ready to go on with script in hand during those last two weeks.

BALLET OF VERBS

Rehearsals were astonishing. Again, the physical work was intense and at times a little insane. This wasn't an adaptation of a novel as so many of Shared Experience's productions were. This was a play, a brilliant play, already whittled down to spare poetic language, and very little seemed to be required physically. I was nervous that the company's method of rehearsal could jeopardise the play's poetry by suffocating it with too much physical acting (or 'wanking about' as a friend of mine put it). One day of rehearsal, where we spent an hour or two becoming the wolves surrounding the farm, had me especially nervous!

I needn't have worried; Polly took us to an extraordinarily physical understanding of the play and our parts. We 'actioned' every beat of every scene so methodically, and repeated out loud what actions we were playing so often, that we were eventually able to perform an incredibly intense run-through of the entire play, physicalising every single objective of every beat of every scene, without using any of the dialogue. Not a word of script was spoken and yet we all knew exactly where were as we roared, wrestled, licked, kicked and scratched our way through the play. Please, try to picture this, I'm not exaggerating: a two-hour play run straight through as a kind of mad ballet. Before each scene, we stated out loud our objectives and the key verbs we would be using to achieve them, then we let rip at each other on a primal, animal level.

After this extraordinary event, Polly trimmed away almost all of the physical life we had created, until what was left were sometimes incredibly static scenes.

To the very end of the run, the physical energy from rehearsals was intact. One particularly static scene where Aislín McGuckin, playing my wife, Madeleine, had to beg the Governor, played by Richard Attlee, for her brother's life crackled with electricity. The ghost of the rehearsed version of this scene, where the two actors had attacked each other like feuding lions, seemed to be always vibrating just beneath the surface.

'STOP BEING SO FUCKING POLITE!'

We opened with a short run at Birmingham Rep, before a tour of the country, followed by a six-week run in London at the Tricycle Theatre and then, strangely, back on tour just for a couple more weeks (these being the weeks the baby was due).

I'd been at drama school with Aislín, in the same year, often in the same classrooms and productions, but really didn't know her well. I'd been both intimidated by her beauty and her brilliant work, so it was nice to get to know her now, in the real world.

For years, I simply couldn't talk to really beautiful women or, if I did, it came out not at all as planned. It was like a kind of Tourette's. One of the few times I tried to strike up a conversation with Aislín during our time at drama school was in the pub opposite. I was teetotal through all my years there so wasn't a regular in the pub, but it was some kind of special occasion and I found myself sharing a few feet of sawdust near the bar with her; her boyfriend was hovering nearby. She was looking particularly dazzling, really, like a kind of Rossetti painting, so I opened with, 'Hello, Aislín, you're looking rough, as usual.' To my nervous, panicked mind, it was intended as a witty and ironic statement of high flattery. It wasn't taken as such, especially by Mr Boyfriend who promptly offered to smash my face in. I wasn't one of the cool kids or tough guys in my year, but it didn't touch me because I was happy, deliriously happy with the work and quietly twice as useful in a fight as most of those lumps.

Also in the company of *The Clearing* was Pip Donaghy, who I'd loved working and exploring America with on *Mill on the Floss*. We booked digs together for our few weeks in Birmingham. A strange granny annexe over the gatehouse of a very grand house on the edge of town. All seemed well, I adored Pip, and he seemed to like my company too. We would travel in and out to the theatre together and often stay up late, drinking wine, eating unhealthy snacks and talking shop.

One night, early in the run, we were back in our digs and Pip suddenly turned on me. From out of nowhere, he tore my acting to shreds! For what felt like an hour, this man who I adored and thought of as a friend skewered my performance in *The Clearing*. He was vitriolic, passionate and, at least eighty per cent of the time, right...

'You're so fucking POLITE! Stop being so fucking POLITE! I know you lost your father recently, but, I AM NOT YOUR FUCKING FATHER! I don't want to be your father. Stop giving me so much fucking RESPECT on stage! You keep moving out of my way and going down-stage for me when it's "my bit". FUCK THAT! FUCK IT! It should be like a boxing match, not a tea party. *You* want to *win* the scene, *I* want to *win* the scene. Give me something to act against, you little bastard! If I ever catch you clearing my light, or moving so more of the audience can see me one more time, I will knock your teeth through your arse!'

Anyone who knows the delightful, sparkly-eyed, kind-hearted Pip Donaghy may find this hard to believe but it's absolutely true and it's to his undying credit that he set me straight that night. I had, in my brief career, done a little too much 'polite' theatre and had loved learning old-fashioned 'stagecraft'; it was invaluable but, as I lay awake that night, I started to realise that it had perhaps left me diluted and not nearly dangerous enough for the magic of theatre that this wonderful man still believed in.

I also wonder if I was over-compensating after my experience on *Mill on the Floss*, desperate for no one to ever think I was upstaging them.

Pip was beside himself with remorse the next morning. I had trouble persuading him that it was fine; more than fine. That he'd had a point. All day I studied my script to remind myself of my journey through the play and, that night, I let him have it. I let them all have it. Scene by scene, I concentrated purely on the task and objectives in hand rather than on what the audience were seeing – and everything felt sharper. I'm eternally grateful to Pip for nudging me out of the boat and into the water.

SILENT DARK CORNERS

There's something delicate and ephemeral I want to touch

199

on here, if I can find a way to express it. On almost every job, private moments develop around the actual performance on stage that are often more lasting ... sacred even. For example, every night during the second half of *The Clearing*, I made a complete costume change. Robert finally had to turn his back on his own wife after she'd run away with his beloved son; trust and love had been replaced by fear and hate. I very consciously elected to make this change entirely alone, in a dark corner of the wings.

Robert's homely, unexceptional clothes were all soft, cotton and moleskin. I used to draw so much from this change every night, as I shed his old self and replaced each garment with the strong, dark, hard leather of his new uniform as one of Cromwell's *Ironfists*. I would finish by slowly pulling on his leather gloves, feeling as if I'd grown new skin; that I was now strong, invulnerable, heartless. The five minutes or so that I had alone in the wings at this stage of every performance was always magical. I would enter the final scene infused with his new rocklike strength. It was play, make-believe in its most pure and childlike form, utterly private and fun!

In the last scene, after many years, Robert and Madeleine finally meet again in a forest clearing. He believes she is there to return his son to him. Instead, she tells him that he has died. He doesn't believe her, it must be a trick. She wants him to take the boy's favourite rag doll. For a long time, he resists, but eventually her words ring true and at last he takes the doll. I had given myself so far to go; pure father's grief had to filter through the construct of strength and invulnerability, which had galvanised in that costume change.

The smell of the boy on the doll unlocks everything. It

was big stuff, Greek-drama-sized stuff, imagining the death of a child while ironically, in the real world, I awaited the birth of my first baby.

Almost every job has one of these private rituals, a private binding of courage and cause. They sneak up on you. It's often only near the end of a job after the backstage journey has become rooted with repetition that I realise how frequently I linger in a certain place at a certain time. I relish these slow-burn conversations with myself. In this often hectic western world we live in, it's sometimes only our work that can afford us such luxuries.

EastEnders
BBC Television

Somehow or other, during rehearsals for *The Clearing*, I found myself auditioning for a proper soap opera for the first time in my life. It was a strange, last-minute thing. One of the regular actors on *EastEnders* was rumoured to have been sacked and scripts were being hastily rewritten for a different character to arrive and cover the parts of the storyline that had previously belonged to him.

My agent wasn't too keen on my next significant television job, after the heights of *Peak Practice,* being a soap opera, but I was far from proud. I also had it in mind to take as long a break from work as I could after our baby was born, so any extra money I could bring in would be wonderful. The dates were almost perfect. I'd be in a dozen or so episodes, scheduled to film during the exact weeks I was in London doing *The Clearing*.

I had nothing to lose, so of course the audition went well and I was offered the job.

DURACELL BUNNY

Apart from the time when I'd rehearsed *The Rivals* by day whilst still performing *The Fantasticks* by night, this was the first time I'd really done what I call 'double banking' – burning my candle at both ends, performing one job by day and another at night.

The *Clearing/Enders* combo was a particularly tall order. You may have gathered that performing *The Clearing* was no walk in the park, and my schedule on *EastEnders* was incredibly tight as I had to wrap early enough to get to the theatre. Many concerned parties (agents, wives, theatre companies, casting directors etc) were just that – concerned. But I was indefatigable, fearless and bulletproof. I convinced them all that it was simply not a problem, and, do you know what? It sort of wasn't. Besides, I still couldn't really comprehend the idea of saying no. I was too grateful, essentially still too surprised that I was doing this for a living at all. When people said they wanted to pay me to act, I asked where to sign. With the added impending responsibility of a new mouth to feed, I was making hay while the sun shone, even if it cost me some exhaustion.

Almost every day of the six-week London run of *The Clearing* went as follows:

Wake early, 5.30 a.m. or so, wash, and then, come rain or shine, drag my trusty but ancient mountain bike out of its shed and cycle to Kentish Town train station.
Catch train to Elstree and Borehamwood Station, cramming the day's lines into my head from tattered scripts and complicated schedules as I go.
Cycle down through the town to the gates of Elstree

Studios, feeling a very definite thrill every time I passed through them.

Get into dressing room by 7.30 a.m. after grabbing some kind of breakfast from the canteen.

On set by 8 a.m. and usually shoot all day.

Wrap by 4.30 p.m. although this was often pushed to 5 p.m. Change and cycle back to station, praying the trains were running on time.

Catch train back to Kentish Town, organising the following day's scripts as I travel.

Cycle three or so miles from Kentish Town to Kilburn High Road through rush-hour traffic, running lines from *The Clearing* as I go, to get my head back into that space.

Get to theatre by 6.30 p.m. if lucky in time to grab some chips or rice for my dinner before the half-hour call for the show at 6.55 p.m.

7.30 p.m. perform *The Clearing*.

10 to 10.30 p.m. finish show, sometimes visit theatre bar briefly to see friends, then out to unlock that bike and get back on the road.

Cycle three miles home, arriving around midnight, put bike back into its shed, then crawl into bed in whatever space was left by my now very heavily pregnant wife.

Caroline was very patient and forgiving about my nineteen-hours-a-day schedule. I think she knew it was designed to ensure I could afford to really take some proper time off once the baby was born and that I was going to move heaven and earth to be at the birth. We were supremely excited about it and this was unquestionably among the happiest times of our marriage.

But, holy moly, I remember those bike rides through

London between those two jobs. That rare, luxurious, vital and slightly lunatic feeling of being *used* on this planet; used to the very edge of your strength, intelligence and stamina. It was exhausting, of course, but as I felt the cold air rushing into my lungs, I knew I was alive. To quote old Hamlet-pants, I was 'eating the air, promise crammed'.

'MOVING ON'

If filming *Peak Practice* was like preparing a carefully made roast dinner, then *EastEnders* was like working as a burger chef at McDonald's. That's not meant to sound disrespectful. If anything, I grew to admire the actors and crews of soap operas enormously. They shoot everything *so* quickly; the actors popping up night after night in these programmes are warriors.

On *Peak Practice* we averaged four to eight pages of script shot each day; *EastEnders* averaged perhaps twenty pages a day. These are normally spread amongst many actors on many story strands but, due to my having to wrap early and their wanting to tie up a fairly large storyline as soon as possible, I worked at an incredible rate. We once completed twenty-five pages of dialogue in a single day. Still my personal record.

My character, Jason James, was, as they say, a bit of a 'douche'. A flash, cockney, wide-boy charmer, who was in Albert Square to take his ex-girlfriend for a whirlwind romance and as much of her money as he could get, not caring a jot for the fact that she was now married. Tired as I was, I would skip into make-up each morning and see if I could make Barbara Windsor giggle (succeeding on several occasions), then skip onto set with my lines tenuously learnt. This thin thread of certainty about the script, if I relaxed, could be liberating. I was forced to listen properly to the other actors to know where I was in the scene. Most of them had a similarly tenuous grasp on the text, so it sometimes felt more like improvising. There was no time to prepare, or overthink or to worry. Just dive in and commit. Commit from the second you were up on your feet.

My scenes were almost all with the infamous 'Slater' family, including the brilliant Jessie Wallace, and future *Wonder Woman* Michelle Ryan. Was my character romantically involved with either of these ladies? No, no, no. Good old Jason James was getting it on with Lynne Slater, played by Elaine Lorden. Now Elaine is a good actor and was very nice to work with but, at this point in her life, she was also a chain-smoker, fond of a tipple and, I suspect, a little bored. From lunchtime onwards, it was like doing love scenes with Oliver Reed: a rollercoaster ride of booze-tinged unpredictability and over-eager ashtray kisses.

My crowning moment on *EastEnders* had to be a scene that ended with Lynne Slater's husband catching us in bed together. Through tears he asked me: 'How do you sleep at night?', to which good old Jason James replied, in his best mockney accent:

'Wiv her.'

Duff-duff-duff-duff-duff-duff-duff-duff-duff…

BEEPER IS BORN

We sailed past our due date with no baby born. *EastEnders* finished the same day that the London run of *The Clearing* finished. The following week, I went back on tour with the play. We were performing in Oxford and I left home in my car as late as I possibly could every day and raced home again straight after the curtain call. The little creature was hanging on in there.

We finished the tour without needing my standby under-study. Almost another whole week later, two weeks after our due date, Caroline and I left our flat in Kentish Town and took a taxi to the Royal Free Hospital in Hampstead to have our baby induced – awful word, let's say … 'encour-aged' – into the world. It was the 6th of June. D-Day.

The labour was long, traumatic, frightening, messy and complicated. It was also cataclysmically beautiful and utterly life-changing.

My desire to become a father had been so strong, I knew I had a reserve of paternal love running inside me as hot as lava. The reality, though, of finally meeting my own child for the first time was like being scooped up and tickled by the hand of God. And she was a girl. A beautiful, beau-tiful girl.

Due to complications after she was born they both had to stay overnight in the hospital. I stayed as long as I was allowed, but was eventually persuaded to go home by the nurses. As I walked down the long hill from Hampstead to Camden in the middle of the night it was like walking in another world. *Everything* felt different. Everything *was* different.

She had no name yet. We hadn't known whether we were going to have a boy or a girl and enjoyed the element of surprise. We did, however, have a shortlist of two names agreed for each sex, and a plan to wait a week and see if we both felt the same about which name suited best. It was wonderful to have these few days of getting to know her, as a human being – just her essence with no name or label attached. She was 'baby', she was life, she was ours.

Our daughter's first name was probably 'Beeper' as, after we eventually brought her home, she slept in her swaddling remarkably well but emitted a constant tiny beeping sound. Right through the night. Before long it was clear that she was a Jessica and not a Tabatha (the other name on our shortlist), and she is, of course, my constant pride and joy.

Holby City
BBC Television

EastEnders didn't pay a fortune but the fact that it had been combined with my theatre wage meant I was in the luxurious position of being able to tell my agent I wasn't available for work for the three months following Jessica's birth. I gave myself paternity leave. Three months without even looking at the phone!

I had been gestating an idea for a one-man show for some time and had tentatively planned a first stab at actually performing it but, just before that began, I got the welcome offer of a guest role in *Holby City* for the BBC.

I jumped at the chance to earn a few quid and to finally get to wear the guest actor's shoes on a medical drama, after all those endless episodes on the other side of the desk during *Peak Practice*. It was my turn to do the twitching and the crying. Or so I thought … before I got on set and found out almost all of my scenes were with Tina Hobley, the female heart-throb of the show.

I gave it my all. My story, ironically, was something to do with having to visit my dying baby's cot in intensive care. My last scene included a long speech during which I cried in every take. Months later, when the episode aired, I tuned in to watch, and realised all my efforts had been in vain. Ten seconds into my speech, my face went soft and blurry in the foreground as the camera racked its focus sharply onto Tina Hobley, who was standing in the doorway watching me whilst thinking about how this poor man's suffering reflected her character's love life (or some such guff). Oh, well, you live and learn.

It was an enjoyable enough job, though: a day or two of filming and at Elstree Studios again, where I'd only a few months previously filmed *EastEnders*. Little did I know how important a role those studios, and indeed *Holby City*, were to play in my life a decade or so later.

The Lifted Veil by George Eliot
Adapted by Joseph Millson and Tim Heath
Yvonne Arnaud Theatre, Guildford – National Tour

A couple of steps backwards in order to move forwards if you don't mind.

An idea had been quietly but consistently knocking at one of the lesser-used doors in my brain for a while. During the long tour of *Mill on the Floss* in 2001, I'd taken a biography of George Eliot's life with me on the international leg of the tour. I also took another couple of her works: *Daniel Deronda*, and a thin little thing I picked up in a second-hand bookshop, called *The Lifted Veil*. I never got around to reading *Daniel Deronda* and read the wonderful biography only until it took me to the point where George Eliot had written *Mill on the Floss*. But I must have read *The Lifted Veil* four times, back-to-back. I loved it. I mean really *loved* it. It was unlike anything I'd read before. Some of the prose was so beautiful it knocked me out of my socks, and my desire to play the strange central character of the clairvoyant, Latimer, was immediate; as was, aptly enough, a 'vision' of how it could work as a one-man show.

Entrenched in Shared Experience Theatre's expressionistic adaptation and performance style as I was, my mind was adapting the book as I read it. However, seeing something in your head is a very, very different thing from dragging it out of your mind and into reality as an adapted, designed, rehearsed, and performed *thing*, that people actually pay money to watch.

I'd recently been part of an evening of war poetry and readings at the British Library for a director by the name of Tim Heath. Tim was a delicate soul from another time. He looked like a tall, thin teddy bear and dressed like Alan Bennett in cords and tank tops. Incredibly well read, he didn't own a television and had a strong aversion to the 'musak' that played in cafes. Tim had himself written and performed a couple of successful one-man shows.

After finishing my episode of *Holby City,* I knew that, as far as auditions were concerned, I was out of the game for a few months on self-imposed paternity leave. So now, with a little money in the bank and a free calendar, perhaps I could have a crack at this *Lifted Veil* thing.

I approached Tim to discuss the idea. I'd thought he would be a good person to turn to for advice as he was so well read and knew the pros and cons of one-man shows. Tim didn't know *The Lifted Veil* but agreed to read it ahead of a meeting with me.

I explained my ideas for adapting the book into a play, starting at the end of Latimer's life then moving to the beginning of the story to create a circular feel. I knew I wanted minimal props and set and strong sequences of movement, but an outside eye in rehearsals would be essential.

Well, Tim rather took the bull by the horns. Before I knew it, he'd not only booked a week's run at the Yvonne Arnaud Studio Theatre in Guildford, but also sent me a fully edited script/adaptation, a fairly substantial invoice for the writing of it and a contract for his work as director!

I was more than a little taken aback by this – particularly the adaptation bit, which I'd been looking forward to doing myself. And I hadn't specifically 'commissioned' anything. But, sleep deprived as I was, I agreed to it all and we booked a week of rehearsals in a church hall in Clapham. A week is a ridiculously short time to rehearse a new piece of theatre but I vowed to arrive with the whole thing learnt and I had a real vision for how the show would work. With Tim as an outside eye and a captain to get it through technical rehearsals, I felt we could do it.

It was an incredibly exciting feeling, to be producing something entirely my own. I'd learnt a lot from my on-and-off involvement as Associate Director of Pursued By A Bear Theatre Company and I knew the world of mid-scale touring theatre well. So I got to work, hurriedly designing and printing a run of publicity flyers and posters, and contacting theatres here and there to book a few extra tour dates for the week or two after Guildford, to try to recoup some of the production costs. To my surprise, and dread, several said yes and booked the show. This thing was happening!

PREPARATIONS
We had perhaps three weeks to get it all ready before

rehearsals. I knew there would be minimal set; everything had to go into one huge suitcase. The period setting was to be created by a decent period costume, which we bought from 'Angels' (the costume warehouse so vast it has to be seen to be believed). I bought dust cloths, which would be thrown over whatever plastic furniture we could muster at each venue. We had a hatstand, a metronome, one large, beautiful antique rug, some custom-made lighting gobos, and music!

One of Tim's greatest contributions to the show was choosing the music. Schubert's *Winterreise*, performed by Dietrich Fischer-Dieskau, was to be a perfect soundscape to this peculiar tale and Latimer's interior life, in particular a track called 'The Hurdy Gurdy Man'. Extraordinarily beautiful and apt.

Eventually, I ran out of excuses and, with our tiny rehearsal period approaching, I had to get on and learn it. I went into my bedroom with a stop-watch and read the entire text out loud straight through as a test. It took nearly an hour and a half – gulp! We would of course trim this, but it was time to get to work. I'd never learnt so much text on my own. There was nothing to do but get on with it.

A couple of quotes from the very text I was learning could not be more apt:

'There is no short cut, no patent tram-road to wisdom: after all the centuries of invention, the soul's path lies through the thorny wilderness which must be still trodden in solitude, with bleeding feet, with sobs for help, as it was trodden by them of old time.'

'We learn words by rote, but not their meaning; that must be paid for with our life-blood, and printed in the subtle fibres of our nerves.' George Eliot, *The Lifted Veil*

HOW DO YOU LEARN ALL THOSE LINES?

'How do you learn all those lines?' is famously the question most asked of actors. There is no answer other than, 'Well, you just learn them.' It's a slog. The process by which I committed *The Lifted Veil* to memory became a template for how I've subsequently learnt all large parts.

Sometimes the hardest part is to start; it can seem an impossibly large hill to climb. But once parental duties were done, I would grab a cup of tea, a large glass of water, then shut myself in a room for a couple of hours at a time and just bloomin' *learn* it! One sentence at a time. One paragraph at a time. One page at a time. Then, always test that the new page is known, without peeking, and can be repeated the magic three times through before moving on to the next.

As I progressed, I would torture myself by always returning to the very beginning of the entire piece and going through everything I'd thus far worked on, before testing the new section. It was a slow process but, by always returning to navigate the journey again from the beginning, the pathways in the brain were deepened. This must be slightly akin to how pianists learn whole sonatas by heart. It's a form of marathon training, slowly increasing the distances I could 'run' each day.

After a couple of weeks of arduous work, day and night grappling with the pages and George Eliot's incredibly beautiful, but *long*, sentences, I had in theory learnt it. Just in time.

MADMAN ON THE COMMON

I left the script alone for the Sunday before rehearsals began so I could concentrate entirely on our family. But all of a sudden an alarm went off – and it was Monday.

A first day of rehearsals is always nerve-wracking and exciting in equal measure, but this was crazy. I had one week! I was the only actor in it and the thing was going in front of a fucking audience next Tuesday!

I set off ridiculously early; I couldn't risk a minute of rehearsals being lost due to unforeseen travel problems.

On my journey from Camden to Clapham, I went to reach for the script in my bag to go over the lines, but stopped. Something told me to leave it where it was.

In my bedroom, I'd naturally been checking my script every time my memory ran aground. I decided to take my armbands off and push my way through the entire script without any help.

I sat on the tube, closed my eyes and began to mumble quietly. When I arrived at a section I couldn't remember, I would resist the urge to look at the script in my bag and, instead, stay with it, chew on it, work ahead and ask myself what section might come next; or sometimes work backwards in my head a page or so, and 'take a run up' to the problem section. Many times my subconscious would kick in and hand me the words that had previously disappeared into a black hole, and, if it didn't, then I knew which sections I had to stick a mental red flag in and rework.

By the time I reached Clapham Common Underground Station, I'd stumbled blindly through it all and was alarmed at how many black spots there were. I was, of course, nearly an hour early.

I went to a cafe, bought a little breakfast, took my

script out, looked at a couple of the memory black spots, then put the script back in my bag and set off onto the Common. The freedom of walking in the open air, away from any observers, allowed me to talk out loud instead of mumbling. I went back to the opening sentence.

'The time of my end approaches...'

The combination of fresh air and the exquisite concentration required to run a large part from start to finish, with no prompts and no other stimulus, is extraordinary, and wonderful. This was how I was going to crack it. Each concentrated attempt taught me more than any rehearsal and the feeling of independent concentration was addictive.

This outdoor, walking rehearsal test has been an important part of my learning process for large roles ever since. It's a level of application and concentration which is satisfying beyond words. As if you've stolen a formula, a code, and it's in your brain, where nobody can steal it from you.

I'm not sure Tim knew what had hit him! By the time I arrived at rehearsals I was wild-eyed with perspiration and inspiration. I insisted on going for it *all,* at once, there and then.

What followed was one of the most exhilarating and fruitful (if high-pressure) weeks of work I've ever known. Tim was patient, appreciative and enthusiastic. I had four or five ideas for every moment, many of which I found hard to explain to him, so would just show him. My vision for the piece was so full and *physical.* I was hurling myself around on the floor at points, sometimes with accompanying grunts and wails, shortcutting my way to a physical connection with the piece, completely uninhibited and uncensored – but possibly a little alarming to a teddy bear like Tim. He would smile and support all my strange behaviours. I effectively directed and shaped the entire piece myself but, without Tim there as a board to bounce my sometimes inspired but sometimes terrible ideas off, it wouldn't have worked.

BILLY NO MATES

Before I knew it, we were at the Mill Studio Theatre, which is part of the wonderful Yvonne Arnaud Theatre in Guildford, and had finished our brief tech and dress rehearsals. I was stage managing the show myself so had triple-checked every prop and costume. Then I was alone in a dressing room. Tim had given me some notes, wished me luck and left me to it.

Twenty minutes before the show began I headed to the stage, lit the candle on a small side table, took my seat in the dust-cloth-covered chair nearest to the audience and closed my eyes.

Never my favourite thing, but it was essential that I was already on stage when the house was opened and the audience began to enter the theatre. Though I was only a few feet in front of the seats, I tried to seem as if I was genuinely asleep; made myself as uninteresting as possible as they came in and took their places. I also tried to keep my light bulbs turned off: no 'sleep acting', twitching, snoring or whimpering. It seemed to work. I could hear the surprisingly large audience enter quietly as they noticed me, and then relax and begin chatting amongst themselves again. I didn't open my eyes at all. I knew it was time to begin when the audience went extremely quiet and I felt the first lighting state warm my face.

Even then, I stayed perfectly still, stretching the moment

out, long enough so that people might just begin to wonder if the actor had genuinely fallen asleep, and then – *WHAM!* I woke with a sudden start and forward movement in my chair, as if from an awful but familiar nightmare.

The instant shock in the audience was glorious. They were in, and we were off!

It was an exhilarating experience. That we'd made this thing in the time we had was something of a miracle, let alone the fact that it seemed to hold, shock and sometimes amuse the audience. I was thrilled.

NIGHT NURSE

Solo shows are bittersweet; when things go wrong you've no one to blame but yourself and no one to turn to for help but yourself. When things go well, it's all your own work and the reward is enormous. But returning to the dressing room after the performance and having nobody to share the highs or lows with is a strange and singular thing.

As the week went on in Guildford, and even more as I embarked on my little tour, the highs and the lows became even more polarised. And as time went on, I would talk out loud to myself in the dressing rooms after the performances.

I also developed my first chemical addiction!

In *The Lifted Veil,* Latimer is rather keen on drinking absinthe, and at points it was essential that he was seen to do so. Absinthe is a unique shade of green; half-decent stage manager as I may be, it proved impossible to recreate with food colouring, or mint cordials. No, the only real visual substitute for a crystal glass of absinthe – was a crystal glass of *Night Nurse.*

Well, it's good stuff, man! I'm not sure of the ingredients

but, watered down slightly though my on-stage glassfuls were, after a week's rehearsal and a few weeks on tour, I found it rather hard to give up. I'm clean now, though, honest!

Writing about *The Lifted Veil,* I've been reminded of the incredible feeling of productiveness and ownership it brought. As actors, we're so often beholden to a source outside ourselves. We long for someone to give us a job, to commission us to act. But this was something I brought into the world. An endeavour so worthwhile that success or failure was irrelevant. I'm inspired as I write this to take a leaf out of my younger self's book and bring Latimer and his haunting tale back into the light.

THE DRACULA SOCIETY

As a footnote to this tale I'm proud and more than a little amused to tell you that the show won an award: The Hamilton Deane Award for best performance in a gothic drama 2002, voted for by the wonderfully named 'Dracula Society'!

Not many people have got one of those.

Not many people have heard of one of those, but that's by the by.

2003

Kids all over the world were busy in cinemas *Finding Nemo,* or falling in love with Will Ferrell in *Elf;* their parents, meanwhile, were busy reading *Eats, Shoots & Leaves;* as a distraction from the enormous and spuriously titled Liberation of Iraq, London drivers learned to wrestle with the new London Congestion charge, while their radios played 'Hey Ya!' by Outkast; *Lord of the Rings* swept the Oscars, Bob Monkhouse cracked his last joke, Concorde took its last flight, and soap opera *Brookside* aired its last episode after twenty-one years.

As You Like It – Peter Hall Company

The Seagull by Anton Chekhov
Cold Meat Party by Brad Fraser
Royal Exchange Theatre, Manchester

Tremulous times globally but we were insulated by the constant joy that it was to watch our baby girl develop and engage in her world. That garden flat on Prince of Wales Road, Camden, was a hope-filled corner of London.

A few months followed without solid acting work but fairly regular workshops as part of Shared Experience Theatre's core company. I helped workshop new ideas and road-test shows including *Gone To Earth* and *After Mrs Rochester.* But by December, I was in need of a job and was beginning to audition again.

For a long time, I'd had a strong yearning to participate in genuine repertory theatre; to undergo that treadmill of experience; to play one show by night whilst rehearsing the next by day. I had somewhat overdosed on biographies and autobiographies of actors from the generations before me, and had read Michael Blakemore's fantastic novel, *Next Season,* set in a slightly toxic and incestuous regional rep, a few too many times.

There were very few theatres left in the country working this way, apart from the giants such as the Royal Shakespeare Company, which still felt out of my reach. I thought I would have to go knocking on doors as far afield as Perth in Scotland, or pack my bags for one of the two remaining summer season theatres in Southwold or Frinton to experience 'rep'. So I was thrilled to get an audition for the Royal Exchange Theatre, Manchester, who were planning to reintroduce a repertory company and a repertory season with multiple plays running simultaneously.

It was variety I wanted; 'rep' asks so much of actors, playing against type, against age, stretching yourself to stretch the company. And the two parts I eventually won could not have been more contrasting: Medvedenko, the shy, penniless, lovelorn, brow-beaten schoolteacher in *The Seagull*, by Anton Chekhov, and Brynn, the open and outrageous gay lover of a rock star in *Cold Meat Party*, a new play by Brad Fraser. I would be in these two plays, in totally contrasting roles, sometimes on the same day – I couldn't wait.

Rehearsals began on New Year's Eve, bizarrely, and after the first day's work on *The Seagull,* I went back to my digs. I'd chosen the only self-contained property big enough for family visits that I could find in Manchester for the £90 a week we were allotted: a flat on the ninth floor of a very run-down, high-rise block in one of the less attractive parts of Salford. It was bare and cold, the front room had been painted fluorescent orange with matching orange furniture, the lift was often littered with human fluids, but I enjoyed living there tremendously.

That first night, I made a cup of tea, prised open the long-sealed patio doors and sat on a plastic chair on the concrete balcony. As a cold northern wind blew in my face I looked out on the various firework displays erupting across Manchester.

I was employed; I was doing a bloody Chekhov at the Royal Exchange; I was paying my mortgage (just); I was happy.

MANCHESTER ... SO MUCH TO ANSWER FOR
Chekhov is often cited as 'the actor's playwright', and it's not hard to understand why. Every role seems to be

infinitely rich with layers and layers of character to dig into. The stakes are always high – love, life and death – but often played against the inertia of ordinary life and financial struggles. Characters swing from tears to laughter at the drop of a samovar. From drama school onwards, actors yearn to lose themselves in one of Chekhov's plays.

Medvedenko was not a showy role but I couldn't have loved him more: put upon, stoical in the extreme and *hopelessly* in love with Masha, who is blatantly in love with another man and treats Medvedenko with utter disdain or, worse, indifference.

Knowing I would later in the season be playing the clean-cut, attractive role of Brynn, I went to town on my transformation into Medvedenko. As rehearsals went on, I began to morph into our director Greg Hersov, who I adored. I found the same style of spectacles, made my hair into a similar nest of craziness and even copied his walk. I'm not sure if he ever recognised himself but it all fitted Medvedenko. By the time we went into production, the designer and I had added a beautiful fake moustache, which changed as the acts progressed. I topped this off with a slightly hunched back, and a Welsh accent to complete the already overripe picture.

It may sound daft, but everything worked. He felt like a complete story, which I could step into easily.

EUREKA MOMENT

A Chekhovian moment of moments at the dress rehearsal for *The Seagull*: it was during a tiny scene towards the end of the third act, where Medvedenko enters, waits for a polite break in conversation, tells all on stage that he has to hurry or he will miss a train, and leaves. This is almost all the audience see of him in this particular act, but in the next act, when we've jumped a few years, we see Masha has married him – or settled for him.

In rehearsals thus far I'd been serving the scene as best as I could, with Medvedenko feeling weighed down by life and yet another task that nobody was going to thank him for. But, in the middle of our dress rehearsal, as I stood outside the doors to the stage waiting to make my entrance for this little scene, I put my imagination firmly into his world and played around with his sadness and pain. I thought about exactly where he was in his story at that point. Suddenly, with only seconds to go before I was due on stage, I was struck with absolute certainty that, at this point in the off-stage story, Masha had just told him she *would* marry him. Far from his usual weighed-down sadness in this little scene, it is actually the greatest day of his life. He is bursting with joy and love for his fellow man.

My cue came, the doors opened. Thus far, in every other performance of this scene, I'd walked in at a slow pace, hovered nervously, waited for my moment and said, 'Yes, and I'm going to walk to the station … see you off. I'll have to look sharp,' perhaps hoping someone might offer to lend me a horse, or a little sympathy or thanks. I was always almost totally ignored, then sadly wandered off.

But not at this dress rehearsal!

I walked on stage, stood where I always stood and waited quietly, bubbling with excitement. Then, smiling like a loon from ear to ear, I said loudly, 'Yes! And I'm going to walk to the station … see you off!' I then *kissed* and embraced the grumpy Shamrayev, my unknowing, soon-to-be father-in-law. He stood, flabbergasted. I shook all the others firmly by the hands, paused as if I'd won the lottery, then said, 'I'll have to look sharp!' And walked away, floating on air.

In the almost empty auditorium, a bark of adoring laughter and a solo round of applause rang out from our director. He later said it was the most Russian thing he'd seen in an English production. It was a tiny moment, but provided a wonderful artistic 'pop' just before opening the show.

CHEKHOV – WHO CARES??

The Seagull opened to universally rave reviews but fairly quickly emptied the theatre! Chekhov, and especially *The Seagull,* appeals so strongly to actors, writers and directors. It is one of the finest plays ever written about why we do what we do. It's hugely appealing to artists of almost any kind but, it turns out, most men and women from other walks of life couldn't care less.

We didn't mind. I don't think any company performing a Chekhov play minds. I'm fairly sure they'd perform it to an empty room.

LOVE IS ALL AROUND ME

As soon as *The Seagull* was up and running, we began work on *Cold Meat Party* by day, and even on the mornings of matinée days.

I was being stretched as I'd desired, it was a wonderful company of actors and I loved this new play, but it wasn't always a happy rehearsal room. The playwright, Brad Fraser, arrived from Canada and I'm not sure what went down behind the scenes but he wasn't happy. He and our director, Braham Murray, with whom he had worked successfully many times, fell out.

Screaming rows and thunderous atmospheres were weathered right up until our opening night, when Braham, sipping a whisky and puffing on his traditional press night cigar, gave us the best first night advice I think I've ever heard: 'Listen,' he said, 'the worst it can be, is a disaster.' This may sound counter-intuitive, but, it's actually a wonderful bit of guidance. The stress of opening a new production, particularly of a brand new play, can feel like life and death. *It isn't!* It's just a play. The world will keep turning, there is always tomorrow to try again; 'the worst it can be is a disaster.'

COMEDY FEELS RIGHT, AGAIN

Well, it wasn't a disaster by any stretch; in fact, it was the surprise hit of the season. Not critically, but word of mouth in Manchester is all-important and word quickly spread that there was a genuinely funny show on at the Exchange. We sold out, while the five-star reviewed *Seagull* continued to play to half-empty houses.

Playing in that theatre in the round (or more precisely, in the heptagonal) was addictive. Such a live space and a joy to free myself from entrenched thoughts of upstage and downstage. Now it was all about energy, absorption in the moment and keeping moving. The sound of a full house laughing in that theatre feels like floating in the air.

It's a magical building; the theatre sitting like a space-craft in the middle of an enormous hall which was once the city's stock exchange. Members of the public wander around buying tickets, looking at exhibitions or enjoying tea and cake as you wander past them in full costume to make your entrance.

Comedy felt 'right' again. Both productions gave me that

'centre midfield' craftsman-like satisfaction. I was doing it; I was in *rep*. I would walk to work with the physical gait of whichever character I was playing that day, which meant leaving extra time for poor old Medvedenko and his limp.

DIGGING IT

The family came to stay once or twice in the crazy, orange high-rise flat with me and I remember pushing Jessica around the kitchen in a plastic washing tub for hours on end.

Other times in that apartment weren't quite so jolly... I fell victim to an incredible bout of food poisoning. All alone one night, in the small hours, sitting on a cold toilet seat, shaking and sweating, I passed out and came round on the concrete floor with a bloody nose and an enormous black eye.

VISITATION

My amazing mother came all the way to Manchester to see the shows, which always means the world. What I hadn't expected was a visit from my recently deceased father!

It was towards the end of a matinée of *Cold Meat Party* and I was pacing around outside the theatre before my last entrance, when I noticed, sitting at a table fifty feet or so away, a man who looked incredibly like my dad. Occupied as my mind was by the performance, I momentarily forgot that he was dead. It seemed perfectly natural that he would have popped up to Manchester without telling me to see the show, and I guessed he was early for the evening performance of *The Seagull*.

I walked slowly towards him. His head was tilted down and slightly away from me reading a brochure.

It was my dad.

Halfway towards him, the logical side of my brain put in a strong reminder that it couldn't be him, as he was, you know, dead. I stopped, realising this was a fair point and that it must be a trick of the afternoon light pouring into the hall. But, as I continued looking, the illusion didn't dissolve, it strengthened.

The man picked up his coffee cup and took a sip: it *was* Dad!

I kept walking, slowly. I could hear from the show relay that I didn't have long before I was due on stage, but I had to see his face. Logic and fantasy kept up a perfectly level game as I drew nearer and nearer until I was only a couple of feet from him. At which point, I clearly saw the man's face – which was not my father's. But the strangest thing is, it *was*. He didn't look up at me. He kept reading, took another sip of his coffee and, somewhere inside my head, my father's voice said, 'Hello Joe', clear as a bell.

It was a visitation, a waking dream, and as reassuring and natural as it was strange.

My body accepted it in the same way it accepted the sleeping dreams I often had, where he appeared and we spent time together. It was sad but also welcome, nourishing.

TAKING THINGS IN HAND...

It was a long run, which gave me nothing but joy and I remained happy in the work. I had a long-standing booking for a couple more one-off Sunday performances of *The Lifted Veil* here and there during the run. It was a brain ache re-learning it, re-rehearsing it on my own in the rehearsal rooms at the Exchange and giving an afternoon performance to my cast mates.

In the last few weeks of the run, I began to get some auditions through from my agent. One seized me fiercely. I was asked to travel to London for an audition with Sir Peter Hall to play Orlando in his upcoming production of *As You Like It*. I became obsessed with the play and the part in the few days I had to prepare it. I had checked with the theatre that I was clear to drive to London after a Thursday evening performance for an audition on the following Friday morning, so long as I was back in Manchester by 4 p.m. in plenty of time for the Friday evening performance.

The audition went well (more about that in another section), and I zoomed back up to Manchester in the rattlingly noisy car I was driving back then. I arrived at my digs in plenty of time and noticed I'd missed a couple of calls from the company stage manager. So I text-messaged him to let him know I was safely back in Manchester.

Now, this Company Stage Manager and I had previously toured the world together with *Mill on the Floss* and I thought I knew him, and he me. I was wrong.

At around 4.30 p.m., as I was taking a snooze in my digs, he called again to ask where I was. I told him and, for some reason I shall never know, he flatly refused to believe me. He told me I had to get to Manchester at once. I repeated several times that I was already in the good city of Manchester, but he'd taken it into his head that I was still in London, and was risking being late for the performance that evening. It was odd but not a worry. I simply set off early to the theatre that evening, so I was actually in the building before any of the rest of the cast, and I thought no more of it. Until midway through that evening's performance of *The Seagull*…

Standing in the great hall outside the theatre, waiting for my next entrance, I re-ran in my mind how the audition had gone earlier in the day. As I was indulging in a little light day-dreaming about getting the part of Orlando for Peter Hall, I realised the doors were open, the cue music was playing and I was due on stage.

I made it, just in time, and all was well, until the scene was over and I was back outside the theatre awaiting my final scene.

All of a sudden, the Company Stage Manager hurried over to me from wherever he had been hiding and with an extraordinary amount of venom, whispered, 'You were *late!*'

'I'm sorry?' said I.

'You were *late* for your *entrance!* You need to buck your ideas up, you're already on *very thin ice!*'

His manner was patronising and superior in the extreme, like a school bully operating under the badge of a prefect. It was bizarre and so upsetting. We had toured the world together; and he'd seen me force myself on stage despite extreme food poisoning and never drop a stitch.

More admonishments were hissed into my face about 'professionalism'; he may even have accused me of lying earlier in the day. I'm not sure exactly what he said because an unwelcome but familiar white haze had begun to descend. I could no longer hear his words, just see his mouth opening and closing.

Before I knew what was happening, I'd taken hold of him and pushed him up against the glass wall of the theatre. I held him there firmly while I asked him what made him think he could talk to anyone in a way that, in any other situation, would earn him a smack him in the face. I said something about actors being human, and that if he spoke to me like that again, he'd regret it. Then I dropped him and carried on with the last scene of the play.

The whole thing came out of nowhere, lasted seconds, and upset me profoundly.

IN DETENTION

I've always suffered great sadness from situations where I'm misunderstood by others, particularly when good and kind intentions and best efforts are interpreted as bad behaviour or lack of professionalism.

I had, of course, acted appallingly, no matter how unjust his whining at me had been.

A formal complaint was lodged and I had to go through a process of redress inside the theatre, including being summoned to the Artistic Director's office for a telling off.

Braham and Greg were joint artistic directors and sat there, as I remember, stifling giggles. They'd known far bigger fights in that theatre and both admitted to me that they thought this particular stage manager officious, but would I please behave as if I'd been reprimanded so they could strike the complaint off. This I did, and I apologised of course. We kept our distance for the rest of the run and all was well.

The audition in London for which I'd left Manchester that day turned out to have been a risk worth taking. I got the job. Orlando in *As You Like It* for Peter Hall! Rehearsals started in London in a few months. I was elated, and began to devour the play.

Voices of Angels
BBC Radio Four

Whilst at the Exchange, I received an offer from BBC Radio Manchester to come and play a couple of roles in a radio play. BBC Manchester have a mandate to employ as many local actors as possible. These rules occasionally get bent a little when actors from elsewhere are residing nearby during runs of plays.

I think this also came my way as the director asking for me was Jim Poyser, son of my wonderful pal, Brian Poyser. Jim was as witty as his dad and I had a great time working on my first radio play.

Voices of Angels was a little thriller about a Victorian murderer. I played both a murdered man and a coroner giving evidence at the trial. My chief recollection is being asked at the last minute to play the coroner as Northern Irish, and being highly surprised when a half decent Northern Irish accent rolled out of my mouth and into the microphone. I had never consciously worked on that accent but it seemed my ear had. Some accents just fit better than others.

A real stroke of luck to get a tiny foothold in the extremely small world of radio drama. It's not a lucrative exercise but so enjoyable and was to become a huge part of my life as an actor.

Doctors
BBC TV

There were a few months between the end of the run in Manchester and rehearsals for *As You Like It*. So I threw myself back into the family life with vigour. I was madly in love with my daughter, as was Caroline. Our flat felt full of light and we stayed busy, and exhausted, from new adventures in parenting.

I walked Primrose Hill, Regent's Park and Regent's Park Zoo endlessly with Jess in her buggy, stopping frequently at Blockbusters video store on the way back to gaze longingly at the movies I wondered if I could ever appear in. I wasn't so interested in the mega-budget studio movies but would stare hungrily at the lower shelves, the indie films and low-rate horror films, which I could *just* about imagine I might *one day* see there with my name in the credits on the back of the DVD. I nursed these dreams like a private religion.

Well, it wasn't a movie, but an offer did come in to play a part in an episode of the daytime BBC soap, *Doctors*. It paid terrible money, but I had no other work and it was a 'standalone' episode that read more like an old-fashioned TV *Play for Today* than a soap script. I was far from proud; three or four days' filming and a couple of hundred quid in the bank? Yes, please.

It turned out to be a brilliant week. There was an extraordinary amount of freedom surrounding the production. It seemed that, as long as the producers, writers and directors delivered each episode on time and under budget, they could shoot *anything!*

Our episode was crazily ambitious: three ex-soldiers meeting for a weekend's camping on the moors. Secrets are revealed about the murder of a prisoner one of them must have committed back in Bosnia years before.

It felt more like making a good low budget film than an episode of a soap. We hiked around marshy moorland all day, electing locations as we went. Black and white war scene flashbacks from Bosnia were filmed with our three or four extras running behind trees, to emerge again and again in the same shot! There was a great deal of laughter, and I relished a role different to any I'd played on screen before: a bespectacled, sober, straight-laced man, a voice of reason who turned out to be the surprise baddie.

Lucky and grateful and with Shakespeare in my pocket I travelled back to Camden.

As You Like It by William Shakespeare
Peter Hall Company, Bath Theatre Royal
UK and USA Tour

BY JOVE, HE'S GOT IT

The day I auditioned for *As You Like It* wasn't memorable only because I got in a scrap with a stage manager at the Royal Exchange later that day. The audition itself was a bit of a collector's piece. I'd zipped down to London in my car after a midweek performance and woke early to get across London for the audition, which had filled me with nerves and excitement.

Peter Hall's place in the history of world theatre is hard to exaggerate. It would be ridiculous to try to sum it up here in a few sentences.

I'd prepared myself as much as was humanly possible. I'd learnt the entire opening speech and scene, read the play over and over and really connected with Orlando, an angry, naive young man with a big, bruised heart.

I walked into the audition burning with Orlando's energy at the top of the play. The large hall was filled with furniture and props set out for the play Peter was currently rehearsing; a chaise longue here, a sofa there, tables with telephones and crystal glasses and wine decanters on them. And there, sitting leaning against a table at the front of the room, was the man himself.

I'm not sure which was stronger, my nerves or the need to begin the opening speech of the play. I was a coiled spring.

Peter shook my hand and introduced me to his daughter, Rebecca, who was to play Rosalind. I was absolutely unable to produce small talk. Unfazed, Peter asked if I'd like to have a go. I answered, 'Yes please,' at once and moved to a far corner of the room, where I paced from foot to foot for a few seconds, performing a final internal rev of my engines, of Orlando's righteous rage. I then looked up, charged into the middle of the room and with a clear voice began:

'As I remember, Adam, it was upon this ... erm...'

Silence.

'Sorry, I'll start again.'

Unbelievably, I'd dried up a few words in. I knew the speech inside out. How could this have happened? Furious with myself, I moved away again to a props table and turned my back to gather my thoughts and re-launch. On my way there, I heard Peter say, 'Well, one line in and he's got the job.'

I chose not to process this at all and instead channelled all my frustration at having messed up the first time into a second very strong and clear and, I suspect, rather too loud canter through the speech.

Once it was over, I registered Peter and Rebecca's beaming faces but didn't dare read too much into this. It could be the kind of smile you bestow on a lunatic who sits opposite you on a train. I couldn't tell. I returned to the front of the room and was at last able to talk to them. They were both delightful, kind, and interested. Peter didn't stop smiling. It was infectious. And I left the church hall walking on air.

FINALLY MR SHAKESPEARE
It turned out he really had made his mind up as quickly as I'd heard. The part was mine!

I'd waited a long time to perform Shakespeare professionally. I'd begun a profound love affair with his plays at drama school where I played Bertram in *All's Well That Ends Well* and Romeo in *Romeo and Juliet,* in full productions there. Before that, I'd played Othello as part of a performing arts course, but perhaps the less said about that the better. I'd presumed Shakespeare would be a regular part of being a professional actor. Instead, it had taken eight years to finally be in a professional production, but what a way to start.

'MAKE THE FORM YOUR FRIEND'
Rehearsals took place in the same cavernous church hall as the audition and, to begin with, felt crushingly disappointing. I'd put in huge amounts of preparation, possibly too much, and wanted to delve deeply into this extraordinary play. Peter Hall, however, appeared to be obsessed only with how it sounded. He would listen to scenes with his eyes closed and openly correct stresses actors had chosen, and seemed fussy beyond belief about 'line endings'.

I'd always had a natural aversion to, and a disrespect for, authority figures and especially assumed authority. This may be the legendary Peter Hall but I was a free spirit who could interpret the language however I damn well chose.

I felt strong resistance to being told how to say the stuff before I'd investigated what it was the scene was about; it seemed so result-orientated, so uncreative.

'Sow an expectation and you reap a disappointment' goes the old saying, and perhaps I'd expected too much from rehearsals. I began to write Peter Hall off as a formerly great director trading on his name and only paying lip service to current work. What I began to worry about in earnest was how I was to stay happy in this rehearsal room and, more importantly, on a very long tour both in the UK and the USA.

One evening, I telephoned my friend from Shared Experience times, Pip Donaghy. You may remember Pip as the cast mate who drunkenly tore my acting apart in Birmingham whilst on tour with *The Clearing* (or you may have spilled coffee all over that page). Anyway, I knew Pip had worked with Peter Hall many times on all sorts of material. I trusted him and wanted his advice. How glad I am that I made that call.

We had a long conversation. I explained my frustrations and my stance on owning my own work to Pip, who listened patiently before giving me the following nugget of gold:

'Make the form your friend,' said Pip.

'Do what?' said I.

He gave me some analogies about jazz musicians needing to be expert at playing written music 'straight' before they could bend things into jazz, which I didn't really understand that night. But crucially, he gave me a suggestion, a dare, which ended up changing everything.

He asked me how long I had left in rehearsals. I told him nearly three weeks. He suggested I explain to Peter that I wasn't really understanding how he wanted the verse spoken and ask him to clarify things, then, and this was Pip's dare, I must absolutely commit to obeying the 'form'; to doing things Peter's way for precisely two weeks. If I still hated it after that, I would have a week left to say, 'Fuck that' and go back to doing things my own way.

The following day, I found a moment to grab hold of Peter and told him I was having trouble grasping what he was after with the verse speaking. I asked him if he could find some time to clarify things for me. He seemed genuinely thrilled by the idea and a 'solus' call where just he and I could work together for a couple of hours was added to the end of the following day's rehearsal schedule.

That two hours alone with Peter Hall working on Shakespeare's verse is one of my most prized possessions. To have someone with that level of knowledge and experience focus their full, laser-like attention on you at a time when you are ready and able to absorb it was an electrifying experience. As doors of understanding started opening in front of me, I would laugh with joy at the sheer fizz of it all and Peter would giggle with me.

Pip was right. What I'd resisted as arbitrary, imposed rules were simply a true understanding of the music. As I began to observe the end of every written line, by 'taking my foot off the pedal' as Peter called it, even for a sniff of a second, and cutting out any breathing mid-written line, the verse began to sound much more modern, interesting and digestible. Though simple enough to grasp, I won't go into all the details of this approach to verse-speaking; Peter went on to write a wonderfully clear book on the subject called *Shakespeare's Advice To The Players*, which I would urge any interested party to swallow whole.

This solo session acted as a kind of speed date for our professional relationship. We quickly began to communicate more in other rehearsals and enjoyed polite arguments often.

'IT'S NOT GOING TO HAPPEN'

I was still able to get my knickers in a fair old twist, of course; I didn't need anybody else's help to find something to keep me up at night.

One scene in particular felt so very wrong in rehearsal. The scene is known as the 'teaching scene'. Rosalind, disguised as a young man, takes poor Orlando to task for his approach to loving and sets him straight in no uncertain terms, all under the guise of pretending to be 'his Rosalind'.

I thank all my atheist gods that I've learnt to be a little better now but, back here in 2003, my inner director / artistic-know-it-all was speaking in my ear rather too often.

It all came from a good place. I'd investigated and invested in the work so deeply, it was life and death to me. If a scene spoke to some, it would scream to me. This scene in particular leapt off the page as a glorious, tragic, comic thing, and it required Rosalind to metaphorically drag Orlando around by his hair – to slap sense into him. All the text seemed to indicate an eruption from Rosalind, which surprised and chastened Orlando. It seemed to me such a clear stepping stone in their relationship and the journey of the play.

Rebecca Hall was, even in full run-throughs, playing this scene in a relaxed, almost resigned manner. It felt upside down to me. At the part of the scene where I felt tensions had to rise, she was cool, calm and collected. I found myself building extra energy into my performance to fill the void. It was all topsy-turvy.

It is, of course, very delicate territory when the way another actor is playing a scene feels uncomfortable to you, and it is *never* a good idea to say it directly to them. One can only pray the director spots your problem, and if things are really difficult, it should be possible to speak to the director privately to see if they agree, and then let them begin to steer the scene a little more in that direction.

When the star of the show playing opposite you in the scene in question is the incredibly famous director's beloved daughter, things becomes a little trickier.

I was enjoying the part so much, but this scene was beginning to feel like a real fly in my *As You Like It* ointment. I didn't feel I could say anything, although I often came close.

After a notes session at the end of one of our final run-throughs, where again I'd sat praying that today would be the day Peter might mention it, and, again nothing had been said, Peter asked if I'd stay behind to have a little chat to him.

The room cleared. He finished sorting a few details with the stage management, then turned to me and looked up at me with that famous 'twinkle' in his eyes.

'It's not going to happen,' he said, and twinkled even more.

'What's not going to happen?' I asked.

'That thing you're waiting for. It's not going to happen.'

My heart pounded. Was I that transparent? Was he clairvoyant?

'But it's OK,' he continued, 'in fact it's really very interesting. It works.'

He maintained the twinkle until he was sure we understood each other, and left it at that.

He was, of course, absolutely right. I remained unsure a while longer; it still *felt* wrong. The combination of my inexperience and arrogance couldn't see how it would work.

The time to open the play before an audience at the beautiful Theatre Royal in Bath arrived. Previews flew by in a blur of technical adjustments and staging and suddenly, it was time to let the national, and indeed much of the world's, press see it and judge it.

I was convinced that the critics would see how there was a gaping hole in the dynamic of the central relationship; that it was, as I felt, upside down.

Well, it not only received almost unanimous rave reviews but Rebecca in particular was singled out in several papers for her revolutionary interpretation of the role. I couldn't believe it. I couldn't see the wood for the trees. This is another of those moments I've experienced while writing this book, when I find myself embarrassed by my younger self. I had so much to learn about acceptance, issues with control and such peculiar high standards.

Rebecca Hall has gone on to become one of the most watchable screen actors of her generation. She is unquestionably brilliant. I know now that if I had a time machine and could go back to watch her in our production of *As You Like It*, I would love her performance.

HE'S YOUNG!
Any scenes not shared with Rebecca Hall were played opposite the legendary comedian Eric Sykes, who, at the tender age of eighty, was giving his first ever Shakespearean performance as Old Adam.

Orlando and Old Adam journey through the play together; Orlando is Adam's eyes and ears and a physical crutch, while Adam is as close to a loving parent figure as Orlando has known and their symbiotic relationship is surprising and affecting. Art imitated life to a ridiculous degree in our production. Eric actually *was* almost entirely blind and deaf. He had, for many decades, worn his trademark spectacles that had no lenses but housed his custom-made hearing aids. If conversations ever got too serious, he would delight in putting his fingers through the frame of his glasses to rub his eyes. I would guide him on and off the stage, then steer him to the positions he needed to stand in to hit his light.

We were firm friends offstage as well as on and went for a meal together at some point most weeks. I was a willing audience for his limitless jokes and stories. I even loved Eric when he would merrily drop me in shit on stage when he forgot his lines. When this happened, his solution was either to make up absolute and utter gibberish, which somehow stayed in the rhythm of the Shakespearean verse but made it hard for me not to choke on my own laughter or, if the dry was more serious, he would stop, clap his hand on my shoulder, turn to the audience, stopping the play for a several long seconds, then say...

'Now then, ladies and gentlemen, this young man's forgotten what it is he has to say. Now, please, he's *young*, he's very young, and it's not easy this breakspeare stuff. Just give him a minute...'

(Audience laugh long and loud and not unkindly.)

I would then whisper his line into his ear, after which he would loudly say something like, 'You want to go from there? OK, lad, if that'll help you, let's go from there.'

It didn't happen too often, thankfully, and only ever thrilled me when it did. I felt honoured to be working with such a master of the relationship between performer and audience and always enjoyed the ride. Sadly, Eric was not in good enough health to take part in the tour of the USA and bowed out soon after our month at Bath Theatre Royal, to be replaced by a less exotic model. I missed Eric out there every night.

POOR ORLANDO

The tour of the USA was extensive, ten weeks or so in and out of major cities on the Eastern seaboard, finishing with a long run in Boston over Christmas.

I wasn't looking forward to all that time away from my gorgeous daughter but aside from it being a decent way to pay the rent, I felt a real sense of what this job could mean in the big picture of my life; a sense even this early in my career, that it was a chapter I could look back on and learn from, an historic production to be a part of. I was also more than happy to be paid to get to know more of America, a country I was always happy to wake up in.

I took myself off for exploratory walks or jogs around every city we visited, wrapped up warmly against the various eastern chills. I almost always elected to take such adventures alone, experiencing the delicious combination of isolation without loneliness. I also began a dangerous, life-long love affair with American diner food and visited both Harvard and Yale Universities, watching and wondering what life inside such expensive establishments must be like.

I went on my own to watch a final production by the graduating drama students at Yale, curious to see how the American equivalent to drama schools compared to England. It was a production of *The Black Dahlia* directed by the wonderful English theatre director, Mike Alfreds, who I knew all about as he was the founder of my beloved Shared Experience Theatre Company. The show was terrific, daring and unapologetic and the young actors seemed entirely committed to it.

The next day whilst wandering in a New Haven bookshop, I recognised Mike Alfreds and, taking my courage in my hands, introduced myself. I told him how much I'd enjoyed the play; he seemed pleased and took great interest in me and why I was in New Haven, of all places. When I explained, he said he would come along to see *As You Like It*. Little did he or I know that we would be working together within a year.

I wasn't a total lone wolf. I joined many a night out, often in the company of James Crossley, who was playing Charles the Wrestler. James was a former Mr Universe and had known great fame as 'Hunter' from TV's *Gladiators*. He was a six-foot-five giant of a man, who, hilariously and perhaps not always believably, I had to defeat every night in a wrestling match. Orlando somehow managed to strangle Charles despite having recently been 'bench pressed' above this opponent's head, then thrown to the ground.

James was a lover of life and a dear pal on that tour. By night we would visit cocktail bars and clubs, where James drank cocktails the size and shape of goldfish bowls. By day we would visit gyms together, where he would introduce me to the rudiments of weight training, and only occasionally laughed at my puny efforts.

We made each other laugh a lot, which caused us real

problems on stage when giggles descended just before we had to wrestle each other. Have you ever tried to wrestle someone whilst giggling? Try it … it's impossible. Like trying to whistle whilst laughing. More than once, we were totally unable to hold on to each other with any strength, and Orlando found himself victorious only because Charles the Wrestler eventually just keeled over, as if he'd had a stroke.

It wasn't all plain sailing. The company was infected with some strange atmospheres at times. Two of our older and most experienced actors developed a profound loathing for each other, and engaged in 'acting battles' on stage a few times each week, trying to outdo, undermine or upstage each other.

We also had an aged lothario in the company, who was slowly working his way through a section of the younger, impressionable actresses and breaking hearts as he went.

I continued to find the balance of the energies between my Orlando and Rebecca Hall's Rosalind hard to relax into, and I fear my face often betrayed my feelings. I still hadn't learnt the liberating power and freedom that comes with acceptance. I wasted endless energy focusing on how scenes *could* be rather than accepting how they actually *were*. My cheeks redden now as I imagine what I must have been like to be around sometimes, tied up in knots searching for a perfect performance.

The lessons I needed to learn were closer than I'd have believed, and the teacher who would teach them to me – the man whose work would lead me to real freedom on stage – had already shaken my hand in that bookshop in New Haven.

BOSTON SNOW PARTY

As November arrived, the production settled in for its extended run in Boston. We were given our own wonderful apartments to live in about a mile's walk from the theatre, which happily included a stroll across the beautiful Boston Common.

Caroline and I had arranged for her and Jessica to fly out to Boston together to stay for the entire six weeks. This had kept us all going during the long separation but, just before the date of their flight, young Jessica came down with chicken pox, a condition airlines frown on somewhat. So we had to wait until she was better before she could fly.

We'd been performing for a week or so when I woke up one morning to see nothing but white outside my windows. An extraordinary amount of snow had fallen overnight. More than I'd ever seen. I presumed we would enjoy a luxurious night off, but, no. Bostonians were used to this kind of thing. Roads were cleared, snow shoes put on and the theatre was as full as ever.

The deep snow and equally deep chill remained throughout December. But, even so, my mum agreed to come and visit. This turned out to be a brilliant week and a really important time for the two of us, together properly for the first time since we'd lost Dad.

Mum was such fun, and game for anything, as was proved the night she joined with the company when we were invited to attend a post-performance drinks reception at the British Embassy. It was a mission getting there through the snow; a gang of us arrived on foot eventually, after failing to hail taxi cabs. We were soaking wet, freezing and must have looked a motley crew.

The house was lavish; diplomats and well-dressed pillars

of the city huddled in room after room; champagne flowed freely – but there was no food. By the time we all staggered back out onto the frozen street, Mum was as sozzled as any of us. I held her arm as we swayed through snow and slush, trying to find a way home, and I felt so happy to hear her laugh. Neither one of us could quite remember how we made it back to my apartment.

It was a new experience, out together without my dad, as equals, as friends. We hadn't really spent time alone together before. We'd also had an interesting relationship during my teens up until I left home, where I suspect I often, to put it frankly, did her fucking head in. There was also a strange, unspoken prickliness between my wife and Mum, which I was yet to understand.

A MESSAGE FROM 'YOUR AGENT'
On arriving at the stage door one day, I was handed a note which read, 'Call your agent soon as possible' followed by an American telephone number. I was confused by the American number. My agent had no US base that I knew of, or plans to be in America to see the show. I knew it was the middle of the night in England at that time so waited until the next day to call. When I spoke to my agents in London, they knew nothing about it. I shrugged it off as some kind of mistake and soon forgot about it.

A few days later, I was given the same message: someone had called, left their number. They'd sounded to the stage door keeper like they were *my* agent. So, I called the number. It was answered almost immediately by a man who at first had no idea who I was either.

Then, just before we were going to end the call, he said, 'Oh, wait, are you in the Shakespeare in Boston?'

'Yes,' I replied.

'Oh, OK. What took you so long to call?'

A slightly strange conversation proceeded. It transpired this wasn't *my* agent, but *an* agent or manager in Los Angeles called Robert Stein. His sister lived in Boston, he'd had an afternoon free whilst visiting her recently and had caught a matinée of *As You Like It*. He wondered if I had American representation. I told him I didn't. He then said he'd be happy to represent me and that I really ought to get out to LA because I could make a heap of money out there.

I took it all with a pinch of salt, thought it all sounded a bit fishy, but told him I'd keep his details and get back to him.

'Make sure you do,' he said, and ended the call.

It would be nearly two years before I called him back, and he would become a significant and eventually sinister player in my story.

NUTS!

I was missing my little girl terribly by this point, but still felt some kind of pride in honouring the play, the part, the production, or perhaps it was Shakespeare. I would walk through Boston Common to the theatre every evening, full of gratitude for my extraordinary luck … to be paid to travel, to act, to play such a wonderful role. But secretly, kindling a new level of ambition; of certainty about my potential. I felt I'd only scratched the surface of what I had to give, and had only just begun to understand the addictive juice of playing Shakespeare – the highs that were on offer. I wanted more and I was determined to get more.

The chickenpox eventually passed and Caroline was able

to fly out with Jess for a wonderful week or so. We walked her in her buggy all over a snow-covered Boston Common, where she would shout, 'Nuts!' to every passing squirrel. They were on their way home again all too soon, and I stayed on to finish the last dozen or so performances.

I awoke on the morning of a day off with excruciating pain in my leg. Upon examination, I discovered my right knee had swollen to the size of a honeydew melon. I'd been experiencing twinges in both knees for a while but had no idea what had happened. I called the company manager, who helped get me to a nearby hospital. Before anyone would look at me, they had to know who was paying for it. I was assured that we were on an American Equity contract and everything was covered by either the union or by Theatre Royal Bath, who ultimately were the producers of the show.

Once I was rubber stamped by the front desk, I received the most wonderful day's medical care. Handsome doctors, wearing running shoes and stubble, inspected, scanned and stroked my knees. I was placed in a private room with a view of the river and fed fresh orange juice. I didn't want to leave, but I did want the pain to go away and to be able to perform the show.

It transpired I had acute bursitis in both knees but the right knee had 'blown up' before the left, although the left was due soon. Bursitis, better known as housemaid's knee, is far more common in the elderly. The bursitic sac (sexy, I know) is an amazing piece of kit we all have in our knees, which inflates, deflates, hardens and softens as we require during normal usage. Problems occur if somebody repeatedly bends the knee fully, makes contact with a hard surface and places weight directly onto the 'sac'. It gets confused after a while and inflates a little like an air bag in a car, only this air bag eventually fills with fluid, hardens and burns with pain.

I ticked all the boxes: years of falling to my knees on stage, decades of skateboarding and, more recently, a year or so of playing non-stop on the floor with my baby daughter. This being followed swiftly by over a hundred performances of *As You Like It,* during which I nightly crashed to my knees from silly heights during a wrestling match.

A George Clooney lookalike stuck an enormous needle into my knee and drained the fluid. I managed not to faint for once (*not* a fan of needles) and was sent away in a taxi with strong painkillers and a shiny pair of crutches.

We adapted the show so that I stayed on my feet a lot more and, despite discomfort, all was well. But I've forever since had to wear knee pads on stage, on screen or at home if I want to kneel on a hard floor for more than a few seconds.

It had felt like a long tour. When eventually the last performance arrived, we were all ready to go home. There were rumours that Peter wanted to take the tour to the West Coast of America the following year, with an extended run in Los Angeles, but they were only rumours at this point.

Our last night party in Boston was attended by Peter Hall and his old friend Peter Shaffer; I'd met Peter Shaffer once before after my first night in *Real Inspector Hound / Black Comedy.* He was very taken by my performance as Orlando, we shared a cab after the party at the theatre, he was extremely friendly in the taxi, and keen for me to go back to his hotel with him for another drink; I was flattered but shattered, not that way inclined, and declined.

2004

MySpace was the talk of the internet, although a little-known company called *Facebook* was registered this year; *Friends* aired its last ever episode, but *Strictly Come Dancing* and *The X Factor* were born; an enormous earthquake under the Indian Ocean and the subsequent tsunamis took over 230,000 lives; Ken Livingstone became Mayor of London and a young lady by the name of Amy Winehouse released her debut album, *Frank*.

RSC
Spanish
Golden Age
Season

The Spanish Golden Age Season
Royal Shakespeare Company
Stratford, Newcastle, Madrid

Early in the New Year, we discovered we were pregnant again. It was as monumental a moment as the first time around, if not more so. I was ecstatic but nervous. I'd been relatively flush when Jessica had arrived, but was now living month to month with my fingers crossed. Love was the other thing I wondered about. I'd fallen so deeply in love with my first child, felt so *full* of love for her, that I couldn't comprehend how I could make any space in my heart for another. My weak mathematics seemed to suggest I would have to withdraw love from my first child to ration out equal love to a new one. I was yet to learn of the heart's infinite capacity to grow.

As January rolled along, our lives were filled with a very big house move from Camden to Berkhamsted in Hertfordshire. I, in particular, had had enough of London. I missed the countryside and fresh air that I'd grown up with and wanted it for my children. I'd also had enough of the violence I'd witnessed and been on the receiving end of around Camden and Kentish Town.

I'd recently made the mistake of fighting back when I was randomly punched on a late bus. I found myself suddenly fending off two men and, when one of them told me that he was going to 'cut me up', I managed to persuade the driver to open the doors, then broke Olympic sprinting records to get home safely.

We were all very happy in our new home, but it wasn't cheap so a job was required, and soon. Auditions were few and far between. Most of the jobs I did try for slipped quickly into the toilet. It seemed I'd lost the knack for getting television work altogether. But one possibility was still hovering – and what a possibility it was.

I'd recently had my first auditions for the revered Royal Shakespeare Company. Three meetings with the various directors for the season had all gone well and I was nursing strong hopes.

After nearly ten years of the acting for a living thing I was acutely aware that I hadn't yet worked at any of the really big shops. The RSC and the National Theatre loomed on the edge of my horizons always. I lived in a duality of feelings about both of these institutions: little old Joe from Sadgrove Farm, Bucklebury in deepest Berkshire didn't think it could ever happen, but little old Joe from Bucklebury was also a dreamer with ambition.

The season of plays I was in the mix for at the RSC was truly exciting, and unknown not just to me, but to *anyone.* A season of unperformed plays and translations from the Spanish Golden Age. Fantastic leading roles in at least two out of the four were on the table, and glorious repertory work in Stratford-upon-Avon then Newcastle playing 'as cast' in the others. If that wasn't enough, the whole season would eventually be performed in Madrid!

'PETER, CAN I CALL YOU BACK? I'VE GOT SHIT ON MY HANDS'

I was at home alone with young Jessica one day and was just starting a nappy-change on a changing mat on the sitting room floor, when our home phone rang. Mid-nappy-change though I was, I took the call, hoping desperately that it was my agent calling with news of an offer from the RSC.

It wasn't my agent. It was Sir Peter Hall. Of course it was. Sir Peter Hall, calling me at home on a number I'd never given him, in the middle of a nappy-change.

It turned out his famous twinkle was equally powerful down a telephone line. A brief catch-up was quickly followed by talk of how close he was to securing a run for our *As You Like It* in Los Angeles later in the year. In the meantime, he had a wonderful proposition for me. He was preparing his second repertory season at Bath Theatre Royal and wanted me to play the lead role in *Man And Superman* by Bernard Shaw and Don Juan in *Don Juan* that coming summer.

I lost concentration for a moment. Jess wriggled vigorously and, in trying to catch her before she escaped, a decent wad of her poo made its way onto my hand. As Peter continued down the line with an incredibly exciting description of this great, rarely performed play, I quickly finished the nappy change and let Jess wriggle away.

Peter hadn't finished his assault of flattery. He went on to tell me how the role in *Man And Superman* was one of the most exacting and extraordinary parts in the history of theatre and that he could think of nobody else with the intelligence and charm to pull it off. He desperately wanted to work with me again etc etc.

So what did I think?

I told him I'd just got shit on my hand.

Of course I did.

That bloody filter was still missing…

When he didn't laugh, I explained what had just happened in a little too much detail before steering back to the question. I wish I could tell you I said, 'Let's get back to the matter in hand.' But I didn't. Instead, I said I was incredibly flattered, thrilled to be asked, and that I would find and read the plays at once.

That wasn't quite what he wanted to hear. He pressed me to say yes there and then, to take his word for it and jump on board.

Though I was immensely flattered, I was in a bit of a situation. There was real pressure from Peter to accept, without consulting my agent, or knowing the deal financially. I felt churlish, silly even, for not screaming 'yes', but I also wanted to know if I might be offered the RSC gig.

I blushed as I took my courage in my hands and told him I'd love to, but that I was waiting to hear about another big job and I couldn't make a decision until I knew about that.

'Ah, is it a film?' asked Peter.

'No' I said.

'Telly?'

'No.'

'What is it?'

I paused. I realised I was holding Peter Hall off because I was waiting to hear about a job with the Royal Shakespeare Company, a company *he* had created and brought into the light. I was acutely embarrassed and anxious as I nervously explained the Spanish Golden Age season to him.

There was a short silence, then, with absolute charm but a little less love, Peter told me he understood, that he could wait a couple of days, but no longer, and hung up.

I immediately called my agent to let her know what was going on. There was a great deal of tutting and sighing. Peter was being naughty calling me directly and she said he knew it. Circumnavigating agents and casting directors, he could charm a 'yes' out of somebody with a single flattering phone call, which otherwise may take weeks of negotiations. I think he was too old to care and wanted his first choice of actors whenever possible.

I read *Man And Superman* that day and was absolutely knocked out by the play, which was an electrifying dissection of the original battle between both men and women, and man and fate. The play was great but the part was unbelievable. I've never read a character in a play who speaks as much. Some of his speeches went on for ten pages at a time! I was instantly drawn to the character and his struggle to resist 'the life force'. I wanted to play him. But I wanted to play Teodoro in *The Dog in the Manger* (the first of the plays in the RSC season) just as much.

It is a truth universally acknowledged that actors spend a great deal of their lives out of work. We expect it and slowly learn to deal with it. What nobody prepares you for are the bizarre moments when you have to choose between two equally wonderful projects. I know, I know. At this moment, dear reader, I would probably be tossing this book in with the pile of things to go to the charity shop. Poor little Joseph. But it *is* a nightmare, albeit a first-world nightmare. As soon as I read a part I might be playing, some kind of love affair begins.

I hoped a strange hope – that the RSC might come back with a 'no', which would make my decision for me. They didn't. It was an offer. I was going to have to end one of the love affairs before it even began.

I was at a crossroad moment in my career and I knew it. I needed to think with my head as well as my heart. I *had* to go to the RSC. It felt like a step on a staircase that I had to take.

It was awful calling Peter to turn him down, but he said

he was expecting it and was incredibly gracious. After we spoke, I wondered who he was calling at home next to twinkle down the phone and tell *them* that *they* were the only actor he could possibly imagine playing the part.

CLAPHAM BABY

Exciting though it was to work for the RSC, it was also a decision we had to really think about. It was a long contract on a very low weekly wage. We were effectively a single income family as Caroline's pregnancy would make work tricky. The flipside of this was that it was regular money, so with careful budgeting I knew I could just about make ends meet.

What didn't help was a succession of very scary letters sent to my home address from the hospital in Boston that had taken care of me when my knee exploded. I was being asked in very strong language for over $3,000 to pay for the medical care. My agent was trying to get the producers of the American tour to sort this out. They made all the right noises, said they were 'looking into it'. Meanwhile, every week a more threatening letter arrived. The whole thing took most of the year to go away, and only after Equity leaned heavily on the producers.

GOLD!

Soon enough, rehearsals began in the gloriously unglamorous RSC rehearsal rooms in Clapham. Laurence Boswell was overseeing the entire season and directing *The Dog in the Manger* by Lope De Vega downstairs in one rehearsal room, while in another, *Tamar's Revenge* by Tirso de Molina was being directed by Simon Usher.

Laurence Boswell was a naughty, bright-eyed,

round-bellied, torpedo of nerves and enthusiasm, with a sideline in very smutty jokes. I adored him. He had an enormous knowledge of and passion for the drama of the Spanish Golden Age and seemed overjoyed to be sharing some of it with the world. *Tamar's Revenge,* rehearsing upstairs, was the only play in the season I was not to appear in.

For the first two weeks, the entire company worked together on a variety of movement, status games, Spanish singing, flamenco and general mayhem, to fast-track both a sense of the world these plays came from and an ensemble feeling amongst the company. Then, after these sessions, the two plays rehearsed in their respective rooms.

It really didn't seem like we were in the lucky rehearsal room. Often quite the contrary. At tea breaks, actors would emerge from the other room with tears in their eyes, putting hands to their chests and exhaling deeply after another 'extraordinary rehearsal'. Those of us only in the play downstairs looked nervously at each other, as we'd spent the last couple of hours discussing exactly which gag might get the biggest laugh.

I was, however, certain that *The Dog in the Manger* was a fantastic play, and Teodoro an extraordinary part. Lope De Vega lived at the same time as Shakespeare and, whilst we know of thirty-seven plays, a beautiful set of sonnets and a couple of epic poems left behind for us by Mr Shakespeare, old Lope wrote some 3,000 sonnets, three novels, four novellas, nine epic poems and around 500 plays!

It's not all about quantity but, as we were discovering, he had quality too, and real originality. *The Dog in the Manger* is an incredibly rich comedy. The essential plot centres around a beautiful and headstrong countess called Diana, who is beset by wealthy suitors urging marriage, but refuses them all. One night, she discovers her loyal secretary (Teodoro) seducing her favourite lady-in-waiting and is consumed by jealousy.

Diana isn't willing to marry beneath her station but doesn't want to let anyone else have Teodoro either, like Aesop's 'dog in the manger'. Teodoro is catapulted all over the stage like a ping-pong ball as he tries to follow his ever changing fortunes.

It wasn't just funny, it was hilarious, and consistently revealed the painful, soft underbellies of every character as the farce snowballed onwards. Teodoro felt like the bastard child of Malvolio and Benedick.

There was a sense of immersion, of 'mission' in the company, as we moved from the rehearsal rooms in Clapham to the Swan Theatre in Stratford-upon-Avon. *Dog in the Manger* was opening the whole season. It felt like we really did have something extraordinary to share with the world.

I notice that I'm starting to use the word 'we' more than I have whilst writing about other projects and that tells a tale. We were only just finding our feet but this turned out to be a glorious company, possibly the truest ensemble of actors I have ever worked in. Almost all of them are still friends, so I suspect there will be a lot more 'we' before the chapter is out.

FIELD OF DREAMS
Stepping onto the stage of the Swan Theatre for the first time to begin our technical rehearsals felt ridiculously exciting, and not just because the set for *Dog in the*

Manger designed by Es Devlin looked exquisite, with an entire thrust stage and back wall covered in brass made to look like burnished gold, but the theatre itself took my breath away.

Seating just 426, the Swan is the perfect theatre. It is a U-shaped, deep thrust stage, where the audience, seated on three sides and on three levels, are always connected to not only the actors, but each other. It's an intimate theatre that has the capacity to feel epic; made entirely from brick and wood, the space feels natural, organic, alive and has perfect acoustics. It's fair to say I'm a fan.

I knew from the moment I walked onto that stage that I'd found my favourite theatre, and nowhere I have worked in the decades since has changed that opinion. All this was before I'd experienced the place in full sail, rocking with laughter, with audiences hanging over balconies, glued to the story.

The experience of performing on thrust stages like the Swan, and theatres in the round like the Royal Exchange in Manchester, made me so much happier than traditional proscenium arch theatres. There's no possibility of playing any kind of imaginary 'fourth wall' between the actor and his or her audience. In my opinion, nothing has contributed more to actors' anxiety than the ridiculous suggestion that the audience aren't there. They fucking *are* there and the quickest way to ground yourself is to look at them, listen to them and welcome them to the events as they unfold. In any case, at our first performances of *The Dog in the Manger*, there they were, on three sides, large as life and twice as noisy. I felt not fear but a relaxation in my bones. I was home.

I was surprised to discover how comfortable I felt in an

enormous organisation like the RSC. It's hard to describe the scale of that theatre company or how it feels to be part of it. After years of uncertainty, here, for a little while at least, I enjoyed a sense of belonging, and something akin to security. The beautiful surroundings of Stratford-upon-Avon didn't hurt either.

I also felt that what I was doing was for my children's good too, and not just by paying the rent and bills. If I could make a mark, get noticed, as useful, *good* even, the RSC was potentially a regular source of employment in years to come. I was ever aware that actors are all too often beggars; it's hard to have tangible currency. I had a family to feed. My only weapons were a growing reputation, the audience's laughter, and hopefully some good reviews. It couldn't hurt to try.

Press night arrived and we all felt a real liberty in presenting a play that barely anyone knew. We trusted each other, we trusted the production, we flew! The reviews as they emerged were superb. There was a buzz, for the production, for the season and even for the cast, including some for me from critics I really admired:

'Joseph Millson as the bewildered secretary, reminds me of the young Kevin Kline in his ability to mix romantic dash and comic absurdity.' Michael Billington, *Guardian*.

What thrilled me about this most was its specificity. This was what I'd been going for! It also described what were perhaps some marketable strengths, and it was there in black and white. It wasn't my vanity that was smiling, it was my anxious father's heart.

WHAT THE HELL?
Tamar's Revenge took over the theatre to begin its own tech

and previews, which meant *Dog in the Manger* was out of the repertory for a week or two, so it was back to the rehearsal room, this time in Stratford-upon-Avon, to begin work on the next play.

The House of Desires was written by Sor Juana Inés de la Cruz, one of the few female playwrights of the age. She was an extraordinary woman, and this long-lost play was remarkable for its time. It explored the idea of free will for women at a time when a woman's role was subject to a strict moral code. It's a romantic farce, advertised as 'a wild tale of confusion and mistaken identities'. Well, they got the confusion bit right.

The plot was extraordinarily convoluted. During that first week, none of us had a clue how to follow it. In the beginning, this included our director, Nancy Meckler, who I'd last worked with on *Mill on the Floss*. I'm sure Nancy had played a part in getting me in the room to audition for the season.

I liked Nancy enormously and I believe the feeling was mutual. She would sit and stare at us all as we worked on the play, with a furrowed brow but the ghost of a laugh always pulling at the corner of her mouth. She seemed to live at a crossroads of panic and delight.

Those of us not in *Tamar's Revenge* went along to their press night, full of pride and support for our brothers and sisters. There'd been tensions and gossip about various problems, and the press night had been delayed. The big wigs at the RSC were not happy with Simon Usher's production and wanted changes. The actors seemed to love and trust him though. I was fascinated to see it.

It was a cryptic car crash. The play itself was good – in fact when I'd auditioned for the season, this was the play

I'd really wanted to be in. The cast were superb, I already knew that, but the production was beyond strange. It was as if Simon Usher *wanted* the audience to hate it; to feel uncomfortable. The house lights stayed on, actors were obscured from sight or audibility at key moments and a rape scene, which could have made its awful point in two minutes, went on downstage in graphic detail for what felt like ten minutes. You could almost hear the director saying 'fuck you' not only to the RSC but to the audience.

The reviews were, naturally, a tad cool, and the audiences stayed away in their droves. As a company, we tried hard not to let it rock us. Those in the play believed in the production and in their director and the rest of us believed in those actors, so that was that. *Dog in the Manger* went back into nightly rep with *Tamar* as rehearsals for *House* continued by day.

ERIC AND ERNIE, OR ERNIE AND ERNIE

The pressure for the next play in the season to go down well was high. Unfortunately, as we neared the end of rehearsals for *House of Desires,* we were all convinced we were about to score another own goal. Rehearsals were tense, which is never great for a comedy. I was pretty vocal towards the end in encouraging Nancy to let us be bold with our choices. The plot was daft, trying to be all 'truth and beauty' about it didn't seem to serve the play.

As with *Dog in the Manger* I was playing someone who had a servant almost always by his side, and, as with *Dog in the Manger* that servant was played by the same actor, Simon Trinder. It seemed almost everywhere I looked, on stage at night, or in the rehearsal room by day, there he was with his hilarious, imp-like face staring back up at me.

We were an enforced double act. Well, I was the lucky one, Simon is a comedy genius. We both had endless ideas for every scene, so it was a test for us at times in rehearsal, but in performance we were a real team. Towards the end of rehearsals we really went for it; Monty Python would have been proud. My Don Carlos was a ponytailed monster of pomposity and pride who dressed in a blue, flared, suede jumpsuit, boomed his lines in a broad Belfast accent and carried himself like a Russian Tsar.

The first preview filled me with dread. None of us had any sense of how an audience might respond to the heightened, bonkers production. I was certain we were about to play to a sea of confused and silent faces. But as we began to roll the snowball of the play down the hill for the very first time, they went with us, entirely, and continued to do so night after night. Especially after a virtuoso solo twenty-minute routine halfway through the play where Simon's character, with the audience's help, got himself disguised as a woman. It was like a brilliant stand-up comedy routine in the middle of the play. Just fantastic. *House* had none of *Dog in the Manger's* depth, but people really enjoyed it, and the critics were impressed and amused. The season was back on track.

WORLDS COLLIDE

Next door in the much larger Royal Shakespeare Theatre (RST) a separate company of actors were staging three Shakespeare tragedies with starry casts. A backstage passageway was shared by the Swan Company and the RST Company. It was surreal and wonderful at first but eventually totally normal for me to pass Toby Stephens as Hamlet as I dashed from stage left to stage right, or to bump into Matthew Rhys's Romeo coming out of the toilet.

I would sometimes creep into the wings of the Royal Shakespeare Theatre to sniff the atmosphere of that historic place, to catch glimpses of the big boys doing the real stuff. That's the way it seemed, but from my vantage point in the wings I soon noticed bored actors pissing about in crowd scenes, eyes rolling as the leading actors did their longer speeches. The work next door in this larger, more famous space seemed more like, well, work. We were blessed in the adjacent more intimate Swan to be presenting plays nobody knew, to be playing parts that hadn't already been seen and played in that town a hundred times, and to have no 'stars'.

I'd taken digs in Stratford only for the periods when I would be working both day and night so treated myself to one of the RSC's 'actors' cottages' opposite the stage door: a tiny one-bed cottage, which I could never quite stand fully upright in. Japanese tourists would peer through my kitchen window every morning to watch the long-haired Englishman making his breakfast. Whenever there was a day where I had a performance only in the evening and no daytime rehearsal I would commute back to Berkhamsted, a three-hour round trip which I took happily to stay connected to both ends of my life.

TOTAL IMMERSION

It was a time of digging deeper into myself in every direction. I was devoted to being a father, enjoying every single minute of the experience and as all parents know the events and life lessons come quickly and often. The broadening of self was equally strong in Stratford. I was unapologetically losing myself in the work when I was there; I was going to mine this extraordinary opportunity for all it was worth. I was an artist, and just learning not to be embarrassed by that word. I compartmentalised my days; when I was home I was home, putting in as full a shift as possible, volunteering for every nappy change, buggy walk and toddler group going, but when I was at work, I was entirely consumed by the work, and by my work family.

BACCHUS

We were putting in the hours, performing three plays in repertory eight times a week and beginning rehearsals for the final play in the season, *Pedro the Great Pretender*, by day. A spirit of generosity and care pervaded every sweaty moment.

When I was staying in Stratford I would join the company for post-show drinks in the infamous 'Dirty Duck' pub. I felt more accepted and comfortable with this gang than I had with any previous company, which occasionally led to a certain amount of excess. I eventually earned the nickname Bacchus, after developing a strange drunken habit of pouring large amounts of wine over my head. There was a joy in belonging, in shared endeavours, both triumphant and disastrous. I wonder if this inadvertently, without malice, was a seed for some discontent in my marriage with Caroline. She was by now very pregnant, doing the lion's share of caring for Jess, and there was I, clearly having a wonderful experience, which try as I might it was hard to fully include her in. I trusted to time and fate, and got on with my job.

Getting on with my job at this point meant entering a couple of months of the hardest work I'd known to date as an actor but it was transformative for me.

Pedro the Great Pretender was an unperformed, 'lost' play by Miguel De Cervantes who was best known for writing *Don Quixote*. A crazy, sprawling, epic comedy following a loveable trickster, who travels Spain trying to be helpful in order to be liked, before eventually finding his vocation on the stage. We were to be directed by the one and only Mike Alfreds, who I had last seen in that bookshop in Connecticut.

I'd been cast in a couple of tiny roles, but also as the King, who had two great scenes. The play was like nothing I'd ever read, but in early rehearsals we didn't have to worry too much about the script as Mike wanted to break us in to his style of working.

He stood very still, smiling enigmatically at us on that first day, and in his clear, quiet voice said, 'When I go into a restaurant, I want a freshly cooked meal. I don't want to eat exactly the same plate of food somebody ate last night. It may have the same ingredients as the night before, but I want my meal cooked from scratch on the night I'm there, and it's the same with theatre. Nothing need ever be repeated in exactly the same way twice, so we won't be "blocking" rehearsed moves in any of our scenes. By the time we finish our rehearsals you will all be able to move freely, in a way which feels fresh each night, which helps the play and inspires each other.'

Mike has since written a wonderful book called *Different Every Night* which will explain with much more clarity and detail this wonderful philosophy to anyone who is interested.

For me, as we began to work with Mike, with games, exercises and long improvisations, it felt like being given a key to a door I'd always been sniffing at. The unexpected was nothing to fear anymore, not in his world: accidents and surprises were positively welcome; other people's ideas to be taken on at once, not resisted. To quote Mike: 'everything is a gift.' He didn't strive for perfection, but for freshness and originality. Work must always remain true to the play and sometimes the shifts were small but the objective was always the same: see what happens *tonight*.

Our work with him was perfectly timed; we knew each other well, trusted each other, and had been through many ups and downs already so were fearless of judgement. It was idyllic; I played like a child and lost myself in improvisations with absolute abandon. The big surprise for me was that when we moved from the cocoon of the rehearsal room I took this playfulness on stage with me in front of the audience, lock, stock and barrel. Before working with Mike something in me had always wanted to get things 'right', to strive for perfection. Thinking back to those early jobs I can see how much anxiousness I created, both for myself and others around me. I was beginning to understand that theatre isn't about perfection: it's live, it's dangerous and perfectly imperfect.

PILLOW FIGHTS

The entire cast and musicians of *Pedro* stayed on stage throughout the performance, watching each other's scenes and changing costume, hats and wigs in full view of the audience. Pedro himself was played by a glorious actor by the name of John Ramm. John had worked with Mike many times before and I learned so much from his ease on stage, and his ease with the audience.

I played various villagers and sang in various songs until

the King arrived. My King was a jealous tyrant who I played with the exact outlook and desires of a spoilt ten-year-old. For once I had someone other than Simon Trinder playing my servant; Oscar Pierce gamely took an endless stream of abuse, unprompted snogs and nonsense from me as the King, but it was the wonderful Rebecca Johnson as the Queen who I had my biggest moment with.

The scene was essentially one where the King bursts in on the Queen as she is reclining on a bed of cushions being fed grapes by her minions, and accuses her of something. An argument develops, tantrums are thrown on both sides before they storm off. That was the scripted scene. What gradually developed, and I promise it did come from the scene, not just actors titting about, was a pillow fight of epic proportions. It had no rules, no choreography, and I'm sure for some of the cast watching, no end, but by God it was fun.

BOUNCE

Pedro went down reasonably well with the critics; it was a curiosity piece really, but the audiences loved it. It was August now and the season was finally complete: we had four plays in rep in the Swan. The sense of freedom and playfulness spilled over into the other plays. Without changing anything significantly I became more present and more responsive and every night did indeed begin to feel more freshly cooked.

No matter which way you cut it, acting on stage is a peculiar thing for a human being to do. Hundreds of strangers watching you pretend to be someone other than yourself and to publicly have your memory, your physical attributes, your musicality, your sense of humour and your voice judged. The fight or flight reflex is triggered every single time.

Things on stage are going to go wrong. I'd spent ten years trying to prevent the unpreventable. It wasn't that I was now seeking accidents, or doing anything to encourage them, but I wasn't wasting energy worrying about them anymore, and that energy diverted itself naturally into what was happening right in front of me each night. I noticed gifts from the audience and my fellow actors which I'd been blinkered to before.

It was only a beginning of course, it takes work to remain that open, but it was a significant new piece of treasure to have in my backpack as an actor. It's never left me. I would have loved to have worked with Mike again, but sadly soon after this season he felt he'd arrived at an age when he decided he no longer wanted to direct professionally. How lucky I was to work with him. How glad I was to have taken this job.

GABRIEL'S TRUMPET

The four plays continued in repertory for the final six weeks or so of the season in Stratford; I commuted to and from Berkhamsted every day. It had been agreed when I took the job that I would be able to attend the birth of my child. As the due date approached I would check in with Caroline and her tummy before I set off, ready to zoom back should I get the call. One Tuesday morning the signs were clear that I wouldn't be performing that night. I told the company manager, who'd been expecting the news; he told me not to worry and wished me luck. We left Jessica with her grandma, then I drove Caroline and her very heavy load to Stoke Mandeville Hospital's maternity department.

The birth was considerably faster and less complicated than last time around, but no less traumatic or painful for Caroline I'm sure. The midwives encouraged a much more natural position for delivery than our previous experience which meant Caroline was able to squat at the side of her bed and reach across it to hold my hands. In the final moments I stifled a yelp (it really wasn't the moment for me to complain), as I felt one of my fingers crack under her incredible grip, and then, there he was.

He.

I'd been absolutely convinced that another daughter was coming our way. Any worries or fears I'd had about love evaporated the moment I held him in my arms. I felt my heart crack open and expand. It wasn't an extra room, but a whole new house of love which opened up for him.

Caroline was once again my hero in human form for what she did that day and always will be. We had two names ready for each sex, and instantly knew that this wasn't an Oliver, but a Gabriel. Gabriel Arthur Millson. The grandfather he would never get to meet whose name he would carry forever as his middle name was smiling somewhere.

I sent a message to my theatre family, telling them the news. Back in Stratford the company would be performing *Pedro* that evening without me. I was missing a performance for the first time in my life. I was later told that John Ramm stepped forward at the start of the show to welcome the audience, and explained that the role of the King would not be played by Joseph Millson that night because he had to be at the birth of his new baby, at which the audience made sympathetic noises. He then told them he was happy to report that an hour or two earlier Joseph's wife had delivered a healthy baby boy. Apparently the actors, musicians, stage managers, ushers and a full audience of total strangers clapped, cheered and whooped his arrival. I cried when I was told. It summed up everything hopeful and positive about theatre, and I'll always treasure the fact that a loud noise of celebration was made in that space to honour his birth.

ON THE ROAD AGAIN

I was back to commuting to Stratford the next day, but only for a short while as before we knew it the Stratford season was over. We had a week or two off which I spent in the brave new world at home with two children and a whole new face to gaze at. It was a big wrench to have to leave him to take the shows to Newcastle.

The RSC had a long-standing tradition of taking all of their productions to Newcastle for an autumn residency. Shows from the RST went to the Theatre Royal while shows from the Swan usually transferred to the trendy Newcastle Playhouse, but it was closed for refurbishments so we moved all four of our plays into the People's Theatre on the outskirts of town.

The People's Theatre is an amateur theatre with an impressively large auditorium; they were welcoming, happy to have us there but almost nobody came to see the plays and the theatre felt cold and dead after the Swan. I enjoyed Newcastle though, a city I'd toured to many times before. I stayed awake and inspired as best I could with cold autumnal jogs through parks and several phone calls home every day to check in on the brood. The company was exhausted by the time we finished in Newcastle but a very delicious carrot was keeping us all going: we were off to finish the adventure in Madrid!

OLÉ

Travel was a perk I hadn't factored in to my daydreams about becoming an actor, but here I was again pinching myself hard at my incredible luck. I was in *Madrid* of all places to perform in the Festival de Otoño.

We had a day off on arrival while the set was fitted into the incredibly ornate four-tier auditorium of the Teatro Español. Once again I snuck away from the gang to have a long solo wander around the city, walking and walking with a little free map. Then, the day of our first performance arrived.

The Spanish don't have an equivalent phrase for 'taking coals to Newcastle', but that's exactly what we were doing. To get some idea of the high pressure we were under, imagine, say, the Italian National Theatre arriving at Shakespeare's Globe to present *Much Ado About Nothing*, asking English audiences to hear the play in Italian while following surtitles from brand new translations. We performed a dress rehearsal in the afternoon to an audience of thirty or so invited guests and were met with stony silence. Laurence Boswell and our producer Jeremy seemed exceedingly sweaty and nervous as we approached the sold-out evening performance. They didn't tell us until afterwards, but they'd been informed that at least a hundred tickets had been bought by a group who wanted to protest at our being part of the festival, and our outrageous decision to try to show the Spanish how to perform their own national playwright's work. 'It's not uncommon', someone nervously explained to them, 'for Spanish audiences to boo loudly at work they disdain'. We were all bricking it.

Dog was advertised as starting at 9 p.m., an astonishingly late start time to us Brits, but of course this was Spain, where the late afternoons are spent in siesta and life only begins to get going again long after the sun has set. As 9 p.m. arrived, we were all poised and nervously waiting in the wings, but no front of house clearance came. After half an hour we were told to 'relax'; the time advertised on the posters was apparently only a guide; the show would start when the audience had arrived, and not before. 'Relax?' Fat chance. An ominous feeling of impending doom grew with every minute. Finally, somewhere between ten and ten thirty we were given front of house clearance and Simon and I locked eyes before dashing out through the set's big brass doors to start the play.

The enormous theatre was full to bursting; our first laughs didn't arrive in any way, shape or form so we braced ourselves for a tough night, but, as the audience began to get used to reading the surtitles whilst following the action on stage, the tension began to thaw. A polite trickle of laughter turned into a torrent; you could *feel* the audience being won over. We closed to a standing ovation, apparently led by the very faction who had come to the theatre wanting to hate us.

We went on from the theatre to a seemingly endless party at a nearby tapas cavern. Bacchus came out from hiding and I was wearing wine on my head by the end of the night. Far from hostility there was an outpouring of love for us from the local actors and directors which was a little hard to believe or understand, until the reviews came out. Lope de Vega's plays were held in such high regard in Spain that a style of performing them in a very sombre way had developed over the centuries. Lope's spirit had been imprisoned by his compatriots. We had recovered a little of his freedom. A review in *El Pais* summed this up: 'In the RSC's hands, a play whose commentaries on social class can draw actors and directors into grinding solemnity erupts like a geyser.'

The rest of our week in Madrid flew by in a whirl of late performances and incredibly late bedtimes. News of a West End transfer for the season was beginning to filter through to us, but the London run would be nearly three months away, no financial retainer was being offered to keep us fed and watered in the meantime and, with the London season checking our dance cards in the spring, it would be next to impossible to find any acting work between now and then; regular day jobs would also be difficult to find, and set up in time. For most of the company who were childless and self-sufficient this was difficult; for me with two young children and a rather adult mortgage and bills to pay it was frightening. I'd budgeted so carefully throughout the season, each week's wage being divided immediately and sent off to cover our various living expenses.

As we boarded the flight home I was still optimistic, hopeful, high on our achievements, but soon after getting back the reality of an approaching Christmas with no income and no savings hit hard. We tightened our belts. We just had to get through to January. As a home owner now, claiming benefits was not an option. I found a little teaching work, searched my belongings for things to sell, but, by the time January arrived, we were genuinely broke.

2005

A little start-up company called 'YouTube' was founded, Bird Flu flew towards us, Mariah Carey told us endlessly that 'We Belong Together', Eminem thought we were more 'like Toy Soldiers', George Bush and Tony Blair entered their second and third terms respectively, *Doctor Who* returned to British television, petrol cost around 88 pence a litre, cinemas rocked out to *Walk The Line* and Harry Potter's *Goblet Of Fire*, Prince Charles married Camilla, Arthur Miller died, as did George Best, as did fifty-six people in the bombings in London on 7th July.

On set ... somewhere

WHY MUST THE SHOW GO ON?

By the time our London contract started I was chasing my tail. We were running on empty as a family. Caroline had performed in a local pantomime over Christmas, during which I would often be found waiting in the wings with Gabriel in my arms, for him to get a quick breast-feed between scenes; it was a fun job for her but the tiny wage didn't go far. Not only had I been waiting a couple of months or so without work to begin the West End run but we'd all agreed to a cut in weekly wage: our ten weeks or so in London would be on a wage of £485 a week, from which I was to pay tax, agent's commission, a hundred pounds a week travel expenses, mortgage, gas, electric, and food and clothes for a family of four. It was untenable, but it was all we had and they were incredible roles to be playing in London; it was a spin of the dice which had to pay off.

The Playhouse Theatre is one of the more hidden West End theatres; tucked modestly into a corner behind Embankment Underground Station, it receives no passing trade and had established a reputation as something of a graveyard for plays, but the RSC's reputation and fan base, along with our knockout reviews, were enough to make sure we stayed busy.

One of our company had declined to come with us into the West End, as his main role was in *Tamar's Revenge*, which unsurprisingly was not part of our London Season. His roles in the other plays were shared amongst those of us who could carry them. I found myself hurriedly learning the role of 'Blind Man' in *Pedro*, which I ended up having rather too much fun with.

I hurled myself into the work every night, Mike Alfred's playful mantras still fuelling the atmosphere on stage, but there was something almost manic and dangerous in the energy that I was burning out there. There was a dichotomy growing between my on-stage life and my home life, which was beginning to drive me a little insane.

I would wander through my days, adoring my time with the children, but weighed down by a backpack full of worry, carefully considering every penny I spent, denying myself even the tiniest of luxuries and often not eating properly. I would cycle to the train station, then cycle through London to the theatre, find out which of the three plays we were performing that evening and devote myself to it as totally as I could. Laughter would rock the theatre, and, if it was *Dog in the Manger* I would take a solo bow, feeling strong and in the peak of my powers; applause would ring in my ears, the bird of delight would perch on my sweaty shoulders for a moment, and then, she was gone.

I pressed on. One Thursday afternoon after a matinée performance I was out on my usual hunt around the Embankment area for affordable but filling food. I found myself walking into McDonald's; I stared blankly at the thin choice offered to vegetarians when I noticed a man dressed fairly smartly near me wearing a smile and a McDonald's name badge. Before I knew what I was doing I had engaged him in conversation. I asked him if he'd mind telling me a little about how he enjoyed working for McDonald's. I told him I was interested in applying but that I felt a little old for flipping burgers. He said that at my age I'd be an ideal candidate for a swift march through the ranks to assistant manager, the role he was currently enjoying. We were getting along well so I asked him if he'd mind telling me what kind of hours he did, and if it wasn't too rude, what he earned. When I learnt that his hours were reasonable and that his basic wage was a clear hundred pounds a week higher than mine, something inside me snapped. What was I doing? This wasn't a game. I had a family to provide for. I'd tried my best, but here I was somewhere near the top of the theatre tree as far as aspirations went and I couldn't make ends meet. There were other ways to earn a living and I was far from too proud to take them.

I went back to my dressing room, free milkshake in hand and wrote a letter there and then to my beloved agent Jan. I told her without hysterics that I was going to have to find a full-time job away from acting as soon as the contract with the RSC ended. If opportunities were offered that paid well I would take them but as a father I simply couldn't play the waiting game anymore.

The perverseness of having to make this decision while seemingly riding so high was heart-breaking.

Jan was fantastic. She called me a day or two later and really listened. We agreed to play it by ear and see what the last six weeks or so of the run might bring. She told me about an organisation called the Actors Charitable Trust set up to support the children of theatre workers and told me to give them a call, which I duly did. I was embarrassed and certain that I wouldn't qualify for any help; I was gainfully employed, and in a high profile job, but they heard my situation without judgement. They asked to see proof of my outgoing expenses which affected the children, gas, electric, food etc and proof of my income. They came back to me a week or so later and said that as it was winter they would pay the heating bill for January and February for us, as this directly affected the children, and that they hoped this would help. It absolutely did and I was staggered and grateful in equal measure. In subsequent easier years I took great pleasure in donating twice the amount back into their organisation.

The other thing Jan did was to throw me at every possible audition while I was still in London performing. I gave them my best shot, came close to some but nothing was sticking. Three weeks or so from the end of the run I read for the part of Macbeth himself in a BBC television film of the play.

I was sent the script and a scene to prepare. It was a superb adaptation, all set in and around a Michelin-starred trendy restaurant and its kitchen. I loved it, and, as ever, did too much homework. By the time I walked into the room to read with the casting director and the director I was bouncing off the walls with energy, ideas, and, unfortunately, desperation.

Halfway through reading the scene I screamed one of Macbeth's lines so loudly that the walls shook. Brian Blessed would have been proud. When the scene was over nobody spoke. It wasn't the kind of silence you get when you've impressed people. From the pit of my stomach I started to feel a strong feather of laughter rising. Tears began to spring from my eyes and a giggling fit was upon me. Once I was able to speak, I apologised and told them I was sorry but my own ridiculous performance had just really tickled me. I wasn't sure where my eruption had come from; I told them that I may have been doing a little too much theatre and wished them all the best with their film.

I didn't care, it was funny. Life and my profession and the ridiculous way we had to interview for jobs was suddenly clear to me in all its capriciousness. A veil of seriousness had lifted and I travelled back to the theatre to try to enjoy the performance that night, knowing these final weeks on stage may be my last for some time, or possibly ever.

A couple of days later Jan called me to say they loved me!

Unsurprisingly they weren't going to offer me the role of Macbeth; that was going to be given to some young buck I'd vaguely heard of called James McAvoy. But, *but,* they were extremely interested in me for the role of Banquo. Jan did an incredible job of pretending I was in high demand and leaning on them to grab me while they could, and within a couple of days a deal was done and the job was mine. Best of all it would begin shooting before the run in the West End finished – the sooner this very helpful wage could come in the better. My money nightmares were over, for now, I was saved by the knell!

The Spanish Golden Age season ended in a blur of fatigue, with night-shoots and morning shoots around the performances for me. We were all exhausted but after over a year in the company of these incredible people and achieving that rare thing of a true ensemble, it was a sad farewell. More than any company I've been in, this gang stayed in touch, remained close friends, family almost. Several of the company were to become future employers for me, and for each other; the women of the company, the W.I. as they called themselves, still meet several times a year. It was a season of work bathed in a glow which has never left us. 'We lucky few' indeed.

Macbeth, Shakespeare Retold
BBC TV

Macbeth was a feature-length television movie shown as part of a season on BBC1 alongside three other modern interpretations of Shakespeare plays, all with fantastic writers doing the adaptations, great production teams, directors and starry casts. This was my first bit of really classy television work. It was a big leap to be playing a leading role in something like this. Although *Peak Practice* had been amazing for me and had a huge audience it was, to all intents and purposes, a soap opera. Looked at with a cold eye my television career so far had consisted of appearing in a couple of sitcoms, and a few soap operas, my last TV appearances having been on *EastEnders* and *Doctors*. My decision to concentrate on my theatre career had paid off; I wasn't 'that bloke from *Peak Practice*' anymore, I was just an actor the casting director had seen and liked in a play at the RSC.

We had a week of rehearsals and fittings before filming started. I was still performing the plays Monday to Saturday but was happy to work all day either going to fittings, make-up tests, rehearsals, or to chef school!

THANKS SHALLOT

The transposition of Shakespeare's play into the world of a high-pressure Michelin-starred restaurant was a stroke of genius by the adapter Peter Moffat. The discipline and hierarchies in a high-end kitchen feel absolutely military, and ambition and respect are at war every day. I'm not sure if it was the director or James McAvoy who insisted on it but as *Joe* Macbeth and *Billy* Banquo were to be Head

Chef and Sous Chef, and as we had an awful lot of scenes to shoot depicting the full flow of a high-pressure kitchen, we were sent off together, just James and me, to study the real thing.

We arrived at the famous Le Gavroche restaurant horribly early one morning, met the Head Chef Michel Roux who told us we were welcome to be in the kitchen but that we couldn't just stand around getting in the way, we would have to work a full shift. We were both happy to do so; far better than just hanging around like poncy actors observing others working their socks off.

Well, holy shit, we were put to work. I'm certain a bit of fun was had at our expense; no menu could possibly require the amount of shallots that James and I peeled that first day. We were squeezed into a corner of the kitchen, shown the Michel Roux way to peel a shallot, handed an enormous bag of them and told to get going. After a few hours we'd peeled a thousand of the little bastards. We had streaming eyes and repetitive strain in our hands, but it was an excellent way to fast track our friendship before shooting began and we were both eagle-eyed, watching and listening to everything going on around us. So many things we saw there made their way into the film, from the amount of burn scars visible on every chef's arms, to cornflour being poured down the arse crack of a particularly sweaty chef, loud laughter, singing, and the non-stop call and response from the head chef to his army in the kitchen.

'*Two Plateaux de Fromages Affinée and a Filet de Boeuf!*' the Head Chef or Sous Chef might scream as an order arrived. 'CHEF!' would come the immediate shouted response from every single person in the kitchen, including us. The unquestioned chain of command, discipline and strict codes of communication felt like those of an army under fire.

We did a second day at the restaurant with a little less onion peeling and a few more top tips on looking like we knew what we were doing with knives and other equipment. I would arrive at the theatre in the evening, stinking of onions but excited by the new project. It was a brilliant part, both in the original play, and possibly even more so in this adaptation.

STATUS GAMES

The actual shooting began during my last week of performances in the West End. We were on night shoots and it felt pretty darn rock and roll to finish a performance, come out of stage door, get into a car and be driven to some mouldy old car park in East London where the unit base was set up, to begin another day's work, which would only finish as the sun came up. I would then be driven home to squeeze the kids and grab three or four hours' sleep before heading off by train to the theatre again.

It was exhausting, but it was only a couple of weeks of both jobs and then I would just be doing the film. I'd seen how utterly exhausted those mega chefs looked at Le Gavroche and decided there was no harm in using my real tiredness in front of the camera.

It felt good to be filming again, partly as I knew this job was pulling me, at least temporarily, out of a financial nosedive, but I hadn't realised how much I had missed being on a set, in front of cameras and part of a unit like this. The cast were absolutely fantastic: Keeley Hawes playing Lady Macbeth, Vincent Regan as Duncan,

Richard Armitage as Macduff; even the smaller parts had actors who were on the cusp of great careers such as Toby Kebbell, Ralph Ineson, Packy Lee and Barry Ward.

Most of my work was with James, and we achieved real simpatico straight away. In fact all the cast worked incredibly generously and sympathetically with each other, which was lucky, as we all hated our director; or, more precisely, he hated us.

It's thankfully quite rare, but I have worked with a few television and film directors who, for whatever reason, on that particular job, could not communicate with the cast. Our director was a bespectacled and remote man who was clearly very well versed in how to make things look beautiful and exciting in an edit, but seemed absolutely bemused by the behaviours and needs of actors and oozed his frustration with us from start to finish every day. The atmosphere was already tense by the time I started work: Keeley and James had had a tricky couple of days and told me of stand-up disagreements on set with him. They'd remained kind and loyal to each other though and were a great team. I think we all went on our own individual journeys from trying to help him achieve his vision, to finding it very hard to understand exactly what that vision was, to feeling that everything you did disappointed him, followed by getting extremely unhelpful, negative notes from him; then finally starting to talk to the other actors before each take, agreeing on a game-plan to help each other and going for that. We became united in our mistrust.

WAKE UP

Two moments ring out clearly for me. The first was just a few nights in, and a key scene. Macbeth and Banquo return to the restaurant in the small hours of the morning after a night out; they've encountered the three witches (bin men in our version) who predicted that the restaurant would get three Michelin stars, that Joe Macbeth would one day own it, but that it would eventually belong to Banquo's children. Laughing the incident and the predictions off (it's a good restaurant, but not that good), they return to find Duncan still up drinking with Lady Macbeth. We are soon told the reason for their late-night carousing; Duncan has just learnt that the restaurant is going to receive its third Michelin star! Macbeth and Banquo share a significant look before joining the hugs and celebrations.

It was a scene set at a round table, so after the wide shot was complete it took some time to go around getting everyone else's coverage; I was one of the last to get my close-up. Everyone was doing fantastic work but also having a great time between set-ups. I was loving it, cooking on gas, and when it came to the look James and I share after we hear the witches' predictions coming true I was right inside it. The director called cut then came onto set and pulled me aside. He seemed furious. 'Come on, man,' he said, 'you've got to *do* something. I know it's late, we're all tired but for fuck's sake you have to react when you hear about the Michelin star. Wake up!' Now, luckily I had already learnt of his frustration with other members of the cast; had I not known about that I would have felt destroyed by this, but I was able to stay calm and tell him I was perfectly awake, and that I was reacting. I asked him to go back and watch my eyes in the close-up on playback. There was something of a stand-off. I stood my ground and asked him again to please go and look at my eyes in the close-up. I promised him that everything he needed was there.

To his credit he watched the playback and acknowledged that I was reacting but that it had been too subtle for him to see at first. He asked me for a take where I did something bigger, to have the option. I agreed and then proceeded to do exactly the same reaction again and he seemed happy. But he'd lost my respect. It seemed to me that he'd *decided* that because we were laughing with each other between set-ups we weren't taking our work seriously; he'd *decided* I wasn't trying, jumping to a narrative of actors pissing about and not concentrating.

THIS JAMES McAVOY FELLA MIGHT GO PLACES

The second moment was a few nights later. It was around 3 a.m. and we were outside in an alleyway shooting a small but important scene from further along in the story. Duncan is dead and Macbeth is by this point 'king' of the restaurant. He and Banquo have lost their former closeness but find themselves alone with each other as they check over an early delivery to the kitchen. Whilst inspecting the meat being delivered, small talk is attempted and Banquo tells Macbeth that his wife is expecting another child.

We shared the scene with a young actor playing the delivery man who had one line of dialogue relating to the quality of the meat as James was inspecting it. We rehearsed for the cameras, and as usual James and I were in perfect sync with our approach to the scene; it was like Pinter, smooth surface on top with wild currents beneath. Yet, again, our director when he spoke to us seemed tense, but he couldn't articulate why.

When it came to covering the delivery man's line of

dialogue he screamed, 'CUT!' He then proceeded to tear the young actor apart, mocking his voice in front of everyone and bulldozing him with instructions for the next take. He shouted, 'GO AGAIN!' and the shot was re-set. James didn't move. Just before action was called he said, 'No. No. We're not going again.' He asked the director to come out from behind his monitor and told him in a voice loud enough for everyone to hear that his behaviour was not acceptable; if he was frustrated with us he couldn't take it out on this actor who had come out in the middle of the night to perform his one line of dialogue and was doing a perfectly good job. He told him to apologise to the actor there and then; if he didn't then James would be going home, there and then.

I fell in love with the man. It was all done without histrionics; he was reasonable, calm, but absolutely immoveable. James wasn't James McAvoy the movie star at this point. He was doing well, but he wasn't home and dry career wise by any stretch, so this was true support for his fellow actors. I remember thinking he was either going to be a mega star or never work again. My bets were on mega star.

The trouble we had with our director did nothing to dampen a fantastic experience; there was a lot of laughter and friendships were founded. Billy Banquo was a fantastic role and I felt we'd managed to make something special happen in front of the cameras every day. The film was a big success and has since become staple viewing in most schools studying the play for GCSE. Both of my children have had the embarrassment of having to watch their dad in it in class at school.

Monogamy (Again)
BBC Radio Four

With the *Macbeth* film in the bank I was allowing myself to feel positive and hopeful for an upwardly inclined year. Caroline had begun looking for a job again but nothing was forthcoming. The next bit of actual work to roll in was an offer of a radio play for both of us. In a roundabout fashion this was work I'd provided for us myself as it was an offer to perform *Monogamy*, the play I'd originally commissioned and produced with Pursued By A Bear five years previously.

Radio Four had asked Craig to adapt his play for radio. I was thrilled more people were going to hear his brilliant writing and very glad they wanted the original cast to perform it. I didn't know the director, but we knew the play so well, this would be a couple of days of fun. Surely...

The story is told backwards in the play as I described before; Craig, Caroline and I all agreed it would be a wonderful experience and rewarding artistically to switch the order for the recording schedule, so that in the studio we would begin at the blossoming of their relationship and travel scene by scene to their bitter end. The play could be chopped up in the edit and put back together in the opposite order for the listener, but we would have a tremendous continuity of emotions as we worked through it. We were excited heading to the studio to begin work together. It was Caroline's first radio play and she was in need of creative work to balance out the parenting schedule.

There was a hurried read-through where we met our

director. She began by giving us her take on the play, which was nothing like the one we'd found when creating it with Stuart all those years ago, but we shrugged it off as it was all going to be recorded very quickly, so how she had taken the play couldn't really affect our performances; we knew these characters too well.

To begin with it was fantastic; it had been five years since we'd closed at the Riverside Studios but the scenes and characters were still in our DNA and we flew as we performed them, barely needing to look down at our scripts. We had a scene or two under our belts before I started to notice a cloud hovering above our director's head. Before we recorded each scene she would come out to join us in the studio to talk it through. Caroline and I would smile and listen, but had no real questions for her and just wanted to have a go first and discuss it afterwards.

This eventually led to tensions as takes were stopped, and notes would come in through the speakers high up in the studio wall. The director seemed to want to push Caroline as Emma into playing the victim and me as Paul into a much more two-dimensional buffoon; the shades of grey we'd found weren't to her taste.

We tried her ideas, but with increasing confusion; the magic with which we'd begun the day was leaking through the floor as we began to second guess ourselves. A small straw eventually led to a break in this camel's back. I knew the rhythm of Craig's writing so well and had taken a tiny pause in the middle of one of the lines, which left room for Paul to arrive at his next thought in his own drunken way. It also delivered a natural rhythmic laugh for audiences in the theatre and possibly for those listening to a radio play. It was a perfectly valid choice. She couldn't give me an alternative or a decent reason not to do it, eventually resorting to, 'Because I'm the director and I said so.'

Now, if you've read this far, dear reader, you will be aware of my feelings about assumed authority, and can probably guess what happened next. I dug my heels in, vehemently defended my position asserting authority over my work. It could be argued that I was justified, but, what did it gain? It was awkward for Caroline who was already nervous and hadn't worked as an actor for a while, and it created an atmosphere in the studio for everyone.

SOW AN EXPECTATION...

I see now that I'd been tripped up by my own expectations. I'd gone into that job full of ideas about a wonderful couple of days recording *our* play, but it wasn't just our play anymore. Today I would be far more likely to flag up at the read-through how strange it must be to work on a play with two actors who know the material so well, and might have warned the director that it may be tricky in two days to shift some of our performance. Who really knows, but I see another lesson being learnt the hard way and the slow way.

As it was, the net result of the argument wasn't bad for the production. Our director descended into a colossal sulk, meaning we were actually able to whip through the rest of the recording without interference. The final broadcast of the play came out extremely well; it was as moving and funny on radio as it was on stage, if not more so.

Richard II by William Shakespeare
Steven Berkoff Productions
Ludlow Festival, Almagro Festival Spain

What I really needed, what *we* really needed as a family, was a decent television or filming job to get on top of things. None were forthcoming and finances were reaching perilously close to the bottom of the well again. Any idea of shaping a career had been parked by the ever-pressing needs of the family. I knew I was going to grab the next paying job that came my way.

I found myself travelling to East London one morning to meet Steven Berkoff to audition for a production of *Richard II* that he was directing for Ludlow festival, with a possible tour afterwards. I was reading for the role of Bolingbroke, a part I felt I was a little young for but which I adored as I prepared for the audition. I'd learnt one long speech and had got very familiar with the rest of the play; desperate for work though I was, my joy at working with Shakespeare's language again was the stronger feeling as I walked into the room to shake hands with Mr Berkoff.

Steven Berkoff had been a gigantic figure in British theatre, creating his own style of in-your-face physical theatre way ahead of the curve. He'd also had his moments as a bona fide movie star, playing bad guys in Bond films, *Rambo*, *Beverly Hills Cop* etc. He hovered over my time at drama school as a mythical figure, a symbol of incredible times gone by. I'd read his jagged autobiography and sat open-mouthed in admiration watching his solo stage show *Shakespeare's Villains*. His reputation was fierce and he'd burnt bridges with institutions, critics and actors for decades. I was excited to meet him.

My instinct was that I wouldn't be his cup of tea, but he was friendly, and interested in who I was and what I had been up to; by the time I got up to read I felt safe and confident in his company. I read the speech I'd worked on the most and enjoyed it. He seemed thrilled and stood up to work on it with me. His excitement about Shakespeare's language was infectious. We laughed together at the joy of it all; it felt like that solus call with Peter Hall. He offered me the part in the room and I travelled home, smiling loudly.

The smile dropped a little when I learnt how small the wage was, but it was better than nothing, and nothing was my alternative, so I accepted.

LOS ANGELES, BY BUS

There were three or four weeks before rehearsals began. My lovely agent Jan understood my reasons for accepting the job and remained optimistic for bigger things down the road. In one conversation she talked about how important it would be as time went on to establish some kind of agent/representation in America, particularly as the *Macbeth* film was going to be aired there on a major network. I told her about the strange telephone call I'd had with some kind of American manager whilst I was performing *As You Like It* in Boston and promised I'd try to find his name and number.

I called Jan back after I found the scrap of paper which I'd kept in a drawer for two years. I told her it was a chap by the name of Robert Stein and she nearly dropped the phone; she said he was a well-known manager, that he represented actors such as Heath Ledger and that I must call him back immediately. I had nothing to lose, so, after working out exactly what dialling code I needed to make a call from Berkhamsted to Hollywood, I did just that.

The same brisk, dark and sardonic voice I remembered from two years before answered my call. Again it took him a moment to place me, then he gave me considerable grief for having waited two years to get in touch, before we began our real conversation. I explained that I'd been a little busy expanding my family and completing a long tour of duty with the Royal Shakespeare Company; I told him about the *Macbeth* film that would be coming out at the end of the year both in the UK and the USA and how my agent thought it was the right time to get American representation. He said he was still interested in representing me but that I had to prove that I was serious: he wanted me to come out to Los Angeles immediately to meet him and let him introduce me to a few casting directors and studios while pilot season was still going. My stomach sank. I told him I was unable to pay for flights and accommodation in LA as I was completely broke; told him about the theatre gig coming up in a few weeks which I was already committed to. He said it would still be worth coming out to begin making inroads, that I could stay with him at his house if I needed to, and left me with the deal he'd originally made: he would represent me if I proved my intent by coming out there in person, and soon.

A family meeting was hurriedly held by Caroline and me, incomes and outgoings examined in forensic detail, jars of change counted, our secret savings of a few bank notes here and there pooled together, along with a kind offer of a little donation from my mum. We agreed we should try; I was surprised and touched by Caroline's support of such a venture in tricky times.

I exhausted our prehistoric computer and its incredibly slow access to the internet to find the world's cheapest return flights to Los Angeles. It transpired there were incredibly low fares if you were prepared to be an on-board courier, transporting a package which remained with you the entire eleven-hour flight and delivering it in person to the right desk, and did the same on the journey back. The flight was the very next day, the seat would be at the back of the plane with no meal service and none of the in-flight entertainment, I could only take one large piece of hand luggage, but, there would be outbound and return flights which would give me ten days or so in LA for an incredibly low fare.

I told Robert the dates I would be tied to by the flights. He said that would work but that he wouldn't be in LA for the first three days so I would need to find accommodation for those nights. After that I could stay with him. He then reminded me that I would need to hire a car to get around there. I hadn't thought of that. Back to the computer I went to find three nights' accommodation and a car I could afford. I managed to find an incredibly cheap deal for car hire at less than $20 per day, described as, 'super budget'.

I decided I would only need it from the day Robert arrived back in LA; until then I could use public transport or stay in walking distance of wherever I was staying. That was the final challenge. My resources were already stretched. The hotel would eat into money I'd earmarked for food and getting by. I eventually found a suspiciously cheap motel in Hollywood itself. No photographs were available online but its location couldn't have been more exciting: just off the Avenue of the Stars.

I went to Stanfords map shop in London to buy a Thomas guide map of LA, then changed my hundred pounds or so spending money into dollars at the Post Office. We'd done it: a ten-day trip to Los Angeles booked and arranged for under five hundred pounds. I would only have around ten dollars a day for food, so I packed snack bars and a few bags of dried food, bought a pair of sunglasses from a charity shop, kissed the family goodbye and the very next day got on an incredibly early train to Heathrow.

I realise this is a chapter supposedly detailing the lessons learnt from a production of *Richard II*. I promise I'll get back to that, but in the meantime I think it worthwhile diverting to Los Angeles to examine what stayed with me from my first visit to that compass point in all actors' lives.

YOU WANNA WHAT?

After eleven hours in a seat with my knees pressed against my chest I arrived creaking into LAX airport. It was early afternoon; the taxi fare to Hollywood would cost two days' food money so I went looking for cheaper public transport. It transpired there basically wasn't any, the theory being perhaps that if you could afford to fly, you could afford to take a cab or hire a car.

I eventually made my way by two buses and one metro train. My fellow travellers on the buses were poorly dressed, tough and lonely looking. As the sun began to set, I gazed through the windows of the bus watching palm trees and poverty living side by side.

Eventually emerging from Hollywood and Highland Metro Station, I came out into the sticky evening air. Here was tinsel town, and she was doing her best to look exactly like she did in the movies. The Hollywood sign was there, lit up in the distance, the potent opium of hope and promise rising up from the sidewalk itself. It was exciting, but my journey from the airport had already shown me that this was a city with two very different faces.

Thomas guide in hand, I wandered along Hollywood Boulevard and its neighbouring streets until I arrived at my motel. I was thrilled by its grimy, neon-lit appearance; it couldn't have looked more like a dodgy motel from the movies I'd grown up watching. There was even a swimming pool, albeit a very uncared for one with litter floating on its unsparkly surface and the whole thing hidden behind a locked chain-link fence.

I checked in, was handed my keys and wandered out to find my room. It was dark, with exhausted carpets of a colour which could once have been pillar-box red but was now dried-blood brown, a rattling air conditioning unit with no off switch, a double bed covered in dubious bedding, and a thinly lit toilet with a dripping shower. I couldn't stop smiling.

Jet lag woke me early the next morning so I was the first and only guest through the door to eat as many free plastic-wrapped items of food as I could at the so-called breakfast laid on in reception. I popped a few sweaty items of food into my bag and refilled my water bottle for the day ahead, then alarmed the man at reception by asking if I could use the pool. 'What for?' he asked. 'To swim in,' I answered. 'To *swim in*?!' he asked again. I nodded. He shook his head and sucked his teeth, but half an hour later the fence was unlocked. I found a net on a long pole and removed a selection of debris from the surface of the pool, then proceeded to paddle about and lie on my thin room towel, reading *Richard II* and sunbathing as if I were Kirk Douglas reclining at the Beverly Hilton.

I spent the day taking myself off on my usual long walks abroad, wandering street after endless street with no destination in mind, knowing that I had the Thomas guide in my backpack to find my way if really lost. The public transport to Hollywood from LAX had cost more than anticipated and I'd had to buy an international calling card for ten dollars to call home, so I took great pride in not spending any money at all that first day; I lived on food from my luggage, stolen snacks from breakfast and any free samples offered in bakeries and stores.

On the second day I discovered a long avenue with half a dozen warehouse theatres. I took my time studying what was on offer and at what times, choosing my evening's entertainment purely on the basis of price. I eventually plumped for a murder mystery playing at a tiny warehouse theatre for a few dollars. I wasn't going for the play (it turned out to be as terrible as the poster suggested). After a day's travel and a second day without speaking to anyone, I was ready for human interaction and I wanted to meet some of my tribe.

I represented at least a tenth of the audience in the theatre that night so when I stayed in the bar after the show it was easy to strike up a conversation with the actors as they emerged. They were friendly, welcoming, as full of advice and warnings as they were hopes and daydreams. I ended up going to a nearby bar for a drink with them and thankfully a kind actor from the cast offered to buy me mine. Then it was back for my last sleepless night at the motel of dreams.

HERE, WEAR THIS

The next day I got myself to Robert Stein's office to meet him for the first time. It was a small office on the top floor of a large commercial unit, but it was real, with a real secretary and he really did want to take me on.

Robert was a wiry and intense man, small framed but burning with energy, sardonic humour, a lot of smiles and a lot of ambition. He took great joy in ridiculing how much I was sweating (I'd walked a long way in scorching heat from the nearest Metro station carrying my heavy bag). Plans had been mapped out for my week: general meetings at major studios with leading casting directors, an actual audition or two, and I was to be his guest at a couple of film premieres.

We travelled in his vintage Mercedes back to his immaculately kept little house in West Hollywood. We got on well. He was generous, saying I must help myself to anything, showed me the room I was to stay in, and told me to go get something smart on as we were going out in a few minutes to the opening of a jewellery store owned by the wife of one of his clients. Everything Robert did, he did at high speed, from his driving to his conversation.

I hurried to my room and changed into what I thought were my smart clothes. When I emerged he laughed loudly and disappeared into his room. He returned with an armful of folded shirts, some of which still had their price tags and labels on them. He held them up against me one at a time before deciding upon a coral pink polo shirt, which I dutifully put on. It was too small for me, and a truly horrible colour, but he seemed happy so away we went.

The 'grand opening' was for a boutique jewellery store

somewhere in West Hollywood. It was a very small affair; Robert's client, whose wife ran the store, turned out to be Mark Ruffalo, an actor I admired hugely and as charming in the flesh as on screen. Speeches were made and then it seemed everyone was taking their turn to choose a piece of jewellery to buy, as a gesture of support for the shop. I didn't want to seem rude so began looking; I found the smallest item I could, a tiny pin badge brooch to bring back for Caroline. When I discovered even this was over a hundred dollars I smiled and backed away.

The next day was a big day. Not only was I taking my first meeting with an American casting director, it was at Warner Brothers Studios, and I was driving there myself. I'd never driven on American roads, let alone in Los Angeles and was nervous about it. Before Robert left for work that morning he said I could use his other car. I looked out of the window and saw a second beautiful vintage car, this one a Porsche. I told him I had a rental car all paid for which I was picking up in a couple of hours. He said it was there if I needed it then left for work.

As soon as he left I poured myself an enormous bowl of cereal, hoping it might keep me sated until the afternoon, and sat down to study my map, eat and think. If I did drive Robert's car perhaps I could get my money back on the car rental, but as I'd never driven out there I was terrified of damaging it. I decided to take it for a test drive around the block; I was probably worrying about nothing.

I sat down in the leather seat, turned the ignition, listened to the beautiful old engine for a moment then began to reverse down his drive. A horrendous scraping and crunching sound came from under the car. I almost shat myself. Had I run over a bicycle? A child? More importantly, was the car scratched? I stopped. Drove slowly back towards the house and there it was again! I pulled the handbrake on and got out to meet my fate. It turned out to be an enormous piece of palm tree which had fallen into the drive. It was fine, it was nothing, but my nerves were jangled. I'd be much happier in my 'super economy', thank you.

I thought I'd chosen a car rental company near Robert's home when I was on my computer back in England. It was on a road with the same name as one he lived near to in West Hollywood, but I hadn't taken into account how endless some roads and boulevards are in that city. By the time I arrived at the little rental company my smart audition clothes were dripping with sweat and I was behind schedule.

I dashed into the office waving my printed receipt for the car I'd rented online. The lady behind the desk took what felt like forever typing numbers into her computer, before eventually telling me that all the super economy cars were out. She asked if I could I come back later in the day. I told her I couldn't. My stomach went cold. I was already anxious about the journey ahead; to miss my first meeting entirely was just too awful a prospect.

I explained my situation, how important the meeting was and how little money I had. Something in my pitiful manner made her go back to her computer. She then handed me a set of keys and said, 'Here you go, I've bumped you up a bit.' I thanked her, signed the forms and dashed out to the parking lot. I pointed the electronic key fob at all the likely cars I could see and pressed the button. None of them unlocked. I kept trying, standing in front of them one at a time and pressing the button.

Just when I was trying one more time before going back to tell her the key was faulty, I heard behind me the clunk of a car unlocking its doors. I turned and saw lights flashing on a black convertible sports car. I pressed the button again and it locked itself.

I returned to the office exasperated, put the keys back on the counter and said, 'You've given me the wrong keys. These opened some ridiculous sports car, I won't be able to pay for that.' Smiling now she said, 'Uh huh, that's right. Try not to scratch her.'

I told her again that I couldn't possibly afford it and she said there would be no extra charge. I stammered my thanks, tried not to cry, and reached over the counter to shake her hand. I may have even kissed it.

And so it came to pass that, with less than seventy bucks to my name, I came to be driving a brand new, black, anniversary edition, convertible Ford Thunderbird around LA. It was an absolutely beautiful car. I climbed inside and set off with my map open on the seat beside me. Driving in that city turned out to be so simple; everything made sense. I was at the studio on time and did my best to play it cool but, as they waved me through the gates, I was smiling like a child in a bumper car.

The meeting went well; all my meetings that week did, and felt so different to the meetings I was used to taking in England. At that time there was a very serious and secretive atmosphere surrounding most television and film auditions in London; it was as if the job you were meeting for were a rare golden crown which the casting departments stood in front of, guarding it from your view until you had passed a set of secret tests. Then, and only then, might you be allowed to touch the holy treasure. In LA, at every meeting it felt as if the crown were brought straight out to you and placed on your head to see if it looked right, because, it just might, and if it didn't, hey, never mind, come back and see us again soon. It felt so much more honest, open and ultimately efficient to me.

I took the deep interest with which everyone spoke to me with a pinch of salt, already too long in the tooth to believe in any Cinderella stories coming my way, but it was refreshing to be constantly validated; that old feeling I'd felt in England at middle-class dinner parties and school playgrounds that acting wasn't a 'real' job dissolved.

FREE FALLING

My father had been a genuine petrol head, a great mechanic with a profound love for driving, and this must have been why I received a visitation from him as I was driving back across a canyon after a meeting one day. It suddenly felt as if *he* were driving the car through me. We both decided to pull over, put the roof down, hide the map for half an hour and follow the roads which looked the most hilly, winding and fun to drive. I doubt anyone who saw me driving past, laughing out loud and screaming, 'Woooooo hoooooo!' would have guessed it was grief fuelling the joy.

I parked the car at the top of a hill on a small residential road. Through the dry, sun-bleached trees I could see the enormous city laid out below me. It felt like the first time in years that I'd truly stopped, to breathe and take stock. I had every reason to be happy, but like the tectonic plates that hide beneath Los Angeles' sunny surface, the stresses and strains from the last few years of my life finally broke, and as suddenly as any earthquake, I was weeping.

LORD OF DOGTOWN

Robert seemed to be on a mission to impress me and I was more than happy to be impressed. The meetings and auditions would have been enough, but he also took me as his guest to a couple of genuine Hollywood movie premieres (usually wearing clothes he'd chosen for me, which I was less happy about).

The first was the world premiere of *Cinderella Man* starring Russell Crowe and Renée Zellweger at the enormous Universal City cinema. The after-party, in a garden nearby, was like a scene from *The Great Gatsby.* I stood, glass in hand, watching the stars of the film and their entourages wandering past, close enough to smell their glory. I felt neither awed nor awkward. I was left alone while Robert schmoozed and I got busy eating all the free food I could find and drinking a great deal of champagne. I made a policy of introducing myself to anyone else who seemed to be on their own, which worked well on the whole. It was through this that I ended up having a long drunken chat with Thora Birch about Harold Pinter, whose play *Betrayal* she was about to rehearse. Some people were incredibly transparent, cutting me dead as soon as they discovered I was nobody important, but on the whole I had a great time.

It had pained me not to bring my skateboard to Los Angeles. A committed skateboarder since my early years, I'd spent countless hours staring at photographs in magazines, posters on my bedroom walls and videos of skaters living dream lives under the California sun, but I knew this was a trip to further my career so had gamely left my board at home. When Robert told me we were attending the premiere for the *Dogtown and Z-Boys* skateboarding documentary, he had no idea what kind of bulls-eye he'd hit.

I thought I'd died and gone to heaven. As we queued along the red carpet to enter Mann's Chinese Theater, we had to pass a large skateboard ramp set up for the occasion with incredible skaters flying around on it to the accompaniment of a live punk band. The film itself was the greatest thing this skateboarder had ever seen, documenting the birth of skateboarding and following the incredible story of its founding fathers Tony Alva, Stacy Peralta and Jay Adams, mythical figures to me, but now, there they *were*, on the stage, introducing the film.

The after party was in a nightclub somewhere nearby, the entire place extravagantly skate themed. Delicious food was presented on top of brightly coloured skateboard decks. At first I thought they were artificial but on closer inspection, I discovered they were all perfectly decent decks, painted fluorescent colours and being used as serving platters. I hadn't been able to afford a new deck for a couple of years and was struck by this extravagance more than anything else.

Robert introduced me to a few people, and helped me get to shake hands with Tony Alva and Stacy Peralta, but it was a little embarrassing at times, especially when he took me over to meet Owen Wilson, who he knew, then dashed off leaving me trying to make small talk with the most reluctant conversation partner I've ever had. I soon reverted to my policy of speaking only to those who, like me, appeared to be on their own; this was far more successful, never more so than when I spotted an older man standing alone and realised it was Jon Voight. He was friendly and interested and managed to seem pleased when

I explained that I'd partly become an actor after watching and adoring his performance in *Midnight Cowboy*.

To meet my acting and my skateboarding lodestars all in one night was something I could never have imagined being possible. I got fairly drunk by way of celebration, danced frantically to the loud music playing, and when Robert told me it was time to go I marched to the buffet table, scraped a selection of snacks from a bright pink skateboard deck, picked it up and confidently marched out of the door.

A day or two later I was headed home. It had been an incredible week, but also instructive. I'd had a taste of how things worked. I was under no illusions; I knew it was a circus, but there was work to be had, and next time I'd be bringing my skateboard.

I had no idea then that in later years I would end up living in that city for long periods of time, that I would find a lot of happiness there, but also crashing disappointments. It would always remain the city with two faces that I'd seen through the windows of that bus.

DON'T GET YOUR KNICKERS IN A TWIST
OK, back to *Richard II*. Remember him?

We rehearsed in an enormous sound stage at the very rough and ready Three Mills Film studios in East London. Steven Berkoff was incredibly well organised and a dynamo of energy. We worked from midday until 4 p.m., but it was four *solid* hours of work, with no breaks other than a tiny toilet break halfway through. He believed much more was achieved this way than the traditional rehearsal day of 10 a.m. until 6 p.m. with breaks every hour and a half and a whole hour for lunch, and I can't disagree. So much time is wasted rounding people up after breaks, making small talk before finding the rhythm of the work again; it was incredible how much we achieved each day and how quickly the time seemed to pass. Those extra hours gave everyone a chance to participate in their home lives too; school runs could be taken before work and dinner could be eaten with families after. I wish more companies rehearsed this way.

The actual work was a bizarre combination of frustrating and inspiring. Steven was at his best, it has to be said, when he would rise to his feet and give you an unequivocal indication of how he wanted things done by doing it himself. It was a hugely physical production: we moved in large groups in perfect unison like a Greek chorus, we rode imaginary horses, and long speeches were delivered whilst walking on the spot in slow motion as if wading through treacle. The design was minimal, as all his productions were, our Edwardian costumes adding the colour and our walking canes becoming windows, swords, or guns, as the scenes required.

From the very first day we had a keyboard player in the rehearsal room, improvising cosmic synthesised underscore for the scenes as we went along. It was annoying to begin with, but I quickly realised there was no room for baby steps with Mr Berkoff; decisions had to be made and preferably bold ones.

We were experiencing extreme sleep deprivation at home as Gabriel was having a great deal of pain through the night with chronic eczema. The dressings on his arms and legs had to be changed every few hours and his crying was endless. I tried to take the lion's share of the late-night comforting. He seemed to find my voice soothing, so he was forced to listen to all of Bolingbroke's speeches a hundred times over. I was off book by the end of the first week which pleased Mr Berkoff no end.

From the audition onwards Steven and I enjoyed working with each other, but to begin with he simply couldn't learn my name. He'd got it into his head that my name was Phil, and that was what he was going to call me, no matter how many times he was reminded of my real name. At a note session after our dress rehearsal when I was complaining about something or other, he loudly set me straight with, 'All right, Phil, don't get your knickers in a twist.'

REPTILES

We opened the show in the grounds of Ludlow Castle during a heatwave. Lunch breaks were spent jumping into the River Teme to cool off. I hadn't performed open-air theatre for a long time, not since *The Beaux Stratagem* in Wimbledon, and I felt liberated by it. The language of *Richard II* is so extraordinary, and yet again I found that if I underpinned my work by obeying the rules for verse-speaking I'd built for myself with Peter Hall, then everything sailed.

There was an unspoken urge to perform at least in part as if doing an impression of Steven. It was irresistible, seemed to please him, and it did the verse-speaking no harm whatsoever.

The production was occasionally ridiculous (trying to maintain dignity whilst riding imaginary horses was a challenge), but when it worked it really worked. We had a ball, the company were excellent; Timothy Walker was magnificent as Richard and we had a great relationship filled with mutual respect on stage. I had old allies in the company: Julius D'Silva from the Spanish Golden Age Season, Matt Cullum from my drama school, and a new friend and fellow skateboarding actor, Fergus O'Donnell.

What I really gained was another cracking role under my belt and more exposure to Shakespeare's verse with another excellent guide and supporter. However, although picturesque, Ludlow's summer Shakespeare programme had not found an ideal partner in Mr Berkoff. Waiting to go on stage for a gala performance in front of local dignitaries and five hundred school children, we were surprised to hear Steven's voice booming out over the tannoy. He was on the stage with a microphone to introduce the production but instead proceeded to perform an off-the-cuff brutal dissection of the British Theatre industry, with particular venom reserved for critics, or 'reptiles' as Steven called them. The atmosphere quickly sank from festive to frightened. 'Anyway, here it is', he finished, 'Richard, the bloody second'.

The run in Ludlow was over in a few weeks, during which time the weather moved from heatwave to monsoon. We battled on riding those bloody imaginary horses and shouting through the rain as we wandered around in slow motion, then before we knew it, we were on the road, taking the play to Spain to perform as part of the Almagro International Classical Theatre Festival.

After Madrid this felt like a very different type of Spain. Almagro sits in the very centre of the country, real La Mancha territory, rural, sleepy and remote. Almost as soon as we arrived in the town square I bought a tiny framed painting of the theatre we were performing in, the Corral de Comedias; it showed a view from the stage over a ridiculously pretty, open air, courtyard auditorium, with a glimpse of the stars and a perfect crescent moon. Only a few hours later we were on that stage working our way through a dress rehearsal. The sun was already setting when we began and by the time we got to the second half, I looked out and saw an exact replica of the little painting, bright stars and a perfect crescent moon.

Fergus and I took our skateboards with us and scoured the dusty streets late at night looking for skateable spots. Fergus was the real treasure I took from this job, a friend and ally ever since, and in years to come he would be the perfect Horatio when I had a crack at playing Hamlet.

It transpired Steven Berkoff did know my name. We had a drink together in the town square on the last day and made promises to work together again. In fact Steven has become something of an acerbic uncle figure for me over the decades. We've met for dinners or coffee often. He's come to see me in many of my performances, even when he's been unable to hide his loathing for the production.

The Romantics
BBC TV

During the run of the play in Ludlow, I'd managed to audition for a few jobs, including one very early milk train down to London in order to take a morning audition then make it back to Ludlow in time for a matinée performance. That particular journey, on 7th July, took me incredibly close to disaster when a suicide bomb exploded only a few hundred yards from me whilst standing at the end of the platform at Paddington Underground Station. I heard and felt the heat from the explosion of a bomb further down the tunnel. The bomber had chosen the very train I was waiting to board. It gave me a sense of delayed shock for some weeks afterwards.

One job which did come in was an offer to play the part of Lord Byron in a docudrama about the Romantic Movement being made by BBC2 in conjunction with the Open University. The series was written and presented by the wonderful Peter Ackroyd, whose books I adored. He would visit the actual locations from the lives of the Romantic Movement's key players, with actors playing the poets, appearing like ghosts in the same location and speaking in their words either from poems or letters.

WHAT DO YOU MEAN HE'S SCOTTISH?

I'd never played a biographical figure on screen before and wanted to do him justice. I visited the British Library to find any accounts of his speaking voice and his appearance. Though born in London he'd grown up with his mother in Aberdeen and had apparently retained more than a hint of that accent his entire life. He also famously suffered from a deformed (club) right foot, which gave him pain throughout his life but did nothing to hold him back from his heroic adventures. Often referred to as the world's first celebrity, he was famously, 'mad, bad and dangerous to know'.

Our first day's shooting was at Newstead Abbey, Byron's ancestral home in Nottinghamshire. We were given complete access to even the private areas of the beautiful house and grounds. The tiny crew, the director, Peter and I rehearsed the first sequence. Peter spoke directly to camera, then exited frame, and the camera panned round to find flirty old Byron staring out of a window reciting some apposite lines of his poetry.

It all went well in rehearsal I thought, although Peter was having trouble remembering the narration. The director came over to me with a worried look on his face and asked me why I was doing a 'funny accent'. I was a little put out; I wasn't too bad at accents. Surely he'd done his homework and knew Byron had grown up in Scotland. It turned out he hadn't, and he didn't. Peter Ackroyd backed me up, but the director was still nervous and asked me to tone it down by fifty per cent. I had to immediately adapt the work I'd done and take half the strength out of the accent. After a couple of takes I was just starting to get a feel for Byron's new voice when it was announced that the scene was complete and we were moving on. So, that was that.

WHAT DO YOU MEAN HE LIMPS?

The next scene was quickly set up in a new location. Again Peter spoke directly to camera, moved out of shot, then I was discovered walking down a beautiful corridor towards the camera, reciting poetry as I went. As time seemed to be against us the director said we would shoot the rehearsal. I was ready, and afterwards felt that by a miracle it had gone perfectly first take. Then I saw the director coming towards me with that same troubled expression on his face. 'Um, is your leg all right, Joseph? You seem to be limping?' Surprised it wasn't obvious, I explained Byron's famous physical disability. Peter backed me up again, and again the director looked totally thrown and unsure. 'Can you just take the limp down a bit?' he pleaded. 'Fifty per cent?' I asked. We went for the scene again with me rapidly adapting my physicality. He seemed happy and within minutes the scene was done.

NEVER BE SHIT

I realised quickly that this wasn't going to be a job where I could take my time finding my performance. I was going to have to be ready to hit the floor running (or limping, ever so slightly). Instead of frustrating me I found this challenge oddly delicious. I was developing a new creed, a new screen acting philosophy which has stayed with me ever since and can be crystallised into the following easy-to-remember motto ... *'Never Be Shit.'*

I was beginning to appreciate the permanence of whatever the camera caught. Whether you get one take or fifty takes to complete a shot, you can never know which moment, from which take, an editor might pick. You also never know how big a screen it may one day be played on, or who may be watching it. I challenged myself to try to only give performances which, if I were to watch them in the future, I would know I'd done my best in, whatever the circumstances. I wanted to do all I could to ensure that I could leapfrog over embarrassment into some kind of pride.

EVER

I was now attacking all and any filming work as if it were a Scorsese movie; nobody needed to know about this private game, it was just for me. Time on set goes quicker and everything is more enjoyable if you can find a way to get into it, really get into it, and play like a child in the time that passes between the words 'action' and 'cut'. The *'Never Be Shit'* mantra also acts as a small level of insurance, even if the thing you are working on is terrible. Be it a film, or just a scene, there is no reason to be terrible in it yourself, ever.

313

The Romantics didn't pay very much, but it was yet another job with travel perks: we were soon on our way to Venice. Byron had lived in Venice for two years with fourteen servants, two monkeys, a fox and two mastiff dogs; we were there for three days with one sound op, one camera man, one combined make-up and wardrobe mistress, a director, a presenter, and me.

It was a low budget production but nothing about a visit to Venice feels low budget. Our ride into Venice on a speeding motor boat taxi made my smile muscles ache and it is the only place I've ever visited which exceeds all expectations at every turn. I was knocked out by its beauty. We started filming almost as soon as we arrived and finished at around midnight. Everyone was exhausted and headed off to their beds, but Peter Ackroyd knew the city well and had other plans. I found myself accompanying him for late-night drinks with his friend, the historian and TV presenter Francesco da Mosto, in St Mark's Square. They were fascinating company, but by the time Francesco waved us goodbye it was 3 a.m. and Peter was in immediate danger of falling asleep. Our hotel was just a couple of bridges away by foot, a fifteen-minute walk at most when sober. I tried to gee Peter into life but he wasn't having any of it and proceeded to make himself comfortable: he sat back in his chair and began to snore.

I was suddenly overcome with a sense of responsibility; I couldn't leave an award-winning author asleep in St Mark's Square. What if there was a flood? I had to get him back to the hotel; he had to be able to talk in front of camera by the approaching afternoon. I tried to wake him, with only partial success. Once or twice I roused him to his feet but he was soon settling down to sleep again. Eventually there was nothing for it but to manhandle him out of his chair and back to the hotel. To say Peter Ackroyd was a heavy man would be a polite way of describing things. I eventually managed to get him up onto his feet with his arm around my shoulders, and dragged him in that fashion all the way back to the hotel.

The next day Peter was more alert and on form than any of us. I couldn't believe it. He had absolutely no recollection of how the evening had ended. It was soon time to head back towards the airport by water taxi, watching Venice recede into the distance, wondering at its beauty and wondering what lay ahead.

The Ghost Squad
Channel 4 TV

Something about my *'Never Be Shit'* – *'Make every take count'* approach to screen work was bleeding into my auditions. I found myself much more able to listen and 'play' even under the pressure of trying to secure employment. As there was almost always a camera there recording proceedings at TV meetings, I was able to trick my mind into thinking it was a take: that this was *it*, it was time to poop or get off the potty.

Which was good news when I received the material for a fantastic audition to play the kind of role I was never getting to read for: a confident, charming but absolutely evil copper in an edgy new Channel 4 drama about police corruption. For once I loved the audition. I didn't push, got right inside the scene and concentrated utterly on the casting director reading with me. The director, Richard

Laxton, was brilliant and gave me fun things to try; the signs were good.

When the offer came in I was ecstatic; I was finally starting to move into the kind of screen work I'd always wanted: character work in well-written drama. My career was starting to get some colour in its cheeks. Home life wasn't perfect; we still had money worries, sleep was rare, but we were afloat, and the children were blooming. Caroline was finding it hard to get acting work and there were tensions to negotiate there, but she was beginning to perform as a jazz singer more and more which I fully supported, even saving what money I could towards producing her first album.

When the full script arrived for *The Ghost Squad* I began work in earnest. I had a couple of weeks before shooting began. My main concern was the fact that, as a naughty coke-dealing copper, I had to prepare and snort many lines of cocaine both for myself and others. During my years in the entertainment industry this was something I'd witnessed a few times but had never actually done. I wanted to look like I knew what I was doing. When the director called for a chat I explained the situation but he didn't seem concerned.

Lo and behold my very first scene to shoot included me having to set up and snort lines of coke whilst holding a complex conversation. At camera rehearsal where I was handed the prop drugs (glucose) and paraphernalia that went with it, we marked through the moves and dialogue for the cameras. I bit the bullet and said to the props team that before we did a take I would need someone to help me look like I knew what I was doing. They laughed. I told them I was serious; they laughed again and moved off as everyone got ready to shoot. We were about to turn over before I finally persuaded the director that I needed a little help. Nobody could believe a professional actor didn't know his way around a line of cocaine. Eventually a member of the camera team gave me a fantastic and surprisingly thorough five-minute masterclass. After that I was chopping and snorting that powdered glucose like a demon.

It was such an enjoyable role and perhaps a template for several nasty bastards I've played since. What seemed to make it sing was absolutely not labelling him as a bad guy in my own mind; I managed to find a way to really feel like he was a wonderful human being, with no weak spots or faults, even when he was performing evil deeds. I didn't judge him, that was the audience's job, which meant there was no metaphorical moustache twirling. The story was better served that way and I was able to concentrate fully on the actors opposite me, seeing what he could get from them to further his goals.

Before these recent adventures in classy television with *Macbeth* and now *The Ghost Squad*, I'd always believed I preferred theatre work to filming, but I was beginning to understand that when filming was good, it was very, very good. I was working with great actors, a really creative and open director, a fantastic script with adult themes, as good as any new play I'd read, and a crew who responded to what the actors created rather than us having to work around already prescribed camera moves. I felt able to improvise, to contribute more than I had before; even though I had thousands of hours in front of cameras under my belt from my time on *Peak Practice*, this felt like a new playground where I could combine all that camera experience with the

'*Never Be Shit*' policy and a Mike Alfreds level of fresh-ness. It was *fun*.

This year was when I first felt any real grip on the slippery ice rink of our business. I knew nothing was guaranteed, but the nagging shadow of imposter syndrome cast over me by my hard-working ancestors was fading, as was my evil ego's trickling suggestion that fluke was responsible for my earning a living as an actor. I was starting to believe that I knew what I was doing; not in an arrogant way, more as a carpenter who'd been making tables for ten years might be entitled to say that he now knew how to make a table.

The Pillars of the Community by Henrik Ibsen
Translated by Samuel Adamson
Royal National Theatre

The *Macbeth* film was advertised heavily and got great reviews when it aired. I was flabbergasted that things were going so well, especially after the way the year had started. My gast was flabbered even further when the confidence I was feeling about building those tables helped me to secure my debut at the National Theatre, a theatre I'd been haunting since I first arrived in London, drawn like a magnet to that concrete cauldron of creativity and class.

From the moment I moved to the capital, I would find any excuse to waste my spare time in the bookshop, cafe and foyer there on the South Bank. I saw every produc-tion I could, queueing from 8 a.m. to buy day seats for the sold-out productions, or sometimes turning up at the interval if I'd heard a play wasn't doing so well and sneaking back into the auditorium with the audience to enjoy the second half for free; a scheme which worked well with plays I'd read but led to some confusion when I tried to follow the second half of new plays.

I saw truly great actors at work on all three of its stages: Paul Schofield, Ian McKellen, Lindsay Duncan, Richard Griffiths, Ian Holm, Alan Rickman and Judi Dench, to name but a few, and saw the work of incredible directors such as Robert Lepage, Michael Blakemore, Roger Michell, Nic Hytner, Peter Brook, Stephen Daldry and Richard Eyre, among many more. To drag my professional football analogy out again, it felt like the World Cup in there.

Pillars of the Community hadn't had a major London production for decades. The new translation we were to perform by Samuel Adamson made it feel like a topical thriller. The plot centred around Karsten Bernick, a thriving shipbuilder in a small Norwegian town. Bernick built his whole life and career on a network of lies. Fifteen years before the play's action he allowed his wife's brother Johan (the part I was to play) to take the rap for a sexual and financial scandal; when Johan and his sister Lona return from their exile in America, he is threatened with exposure and the noose slowly tightens.

TOE TO TOE
I adored the play and my part in it. Johan is talked about often in the first couple of acts, in hushed and scandalous tones, but arrives on stage only just before the interval. It was wonderful listening to the picture that was being created in the audience's mind of a cad and a bounder, only to shatter it on arrival when everybody meets the quiet, calm, kind and loving man Johan is.

Everything about the National Theatre screamed craft over glamour, function before fashion, its brutal concrete exterior acting as a reminder that the building is utilitarian; the treasure is to be found on the stage, and nowhere else. No frills, just quality.

The RSC sometimes felt like an academy, or a conservatoire, with its drumming workshops, endless compulsory voice calls and movement classes. The National felt like a factory: those resources were there if you needed them, but only if you needed them. You'd been chosen because you were good at your job and were left alone, trusted, to get on with it. As I walked through the labyrinth of backstage corridors to enter our rehearsal room for the first time I was grinning like a Cheshire cat.

It all chimed so perfectly with where I was at in my own development. The large cast around me were incredible, led by Damian Lewis as Karsten and Lesley Manville as Lona. At tea breaks or walking past these people in corridors I found it hard not to feel star struck and awed by their brilliance in performances I'd seen, particularly Damian's work in *Band Of Brothers* and Lesley's in Mike Leigh's film *All Or Nothing*, but on the floor of the rehearsal room and later on stage, I felt utterly equal and ready to go toe to toe with them.

I was freshly interested in acting really, almost weirdly *into* it, like someone who'd just found a new hobby they adored. I was reading Mamet and Steiner for fun! Again, I can see an almost manic intensity to how I was behaving; it was all-consuming. I was cherishing my time with the children but a distance was beginning to grow between Caroline and me, and I was using the addictive thrum of hard work to fill that void.

I'd always understood the concept of playing actions, and thought I had a good vocabulary of transitive verbs knocking around in my head for discussion in rehearsal, but this was the job on which I really harnessed the fun that could be had with precision. It was a route I took from necessity; in early rehearsals Ibsen's language and even whole scenes fell through the floor if approached with a general over-arching scene objective. The surface dialogue was often so very far from what was really going on. I began to experiment with actioning every single line. I'd recently purchased the wonderful pocket-sized *Actors' Thesaurus* book by Marina Calderone and Maggie Lloyd-Williams, an infuriatingly helpful book that I wish I'd had the vision to put together myself; a thesaurus of active verbs grouped into categories, so that if, for example, you find yourself always jotting the word 'punish' on scripts when playing a harming action, you can turn to the word 'punish' and see a dozen related but very different transitive verbs to play: with the same line of dialogue I might find myself trying to 'whip' one day, 'discipline' the next and maybe 'skewer' the day after that. It became a delightful, private game in rehearsal.

TEACHER'S PET

The opening of the second half of the play begins with Johan on stage for twenty minutes or so enjoying a succession of two-handed scenes, as one at a time the key characters come to have a private moment with him, culminating in the all-important showdown with Damian as Karsten. Johan was such a gentle, still presence in this long set of scenes. He didn't say much, but listened intently to each character before asking a few questions of his own. He was hard for the characters to read, and also the audience, but he had a strong agenda and objective beneath it all:

he was back to reclaim his name. Bernick had to redress the past.

Bernick and Johan are alone together for the first time; Bernick is all warmth and gratitude towards Johan, but he's nervous. Why is he back? What does he want? This scene in particular gave me a delicious pleasure to rehearse; Bernick had become a renowned 'pillar of the community', but it was Johan who held all the cards. I was confident and calm. I'd done my work, choosing and repeating actions for each line, even actioning the quality of my listening during *his* lines. I felt like a clean instrument, listening openly then playing actions strongly and experimenting with different ones every few days. I was seeking that golden state that hovers between precision and freedom.

It wasn't a competition. I didn't care what anyone else thought but for my own satisfaction I was demanding my absolute best work, at all times. Our director Marianne Elliott seemed thrilled with progress. We got on fantastically. She was open-eyed and generous but incredibly demanding, which suited me down to the ground. It was a large cast and even the smallest parts were played by wonderful, experienced actors. *This* was the premier league that I'd always wanted to play in.

HATGATE

Early chats about costume with our designer Rae Smith were some of the most inclusive I'd known. Between us we imagined Johan's hard-working life as a rancher in America and what he might be wearing for his return to Norway. Everything we agreed on helped my love affair with the man deepen. Rae's original design included a wide-brimmed rancher's hat, and it just so happened that one of the only items of my father's which I'd been able to keep after he died was a wide-brimmed, suede hat. I asked if I could bring it in and she agreed.

I hadn't spent a lot of time with the hat. I'd popped it in a suitcase in the loft and left it there as buried treasure for later life. When I took it out to try it on I discovered that the tattered silk lining of the hat was saturated with a clear river of his scent: golden Virginia tobacco and another silvery smell that was just, *him*. I pressed my nose against it and inhaled deeply.

I brought the hat in for Rae and Marianne to see and they thought it was perfect. I was so happy that my dad was going to be with me as I stepped out on stage at the National Theatre for the first time, his DNA crowning me with support. As we came to the end of rehearsals the costume department took the hat from me to build into their wardrobe plot. I made sure they understood how important it was and that even though the lining was tattered to please not mess with it. I was assured it would be cared for.

When I arrived in my dressing room the next week to begin our technical rehearsals, my costumes were hanging up and the hat was there laid out on my table to welcome me. I picked it up to take a reassuring sniff of Dad and discovered that the lining had been removed and replaced, and the hat itself had been steam cleaned. There wasn't a molecule left of him. He was gone.

KNOB

The hat disaster broke my heart a little, but I didn't have time to dwell on it. The move into the Lyttelton Theatre was too exciting. I loved the space, a solid funnel of straight lines. The technical rehearsal was an eye opener; everything seemed to be better made, more detailed than any theatre I'd worked in before. Everything that is, except for the door handles.

The first preview arrived; I paced the backstage area for an hour before my first entrance, listening to my character's name being mentioned again and again, and taking real joy in imagining Johan's internal life. It was my own private backstage playground.

After a little too much pacing back and forth in the wings, the moment came. I took Lesley Manville's arm, and on we went. The actioning work I'd done paid off; I felt calm out there with a very specific job to do at every moment. The scenes progressed well, really well, until towards the end of the play when my 'big' scene arrived. Johan is betrayed for a second time by Bernick and feels all the years of rage rise up in him. Through tears I screamed my last line at him, exploding like a volcano before stomping off to open the door to make my exit. I yanked at the door, and … the handle came off in my hand.

None of the other doors made any sense to walk through as they led into the house and I was most definitely leaving. I hadn't prepared any transitive verbs for such a moment so I raged and sweated and huffed and puffed, hoping someone backstage might have the foresight to push the door open from the other side for me. Nobody did. I eventually managed, with some difficulty, to replace the door knob and escape, refusing the offered help of Damian and avoiding his eyes desperately as I knew how close my tears were to laughter.

No other such hiccups attended the previews; the

company were lovely, Marianne kept a tight ship and we sailed into an electric press night. The show was a genuine, five-star hit, going on to win awards. For me it felt like a profound victory. A hill I'd been tilting my head at for so long had been climbed. But now what?

As I hovered on the edges of the incredibly starry press-night party, drinking a cocktail, receiving respect and admiration from members of a profession not so long ago I hadn't dared believe I could belong to, I chewed on my straw and wondered: would I ever *really* belong? The tree-climbing, country boy that I was sat with me the entire night; he laughed at me whenever I tried to sound serious or grown-up, and he insisted we steal a load of food for the train ride home.

New Tricks
BBC TV

High among the long list of things that make working at the National Theatre a total win is the fact that each of the three theatres usually has two or three plays running in repertory, but it's very rare to be cross-cast in another production. So it's never a battering schedule for the actors and there are often significant breaks where you can either enjoy having a life again, or spending time with your family (as I did as soon as I could), or, if you are lucky enough, you can squeeze a bit of radio or filming work.

Über agent Jan had been hurling me at meetings whenever possible. I think she could smell that the iron was as hot as it was ever likely to be; my stock was rising and she had plenty to mention to casting directors when trying to persuade them to see me. She was also bringing lots of people to see the play.

Among the more ridiculous of these was a top-secret meeting with Debbie McWilliams, the casting director of the Bond films. It was common knowledge that a new Bond movie, *Casino Royale*, was being made the following year, and that it would be the first outing for a brand new actor as James Bond, but nobody knew who was going to get the most sought-after job in cinema. Jan had brought Debbie McWilliams to see the play and she'd apparently liked me. A call came in for me to go in for a meeting with Debbie and some of the producers. Jan got a little over-excited and was convinced I was going to be the next James Bond. I was less convinced, but after the meeting I almost began to wonder. It was a very posh chat, with movie-star-level tea and cakes, but nobody would actually talk about the script or what part they were considering me for.

A week or two went by, and I was called back in to audition for the role of 00.........9. I was thrilled to meet for any role in any film, let alone a scene in a Bond film. The two pages I was sent didn't tell me much. I screen-tested my couple of lines of dialogue and heard nothing more about it for a very long time.

One slightly more down-to-earth meeting did eventually come good when I was offered a guest role on the ITV drama *New Tricks*. A few days playing a sleazy wine dealer who gets romantically involved with the brilliant Amanda Redman as Detective Pullman. It was a cracking cast for this particular episode with Frances de la Tour, Richard Briers and a personal hero of mine, Michael Maloney, playing the other guest roles.

I COULD BE SO GOOD FOR YOU

Many of my scenes were with Dennis Waterman. I'd grown up watching him in *Minder* with my dad; it was a big favourite in our house, so I was chuffed to bits to be working with him and even more that we were getting along so well. When lunch was called on my final day and Dennis asked me if I fancied skipping the on-set catering to join him in a nearby pub, I told him to lead the way. He seemed pleased to have someone new to share an illicit mid-shoot pint with. He managed to drink two and sink a whisky chaser before I'd got halfway through mine.

We returned to set and cracked on with the afternoon's work. I was full of the joys of spring, joking with the wonderful director and crew, but Dennis seemed to be cooling a little. As the cameras were turning round and lights were being reset he suddenly barked, 'All right son, a joke's a joke, but fuck a pantomime, you can stop it now.'

I had no idea what he was talking about. 'Stop what?' I asked.

'Come on, you've been doing it since you first arrived. I thought it was funny two days ago, but it's just boring now, so cut it out, all right?'

I still had absolutely no idea what I'd done. Red-faced and confused I sidled up to the camera crew and asked them if they knew what he was so upset about. 'It's the singing,' one of them said.

'The what?' I asked.

'The singing. You've been whistling, humming or singing the theme tune to *Minder* for three days!'

It transpired that every time I'd been on set with Dennis I'd been loudly chirping my way through the theme song to *Minder,* which he himself had originally sung over the opening titles. I was only vaguely aware I had been making happy noises. Dennis being in close proximity must have launched my subconscious into involuntary karaoke. I was mortified, but luckily he saw the funny side and even sang it for me when I wrapped my last shot.

Darkness
Recording for BBC Radio 3 / Open University

The run of *Pillars* continued; I loved it in that building so much, I was wondering which drawer in which office might contain a ten-year contract. I had a fair while left; the run would continue on and off into early February, which meant we had the luxury of paying our own heating bills at Christmas.

Having just scored such a hit with her first production at the National, Marianne Elliott was about to direct her first production for the RSC; she would be helming *Much Ado About Nothing* in my beloved Swan Theatre, in rep with *King John* and *Romeo and Juliet*. She flattered me hugely by saying she was interested in me for the role of Benedick, but said I'd have to audition, not only for her but the other directors, as it would be a cross-cast repertory company. I ended up reading for Benedick in *Much Ado* and Faulconbridge (the Bastard) in *King John* to be directed by Josie Rourke.

I was oddly nervous auditioning again so soon for Marianne. I hadn't had much time to prepare, so concentrated on the play I knew least, *King John*. I thought I knew *Much Ado* well enough and already had the Benedick speech in my pocket, although I hadn't rolled it out since that audition for Mark Rylance years before.

Unsurprisingly, the audition for Marianne went terribly. It was awkward for both of us: we were in a tiny room, and after our fantastic rehearsals for *Pillars* it felt strange to be trotting out an old speech I'd been performing since drama school. It wasn't specific, new, or alive. I thought I'd blown it, but, half an hour later I went in to read scenes from *King John* with Josie. I'd fallen madly in love with the play and the part over the preceding days so was full of energy and ideas; everything in *this* meeting felt new and alive.

Eventually, Josie's desire to have me in *King John* and Marianne's faith in my work after *Pillars* combined to bag me the job of a lifetime: Benedick and the Bastard in the same season at the RSC, in the *Swan*. Rehearsals would start mid-January, so there would be an overlap with performances of *Pillars*. I would be simultaneously working for the RSC and the National Theatre. This was hard for my tiny mind to compute, but my ridiculous run of good fortune wasn't over yet: the Bond film got back in touch, saying I just might get my few days on *Casino Royale,* although they wouldn't be able to confirm until the New Year.

It was as if a gigantic boulder, which I'd been pushing up a hill for the last ten years, started moving forward on its own. I was grateful, but watchful, and far from trusting. I didn't stop pushing for a second; I knew it could begin to roll backwards at any moment.

SPOOKY

It was with this in mind that I leapt at a small gig recording a few poems by my old friend Byron for the Open University. I was to record 'She Walks in Beauty', which I was familiar with, and 'Darkness', which I'd never read before.

Byron wrote 'Darkness' in 1816, which was known as 'the year without summer' after Mount Tambora erupted in the Dutch East Indies, casting enough sulphur into the atmosphere to reduce global temperatures and darken the skies for many, many months. This pall of darkness inspired Byron to write his extraordinary, apocalyptic poem. I studied the poem and its evolution late into the night before the day of recording.

At 6 a.m. we were woken by the sound of an explosion, loud enough to shake our windows, to set children screaming and car alarms honking. There was another a few minutes later and looking out of our bedroom window we could see, to the south, an orange glow burning in the dawn sky. Our fuzzy, dream-space-filled imaginations immediately wondered if nuclear Armageddon had struck London, but news reports were soon speaking of an explosion at the Buncefield oil storage terminal in Hemel Hempstead, just four miles down the road from us.

It was an enormous explosion, the biggest of its kind in peacetime Europe. The facility stored 273 million litres of oil. Two of its largest containers had exploded that morning; the rest were entirely burnt out over the next two days. The explosion measured 2.4 on the Richter scale, the flames were hundreds of feet high, the black cloud could be seen from space, but due to the time of day there were remarkably few casualties, and no fatalities. All I knew was, it was a little spooky. I'd spent the day before working very hard on Byron's poem, which begins:

I had a dream, which was not all a dream.
The bright sun was extinguish'd, and the stars
Did wander darkling in the eternal space…
… Morn came and went – and came, and brought
no day.

An hour or two later as I stood on the platform, going through these lines, waiting to catch one of the delayed trains into London to record them, the low winter sun was completely obliterated by an enormous and expanding cloud of thick, black smoke. We were *in* Byron's 'Darkness', and I couldn't help but wonder what it might portend.

Epilogue

So, this is where the story of my first decade on this roller-coaster ends, but, just in case, dear reader, you think it might be plain sailing from here, let me assure you that what goes up must indeed come down. The only thing an actor can ever be certain of is uncertainty; the decade that followed contained fantastic highs, but also incredible lows. I would continue my love affair with Shakespeare, Benedick and the Bastard at the RSC; I would also have a crack at Hamlet and play Macbeth at Shakespeare's Globe; I would win awards, star in films, TV shows, play leading roles at most of the theatres on my wish list, but, I would also be in some catastrophic flops, fail endless auditions, and be out of work for periods long enough to retrain as a carer for the elderly and work late shifts in bars to make rent. In my private life I would suffer the slings and arrows of crippling divorce, depression and injuries, but, on the upswing that followed I would see my children bloom, and, before the decade was out, I would meet and marry the real love of my life. And if that sounds like an advertisement for the second volume of memoirs you'd be absolutely right.

Living without equilibrium – that seems to be the sacrifice an actor makes. The only constant, for me, the only thing I can trace from today right back to the beginning of my story, has been the relationship I've had with my work. We've been separated occasionally by unemployment, but, when we are reunited it is always the same exciting, respectful, brotherly relationship, based on hard graft and a desire to learn.

Work, my favourite four-letter word.

Thanks

I hope the debt I owe to my family is clear, but it's important to send the love and gratitude on its full tour of duty, so let me take a moment to say that my mother is the best of the best. I want to thank all the early readers, many of whom were kind enough to offer me their responses as quotes for the cover, Sam Carter for his fantastic work, Alexa Tewkesbury for her incredibly generous and detailed proofreading, Anthony Cozens for his early proofread, Jason Bartholomew at the BKS agency for his advice and support, my brother Peter James Millson, my children (both full and step), and last but by no means least, I want to thank my friend and wife Sarah-Jane Potts for sending me off to a coffee shop in Los Angeles to start the bloody thing, and for sometimes laughing out loud when she read it. It meant the world.

Onwards.